A History of Africa
Hosea Jaffe

A History of Africa

Hosea Jaffe

with a Preface by Samir Amin

Zed Books Ltd.

A History of Africa was first published by Zed Books Ltd.,
57 Caledonian Road, London N1 9BU, in 1985.

Cover designed by Andrew Corbett
Printed by The Bath Press, Avon.

British Library Cataloguing in Publication Data

Jaffe, Hosea
    A history of Africa.
    1. Africa — History
    I. Title
    960   DT20

    ISBN 0-86232-274-X
    ISBN 0-86232-275-8 Pbk

US Distributor
Biblio Distribution Center, 81 Adams Drive,
Totowa, New Jersey 07512

Contents

Acronyms

AAC	All African Convention (South Africa)
ANC	African National Congress (South Africa)
APO	African Peoples Organisation (South Africa)
Anti-CAD	Anti-Coloured Affairs Department (South Africa)
ACP	African, Caribbean and Pacific Countries (of Lome Convention of the European Economic Community)
ALEMAKEF	Ethiopian Students Movement Abroad
BPC	Black Peoples Congress (of 'Black Consciousness', South Africa)
BSA	British South Africa Company
CAD	Coloured Affairs Department (South Africa)
CATA	Cape African Teachers Association (South Africa)
CPSA	Communist Party of South Africa
CPP	Convention Peoples Party (Gold Coast, Ghana)
CGT	*Confédération Générale du Travail* (France)
DEIC	Dutch East India Company
ECA	Economic Commission for Africa (Addis Ababa)
EEC	European Economic Community
ELF	Eritrean Liberation Front
FLN	National Liberation Front (Algeria)
FLNA	National Liberation Front of Angola
FRELIMO	Mozambique Liberation Front
FROLINAT	*Front de Libération Nationale du Tchad*
ICU	Industrial and Commercial Workers Union (South Africa)
IFAN	Institut Fondamental d'Afrique Noire (Senegal)
ISL	International Socialist League (South Africa)
KANU	Kenya African National Union
KADU	Kenya African Democratic Union
KNUT	Kenya National Union of Teachers
LMS	London Missionary Society
MPLA	Angolan Peoples Liberation Movement
	Natal Indian Congress

NIC	Natal Indian Congress
NAD	Native Affairs Department
NRC	Native Representative Council
NLL	National Liberation League (South Africa)
NEUF	Non-European United Front (South Africa)
NEUM	Non-European Unity Movement (South Africa)
NATO	North Atlantic Treaty Organisation
NEF	New Era Fellowship (Capetown)
OAU	Organisation of African Unity
OECD	Organisation for Economic Cooperation and Development
PAIGC	African Party for the Independence of Guinea-Bissau and Cape Verde
PAC	Pan African Congress
PCF	French Communist Party
POUM	*Partido Obrero de Unificacion Marxista* (Spain)
PCI	Italian Communist Party
PSF	French Socialist Party
RDA	*Rassemblement Démocratique Africain*
SAIC	South African Indian Congress
SACPO	South African Coloured Peoples Organisation
SASO	South African Students Organisation
SWAPO	South West Africa (Namibia) Peoples Organisation
SOYA	Society of Young Africa (South Africa)
TLSA	Teachers League of South Africa
TANU	Tanzania African National Union
TUC	Trades Union Congress
UNITA	*Uniao Nacional para a Independencia Total de Angola*
ZANU	Zimbabwe African National Union
ZAPU	Zimbabwe African Peoples Union

Preface

by Samir Amin

Many people probably still think that the causes of the economic difficulties which African countries are currently facing, the tragedy of the Sahel Famine and the financial breakdowns, are all to be found in the contemporary local society (the class structure of the power) and/or in the current international world system. Being among those who strongly believe that the roots of much of the present go back to the three or four last centuries of our history, I cannot but welcome this History of Africa which our comrade Hosea Jaffe offers us.

It is not the purpose of this foreword to discuss all the views expressed by the author — especially with respect to the modes of production of precapitalist Africa. These views are indeed stimulating and are often even new proposals which should reopen a discussion of great importance. I only feel perhaps useful to complement this history by some short remarks on the contemporary crisis in Africa.

Twenty years ago when most of the African countries were acceding to independence, the view prevailing at that time, even among Africans, attributed underdevelopment on the continent to an historical backwardness which was to be overcome simply by redoubling efforts aimed at progress in a previously defined and known direction. What the national liberation movement, such as it was, was blaming the colonisers for was precisely the fact that they were not up to the task.

African 'left' and 'right' were convinced that independence was a sure guarantee of and a sufficient precondition for the acceleration of modernisation rates. The liberal thesis considered that maintaining large opportunities for the exterior by becoming integrated into the international division of labour, and recourse to a 'rare input' — foreign capital — were not inconsistent with the acceleration of growth, quite the contrary. The government's role was precisely to create more favourable conditions likely to generate new opportunities for capital investments, by accelerating the schooling and training so feared by the colonisers, in the modernisation of both infrastructure and

1

administration. The socialist thesis of the time, suspicious of foreign capital, was arguing that the government was itself to compensate for the lack of capital, specifically with a view to effectively speeding up the modernisation process. In other words, the socialist thesis was not rejecting either the 'modernisation' perspective or that of integration into the international division of labour.

Both theses shared the same basic views concerning 'technique neutrality' i.e., both were arguing that the direction of modernisation could be and was known: a mere glance at both Western and Eastern advanced societies will convince us of the similarity of a number of objectives in terms of consumption — and means — organisation of production, administration, education. The 'socialists' were probably more sensitive to issues like national independence, which is why they were on their guard against the recourse to foreign capital. They were also probably more sensitive to issues related to income distribution and the priority of collective services. But the 'liberals' retorted that capitalism would also solve these problems and moreover, would gradually lead to a democratisation of social and political life.

Both theses were finally based on the same West-centred and technico-economistic view, the common denominator of a popular version of Marxism and the best of bourgeois social science.

Only 15 years ago protests were still rare and unwelcome, considered as peasant utopias and culturalist nationalisms. It is true that, because of a lack of sufficient support, the protestors were often guilty of such weaknesses. But why then should Africa have had to make itself conspicuous by such fantasies?

The outcome of the real history of the last two decades has been such that the two theses are systematically called into question today. It is this twofold historical 'frustration' that gives the thesis of unequal development the strength it is gaining.

The thesis of unequal development began by the affirmation that underdevelopment, far from being a 'backwardness', was the result of integration into the world capitalist system as an exploited and dominated periphery, fulfilling specific functions in the process of accumulation at the centre of the system. This integration, contrary to superficial points of view, did not date from the colonial sharing at the end of the 19th Century, but from the very beginning of mercantilism in the 16th Century, a period when Africa was 'specialised', through the 'slave trade', in the supply of labour power which, exploited in America, was to speed up the process of capital accumulation in Atlantic Europe. This 'specialisation' which, apart from its horrors, was leading to a regression of local production systems as well as State organisations — and moreover, was to mark the ideology of the societies involved in this shameful trade with features which will remain for a long time — was impoverishing Africa.

The thesis of unequal development proceeded with its analysis by trying to understand the mechanisms by which capital, dominant on the world scale, was subordinating pre-capitalist modes of production while distorting them. Whereas the ethnological main stream was carrying on its research on the singularities of African societies, trying to isolate them conceptually, the thesis of unequal development was laying stress on the integration of apparently 'traditional' rural societies in the process of capital accumulation. It was in this manner that, in the first half of the 1960s, the essential characteristics of the modes of formal domination of capital over the African rural world were defined. It was shown how in the 'trade economy', the technical and commercial systems of supervision were depriving peasant producers of their control over production means of which they were still the formal owners, in order to extract a surplus of labour, transformed through commodity trade into profit from the capital of the dominating monopolies. It was shown how the driving back of peasants into the intentionally small reserves in South Africa and Zimbabwe was intended to supply cheap labour power to industries and mines.

Then, in the second half of the 1960s, the Cultural Revolution took place. The establishment of 'communes' was at last a positive example of a fundamentally new orientation of a development based on an alliance between workers and peasants, replacing the dogma of 'socialist primitive accumulation', i.e. in practical terms, the continuation of peasant exploitation under new forms. A solution was thus found for the dilemma in which all tendencies of the Marxist debate had been trapped since the 1920s. These were the facts which paved the way for the ideological penetration of the theses of unequal development, especially into the liberation of South Africa, until recent years a victim of the narrow limits of the English imperialist tradition.

The way was thus opened for a positive rethinking of all the issues of development: orientations of industrialisation, the question of State and Nation etc. Within this perspective industry is meant to support the technical and social revolution in the rural area. This inversion of priorities also, by the force of circumstances, involved fundamental revisions at the level of reflection on consumption models, the articulation of big and small industries, modern techniques and artisanal and traditional techniques etc. A positive content could be given to a strategy of 'disconnection', i.e. of refusal of the imperatives of the international division of labour, heretofore considered as inevitable necessities.

The seed was sowed. But it could not germinate unless it had fallen on fertile soil. For ideas become realities only if they are supported by effective social forces.

However the ground is becoming increasingly solid. The old movement of national liberation, whose objective was political independence, has exhausted its potentials. The 50-state Africa to whose creation it contributes finds itself in a dilemma: a dilemma of economic development whose contrasted effects are ever more explosive: urbanisation and mass unemployment, agricultural stagnation, soil deterioration, famines and massive imports of food products, growing external dependency; a dilemma of national construction: the artificial frontiers, respectfully sanctioned by the OAU, are splitting under the pressure of the very peoples, ethnic groups and nations; a political dilemma: imitative democracies give way to tyrannies, single parties of national construction give place to military and bureaucratic cliques; an ideological dilemma: capitalist liberalism and bureaucratic social-ism do not answer any needs of the popular masses and ask for external support; a cultural dilemma: imitative education shows all its dis-functionality; the imposition of the foreign languages of colonisation — the corollary of the establishment of state within the frontiers we know — is a vehicle of alienation as ineffective as it is unbearable.

The reason is that the old movement of national liberation was in fact a bourgeois movement even though it was able to mobilise peasant masses and even though its petty bourgeois component had given the illusion of a possible socialist prospect. The newly emerging movement will be that of peasants and workers, by the force of circumstances. It will probably inevitably assume populist forms in a first stage while the seed sowed has not yet germinated, as the events of Iran show, heralding a new popular stream which may once more put the peoples of Asia and Africa in the limelight of the great transformations now taking place in the world.

The present crisis of the imperialist system obviously enhances all these contradictions. The solutions offered by the system — delocation of some industries which will allow monopoly capital to extract from the exploitation of the workers in the Third World the super-profits required for a new start at the centre — are no longer an answer to the questions asked. There is no alternative to a strategy of national and popular reconstruction, which is self-centred and disconnected from the world system.

This solution will make its way, but not without difficulties. In some countries of the continent the old movement of national liberation only achieved its objectives, belatedly, in 1974 or even later and it has not yet achieved them in Namibia and in South Africa. The old ideology of the 'non-capitalist path' which was in the past related to a radical tendency, still has some roots.

As long as the populist stage which is beginning has not generated a new liberation movement based on a peasant-worker alliance, Africa will remain as it is: the underbelly of the system. Then the powers will inevitably be induced to fight on this continent the battles which oppose them and whose objectives are absolutely unrelated to the interests of African peoples and nations. Over the short term, a 're-sharing' of Africa is not excluded. As long as the popular forces of the continent have not imposed their autonomy they will remain, like their adversaries themselves, the stakes in the great powers' strategy.

PART ONE

African Communism and Despotism

African Communism and Despotism

From the 10th Century, during the Crusades — which the South African thinker Ben Kies[1] has called 'the first great plundering expedition of Europe' — learned historians in the African countries bordering the Mediterranean, writing in Arabic, described the civilizations of the Sudan and the regions along the course of the Niger. El Bekri, El Idrisi,[2] Ibn Hawkal,[3] Ibn Khaldoun,[4] Ibn Battuta,[5] El Masudi[6] and Leo Africanus[7] revealed the existence of a series of societies, which were subsequently 'discovered' by European travellers and writers such as Dapper,[8] Lopez,[9] Cresques,[10] Mungo Park,[11] Barth[12] and Frobenius.[13] Since the political independence gained after the war, knowledge of these and similar societies in Central and East Africa has been extended by African scholars in proportion to their ideological independence of Euro-American schools. Only the most generalized data have been included in our brief chronology, with the main object of illustrating the antecedents of the modern liberation movements.

Apart from the well known civilizations that flourished in Egypt, Carthage, Kerma, Napata and Meroe in the pre-Christian era, many societies existed in other parts of Africa comparable with those that grew up at the same time in Europe and Asia. The writings of James Africanus Horton, Edward Blyden and Casely Hayford[14] in the 19th Century, and Nkrumah,[15] Sekou Touré[16] and Amilcar Cabral[17] in more recent times, indicate that the 'lost past' is itself an important 'memoria' for the independence movements. Some of the illustrative examples in this section suggest that for Ethiopia and the liberation movement in Zimbabwe, for instance, the 'lost' — or better, perhaps, 'buried' — past is a vital element of our own times. Mali, Ghana, Benin, Zaire and Tanzania, among others, have taken their very names from this past. Ancient kings' titles have been made into honorific prefixes of the presidents in Ghana, Mali, Zaire and Swaziland and of the former tribal administrators in Ankole, Ijebu, Rwanda and Burundi. Modibo Keita, the leader of Mali's struggle for independence, who died in prison in 1977, laid claim to the illustrious name of the Keitas of the kingdom of

Mansa Moussa, whose dynasty is recorded in Abraham Cresques's Catalonian map of 1375. Cabral, Senghor,[18] Nkrumah, Nyerere,[19] Neto,[20] Keita, Sekou Touré and Samora Machel,[21] each in their own way, have shown how independence movements *are attempting to recapture the origins and authenticity of the African heritage*', as the Nigerian President, General O. Obasanjo, put it when he opened the 1977 Lagos Arts Festival. Kenyatta recalled the old co-operative spirit of 'Harambee' —'let us work together' — for purposes which came in for criticism within Kenya, but none the less he too had recourse to this African 'memoria'. Nyerere, on a different intellectual plane, made the old 'Zanj'-Swahili collectivist spirit of 'Ujamaa', of mutual sharing, cooperative work and mutual respect (based on the ancient family structure of the *gens*), an essential part of his 'African socialism' and of the Arusha Declaration of 1967.[22] Thus the 'lost past' lives again in the thought, the symbolism and the practices of liberation movements and of the independent nations themselves.

The Present as Colonialised Past

The connection between the past and the liberation movements is not only subjective, as in the foregoing examples: above all it is objective, and the factor linking past and present was European colonialism. It is this mediation, with its slave trade, its conquest, dispossession and subjection — material and spiritual — by both secular and religious agencies, that transmuted and then transmitted the essential elements of the ancient past to the present. This mutation and transmission was a real process. What came out of it may seem to be the past, but its essence is quite different, even in quality, from its appearance. The 'essence' may indeed be the opposite of the 'phenomenon', and the latter may invert and mystify the former. The problem of the pre-colonial past cannot be resolved simply by considering this past, but only by considering the whole connecting system: pre-colonial society–colonialism–liberation movements. A single example will clarify this: the colonialists transmuted the role played by African kings and chiefs a thousand years ago, and it is the product of this mutation, not the original role, that in the 20th Century, after the Second World War, became part of the role assumed by the kings and presidents of a number of states after independence. Thus it is not the past that is perpetuated, but its colonialist mutation, albeit in an apparently non-colonialist setting.

The very first modern-style political analyses of the African past (as described by Arabic-language historians in the countries bordering the Mediterranean, from El Masudi, Ibn Hawkal and Ibn Khaldoun[23] of the 10th Century onwards) were made by the Liberian President Stephen Allen Benson (1816–65)[24] who went to Liberia from the United States at the age of six; by Edward W. Blyden (1832–1912),[25] a West

Indian who went to Liberia in 1851; by Alexander Crummell (1821–98), who went to Liberia from the United States by way of Cambridge in 1853; and by the Edinburgh-trained Sierra Leone doctor, James Africanus Horton (1835–83).[26] Joseph Ephraim Casely Hayford (1866–1930),[27] a barrister from Cape Coast, Gold Coast (Ghana), educated at Fourah Bay, a disciple of Blyden, may be regarded as the last of the old school and one of the first of the more recent, if not more modern, African nationalists.

All these political writers and scholars went back to the indigenous culture of West Africa, the 'communism' or 'socialism' of the 'aborigines'. What they studied, however, was not the authentic past, but a version transmuted by four centuries of colonialism. All of them, too, looked at the past through European spectacles of 'race': they all accepted that man could be divided into different racial groups and, implicitly or openly, that the civilization built up by the white races in Europe was superior. The racial classification they accepted, thanks to European or American indoctrination by church, state and university, was that of dividing man into 'white' and 'black' — a racial theory that ran through their study of the communal aspect of early West African societies. Thus, these first African political analyses of the history of West Africa — like those in the autobiography of the Arabic-speaking rebel Tippoo Tib[28] in East Africa, written at the beginning of this century — were already biased by the European-created colonialist concept of race. Hence not only were the objective societies which they studied not originals but colonialist 'copies', but also their subjective view of those societies was, literally, coloured by the racial ideology of colonialism. This combination of obstacles to an understanding of the ancient past has persisted to the present day, albeit to an extent that varies with place and time. The weakness was not peculiar to the African pioneers mentioned above, nor to the others, less well known, who lived a century or so ago. The point here is the way in which objective and subjective changes were made to the old past by colonialism as a mediator between past and present.

One significant difference between Benson, Blyden and Hayford on the one hand and Joseph Kizerbo,[29] Sekene Mody Cissoko[30] and some other modern African historians on the other, is that the former saw mainly the communitarian, collective, 'communist' side of the old societies, while the latter take account of other elements such as hierarchy and private property. And in the final analysis it is this double-sided nature of the past that is most important for a modern reconstruction of it.

The most important societies for the modern liberation movements were: Zanj or Azania in East Africa, the kingdoms of the Sudan and of the Niger in West Africa; Nubia and Meroe in Sudan; Pharaonic Egypt; Ethiopia at the time of Axum and after King Ezana; the Congo kingdoms of Central Africa, and Zimbabwe in Southern Africa. In their

9

territorial-temporal union these cover much of the continent. For the most part their genesis and rise took place in the period that our chronology calls the 'lost past'. The decline of some took place under Ptolemaic and Roman colonialism, but, for the most, mainly in the 'colonial' period from the 15th Century onwards. The whole process spans the millennia of the rise of Egypt, Carthage, the Sudan, Axum, Zanj, the Saharan and Niger–Sudanese, Zaire, Zambezi and Lake kingdoms, and the swift decline of the complex of tribal, despotic and feudalised African societies during the past 500 years. The first phase, of growth, has been described and documented, particularly by Arab–Africans, while Europeans have, in the main, given their own description and documentation of the phase of decline. For an understanding of the original, pre-colonial, societies, the Arab–African sources and research done by a handful of disinterested African, English, French, American and Eastern European, Russian and Indian scholars, since independence, are of fundamental importance. In the accounts of the declining phases by European and North American writers, however honestly intended, the distortions due to their colonialist history are almost inevitable.

The African Iron Ages

By the 1st Century AD a series of Arab–Bantu speaking communities on the East coast of Africa was trading with Rome, Arabia and Asia, exporting ivory, oil, gold and craftware. Iron was the dominant material for tools and weapons in Meroe (700 BC to AD 350) on the Sudanese Nile, in Nok (before 500 BC) and Igbo Ukwu in Nigeria, and later in Zimbabwe, among the Masai of Kenya–Tanzania, the pastoral Baganda and the agricultural Bunyoro between Lake Victoria and the Ruwenzori mountains, and in some Saharan societies. Although some of these societies were classless and hence also stateless, while others had a socio-political stratification, all had strongly communitarian forms of land-ownership, cooperative labour, whether agricultural, pastoral, fishing or mining and crafts, and strong gentile linkages (exogamous with respect to the *gens* 'family', but endogamous within the tribe or federation of tribes). The social cell, as in most of America, Asia and Europe before classes formed, was the *gens*. The gens took many forms in Africa: thus the Masai had an intra-gentile grading of its largely nomadic population, while the Bunyoro *gentes* drew tribute from the agricultural Ganda, whose own kingship, the Kabaka, and Council of Elders, the Lukiko, were drawn largely from the leading *gentes*. Despite missionary 'divide and rule', the Bunyoro, led by the Kabarega, their king, fought by the side of the Ganda against England, thereby overcoming three-quarters of a millennium of tributary inter-dependence. Tribal and gentile inequalities in other African groups either overcame their ancient antagonisms or else were grist to the mill of European 'divide and rule' and 'indirect rule'.

African independence has driven the threshold of the Iron Age and of the Bantu diaspora further and further backwards in African historiography. This itself was a struggle of non-racial thinking and carbon-14 dating against the racist ideas about Bantu iron-users of Inskeep, Dart, Broome, Bleek and Meinhof. By 1940 the Bantu Iron Age was being mooted by Euro-archaeology as having begun about 1500. By 1960 the threshold had moved back to AD 1000; by 1980 it was conceded to be a thousand years earlier. Although Meroe island is no longer regarded by all as having been the 'Birmingham of Africa', Meroe — and Axum — worked iron by about 700 BC.[31] Meroe and Axum followed on the metal-working Nubian Kerma and Napata societies, which provided some of Egypt's Pharaohs. The African scholar, Wai Andah, has shown that the Nigerian Nok people worked iron before 500 BC. From the Niger–Zaire centre, from Carthage after 850 BC, from Meroe, from the ancient haemetite-using peoples of the East African lake districts, from the fragile laterite iron ores in the soil of Zaire and Uganda, came not only the wondrous colours for the San, Khoi-Khoin, Bantu and other rock-paintings and incisions of central Tanzania and other sites, but axes and other tools. By 1000 BC the Bantu diaspora began from the Niger–Zaire Atlantic coast and Benue Plateau region, and 'Iron was in use by those who expanded and all would agree to the rapid, some would say explosive, expansion of the Bantu'.[32] The iron-smiths of Igbo-Ukwu, Nigeria, before the 8th Century AD, continued the ancient tradition in West Africa.[33] In East Africa, from the Cape to the Horn, iron became a daily product, with copper and sometimes gold. Iron production accompanied a transition in which hunting and fishing (once the main occupation, when the lakes were many times their present size, before 4000 BC and again in the 3rd millennium BC) rapidly took second place to nomadic pastoralism. Both were overwhelmed by mixed farming from at least the start of our present era. For some 500 years before the colonial holocaust, the Xhosa and Natal Nguni mined and smelted iron,[34] the Sotho worked with iron, copper and tin, and San hunters, Khoi-Khoin herders and Bantu mixed farmers were co-extensive territorially and socio-economically over Southern, East and parts of West Africa. The tourist-apartheid stricken remains of the nomadic Masai, San, Hadza, Sandawe and of forest-dwelling clients of the Bantu, can give no idea of the social and technological progress made from the time when the first crops were sown about 13000 BC in plateau and lacustrine East Africa, or from the time when cattle were domesticated in Algeria and Libya by 5700 BC.

European 'Africanists' have made too little of the Early (from 700 BC, they say, to AD 400) and Late Iron Age in Africa, but too much, in general about iron, on which Greek and Roman technology rested after iron and iron-working were imported from Anatola, Turkey, where, by 1500 BC, it had been properly mined and worked, and the Hittite expansion, which also struck Egypt for a brief while. China, however, began using iron widely only after about 600 BC, Needham has informed us, but had a highly organized social and cultural life using stone and bronze before that, and iron did not change the basic social formation of China for millennia. The Americans used stone for the 50,000 years before the continent was 'discovered' by Columbus (or the Vikings), yet, with this single material — and wood — they managed to construct several levels of 'primitive communism', as well as the finely and deeply stratified Olmec, Mayan, Toltec, Aztec and Inca forms of the 'Asiatic mode' of production. The similar society of Pharaonic Egypt (3000 BC to the Ptolemaic conquest in 323 BC), used stone and timber as basic materials of labour; bronze refurbished but did not change the mode of production. Tutankhaman (1362–1352 BC) had a gold death-mask, but also an iron dagger (whose nickel content indicates a probable meteoric origin), but the introduction of iron by the Hyksos in no way rewove the fabric of Pharaonic 'communal despotism', as Ibn Khaldoun could have described it.

Gentile Communism

More important than the materials of labour — stone, wood, bronze, iron — was the geo-economic dynamic setting of society. This led, eventually, to the separation of the paths of modal development as between Europe and the rest of the world. The sea–valley–mountain stage, on which the drama of political economy was enacted in Europe, differed from the desert and mountain-bound river valleys of the great Asian and African civilizations, and from the forest–plateau, desert-ocean bound societies whose driving force was not irrigation but production for long-distance foreign trade, such as the Sahara–Sudan, Axum and Zanj societies, the Mayans, Incas and Aztecs, or the Carthaginians — those Phoenician settlers who were Africanized by Roman destruction, tribute and tyranny, after they had themselves exploited the Berbers, Numidians, Libyans and Mauretanians for half a millennium after they came to Africa around 1000 BC.

In pre-class Africa, matriarchy was widespread, but when the *gens* was patrilinear women were clearly exploited and oppressed, even when kingly descent was transmitted through the king's sister. This exploitation and oppression increased with the social division of labour and the growth of a gentile or tribal hierarchy. Among the men, at least, there was a system of egalitarian self-administration, with the king at its head — a logical and natural historical expression of the rule of the family or the clan. The king and his 'court', as Europeans saw them, were not so much rulers as custodians of the common property. In particular, they had no authority or power to alienate the common land. Every treaty made by the Europeans a thousand years later would have been inconceivable and unlawful under customary tribal or *gens* or clan communal law in Africa. The alienation of land, with few exceptions, as in some areas of Ethiopia, did not exist in pre-colonial Africa. The egalitarianism that existed, for example, among the males of a community, was inter-tribal within the *gens* or group of clans having a common ancestor, and petered out towards the economic and territorial periphery of the tribe. Land, being everything at the time, became the main object of conflict, followed first by cattle, then by women and finally by men. In so far as the level of production within a tribal group made it possible for a prisoner of war to create some surplus, a man or woman prisoner preserved his or her life and entered the victorious tribe as a slave. If the productive capacity of the tribe did not make this possible, the prisoner was either released to return to his own *gens* district or, if potentially dangerous to his captors, was killed. Sometimes, as Thomas More recorded in his *Utopia*, and as also occurred in Europe, Asia and the two Americas, he might be executed and eaten instead of being buried, but that was not common. As Marx noted in *Capital* and in the articles he wrote for the *New York Herald Tribune* in the 1850s, it was the Europeans who were the main 'head-hunters and scalpers'.

Doubtless Morgan and Engels[35] would have classified the Batwa or San societies (called 'Bushmen' by the Europeans who decimated them) in Ethiopia, Central Africa, Southern Africa and the lake districts of Ruanda and Burundi as 'savage' communities, in which hunting, fishing and the gathering of food were all-important. Doubtless, too, they would have classified the early, pre-Zanj and pre-Zimbabwean, societies that existed in East and Southern Africa and the contemporary societies in Guinea, Nigeria and the Sudan as belonging to the 'lower stage of barbarism', despite their agriculture, pastoral farming, pottery, some metal-work and a strong social organization based on the firm union of the *gens* within a communitarian but tribally divided society, with each tribal grouping separate from the others and quite often in conflict with them. Communalism, collectivism and cooperation — 'Harambee' and 'Ujamaa' — were not social but tribal (as was the case in much of Europe in the same period), and the situation did not change even with the effects of the transformation of 'pagan' Africa into an organized Muslim society in the 7th Century.

Egypt, Nubia, Meroe, Axum

But in Meroe[36] in eastern Sudan, and in Axum[37] in Ethiopia, as well as in Somalia (which is probably the 'Land of Punt' mentioned in the inscriptions that Queen Hetshapsut of Egypt had carved on the walls of her palaces) there existed something more than a society in the 'lower stages of barbarism', even in the pre-Islamic period. Both in Meroe and in Axum there seems to have been a communal system of usufruct of the land, rather than private property.[38] Communal land ownership did not preclude but did circumscribe a system of slavery, and a hierarchy of caste.[39] The religion, a combination of sun-worship and ancestor-worship, testified to a communal, pre-class or proto-class, socio-economic system based on the *gens*. Slaves were used as communal or, more rarely, family, servants, rather than owned and sold; as property they belonged to the dominant *gens*, or tribal aggregate, and were entrusted to the custodianship of the king (or queen) who (as in the case of the 10th Century tribal Ethiopian Queen Judith) had himself or herself a kinship base in the *gens*. In a society of this type, something akin to the Roman *gens patricia* was developing. The hierarchical clan or caste system combined communal ownership of land, and even of slaves, with exploitation and oppression — a 'tribal' equivalent of the Hindu caste system.

The economy of Axum[40] was a mixture, not a compound. It was a tribal social formation with a proto-class character with little slavery. When, in the 5th Century, the Byzantine Church created the Coptic Church of Ethiopia, a new element was inserted into the system. The new Church, which arose in the time of Constantine's schism with Constantinople, created links between the upper levels of Ethiopian society and the Graeco–Egyptian Church, with its colonialistic Ptolemaic (323 BC to 30 BC) and Roman (from 30 BC) private-property roots in the paleo-racist non-Egyptian social circles in Alexandria, the Byzantine theocracy and, later, the Christian circles in Jerusalem, under European control. As is known, the Catholic Church, both Roman and Byzantine, became increasingly feudal from the 4th Century on, an increasingly secular institution owning vast estates, exploiting serfs and oppressing the minds not only of Europe but of all who came under its sway, even before its colonialist Crusaders and later reign of terror in Africa, Asia and the two Americas. This feudal factor spread within the Coptic Church in Ethiopia in a period in which the tribally based society was itself undergoing social changes towards 'communal despotism'. On fertile highlands the seeds of private landed property, already sown in Mediterranean Africa by Ptolemaic and Roman colonialism, and sown afresh by the Coptic Church, fell on fertile soil.[41] By the mode of production of feudalism we mean here a hierarchical system of exploitation offering 'protection' and vassalage in exchange for labour, produce or money or military service, based on private ownership of the land and private (serf, peasant) rather than communal labour. Whether this land belongs to barons or to a hierarchy of priests within a church, it remains private, not communal, property. Feudalism presupposes a social revolution: expropriation of the *gens* or tribal federation that owns the land, not by an alien conquering tribe but by private individuals, families, war-lords and, later, churches, nobles and kings. Under feudalism both the producers and receivers of the surplus were privatized. Such a social revolution had taken place in Italy even before the Roman republic and in Greece before the slave-based Athenian democracy. It had not taken place even in Egypt before the Pharaohs: in 'classical' Egypt slavery was marginal to peasant or tribal communal labour, combined with communal ownership of the land along the Nile.[42] Babylonia was more Egyptian than Graeco–Roman as far as the form of landed property was concerned.[43] [44] With a few exceptions, the social revolution expropriating the *gentes* did not take place in pre-colonial America, Asia and pre-colonial Africa, or the islands of the Pacific, Indian and Atlantic Oceans. It was limited to Western Europe, and when it spread into other continents — and into Russia and Japan — this was largely due to the prior revolution in Europe; and that occurred specifically before slavery in the Mediterranean basin and later under Charlemagne in central Europe. The European conquistadores in the Americas, Africa and Asia came armed not only with gunpowder and the Bible but also, and above all, with their prior history, based on the experience and the concept of private ownership of the land. The revolution from communal to private land ownership outside Western Europe came largely, if not solely, from Western European influence or from direct conquest and dispossession.

The European and Non-European Modes of Production

Private ownership of the land, and even the idea of private ownership of land, hardly existed in the American continent before the Spanish conquests of southern South America and Mexico, and the Portuguese conquest of Brazil.[45] Until Vasco de Gama conquered the coast from Bombay to Goa, private property in the land was unknown in the Indian state of Maharashtra,[46] nor was it known in Ceylon before the Portuguese came or in the Philippines before Magellan. The Dutch conquistadores introduced private landed property into Malaya and Indonesia, and the British along the east coast of India. China retained its forms of communal property, the 'village lands', even under the warlords. Feudalism in the European sense did not exist in China until the European Opium wars, the crushing of Taiping and the Boxers, when semi-colonial capitalistic exploitation brought it in from the West and it was brought to an end by the Maoist revolution of 1949.[47] With rare exceptions, there was no generalized ownership of land in Africa[48] until the conquests of the European colonialists, who, as an external force, expropriated tribal communities throughout Africa. What Kautsky, Plekhanov and, later, the Marxist school of the Stalinist period,[49] describes as the feudal state did not, properly and generally speaking, exist in Africa, or indeed anywhere outside Europe.

15

Leopold Senghor, former President of Senegal, a self-proclaimed African Marxist, recalls in his book *For an African Re-reading of Marx and Engels* a letter from Karl Marx to the Russian revolutionary Vera Zassoulitch, dated 16 February 1881, in which he wrote:

> The 'historic inevitability' of this movement [of capitalism towards socialism] is therefore *expressly restricted to the countries of Western Europe* . . . The analysis in *Capital* does not provide reasons either for or against the vitality of the rural commune, but the studies I have made, and my researches into material from original sources, have convinced me that this commune is the point of departure for the social regeneration of Russia.[50]

The 'historic inevitability' of the sequence referred to in the *Communist Manifesto* — slavery–feudalism–capitalism–socialism — is thus specifically limited by Marx to a particular group of Western European 'advanced' (i.e. colonialist) countries. It does not automatically apply anywhere else in the world. Indeed, even in Western Europe, as Marx showed in his analysis of its evolution, feudalism did not come out of slavery. In most of Europe — Central and Northern — it came after tribalism ('barbarism'). In Southern Europe feudalism arose from the intersection, collision and resolution of the conflict between northern tribalism and southern slavery, and not simply from the internal dynamics of Roman slavery during the decadence of the Roman Empire. Even here the 'external factor' — the barbarian invasions — was a deciding, if not the fundamental, factor.

The same process did not take place in Asia, the Americas or Africa. The development of tribalism did not generate within society a 'barbarian' feudalism of the Franco–Teutonic type, with an increase in private landed property. What emerged from it was something different — something that, in the case of Asia, Marx called 'oriental despotism'.[51]

Richard Pankhurst and his Ethiopian colleagues have collected an abundant literature from original sources on the peculiar development of 'feudalism' in Ethiopia. It will still be some time before the whole story is told, but what has emerged so far is a moving picture of a society combining classical 'African propertylessness' (Marx) with European-type feudal features, with a strong internal tribal communal influence. In some regions — Wollo, the northern Eritrean frontier area, the Danakil desert and the Ogaden (all cattle and sheep pastoral and mixed farming regions) and in parts of Shoa itself — the tribal factor still remained and, here and there, prevailed. This, even amid a 'feudalism' in which some Rasses (land-barons) owned hundreds of square kilometres of land and, in one instance, something like a million serfs (this is the time of Haile Selassie, before the 'African Marxist' military revolution of 1974–7). But there is no doubt that the dominant form of property in Coptic Ethiopia was increasingly feudal, based on private exploitation of land and on serfdom. There is, moreover, no doubt that this system was fully developed before the first significant European penetration, that of the Portuguese in the 16th Century. In Ethiopia, unlike Goan India and Portuguese Ceylon, Malaya and Indonesia, private landed property existed before the expropriations and massacres of the Portuguese conquistadores. The Portuguese left some traces on the architecture of Gondar and on some forms of land ownership there, but Portuguese colonialism failed in Ethiopia both generally and in this particular respect.

However, the Ethiopian system of exploitation based on feudalized tribalism was the exception in Africa, not the rule. It was not, moreover, of the European type,* which, arising partly or wholly from Roman Teutonic and Slav tribalism, steadily destroyed its mother. In contrast, the Ethiopian variant coexisted with tribalism until it came to an end in 1974; and this tribalism, far from disappearing, coexisted with, and even formed the basic social formation of, the Sudan–Niger–Guinea societies and the societies of Zaire, Zanj, the East African lake kingdoms, Mwene-Mutapa and Zimbabwe from about the time that Africa was penetrated by Islam in the 8th Century.

The chronology of African pre-colonial history indicates the main outlines of the assimilation of Islam by the Bantu- and non-Bantu-speaking tribal societies. This assimilation was facilitated by the common, tribal origins of both Arab Islam and the animist religions of the Bantu, founded on ancestor-worship, and of other African religious beliefs and customs, including communitarian usufruct of the land and of all natural resources — mineral, forest and aquatic. At the same time, trade with Baghdad, Damascus and Cairo brought with it new elements of learning in astronomy, algebra, literature and philosophic and religious thought. Just as it raised Europe out of its medieval darkness and set it on the road towards capitalism, so this Arabian culture generally raised the level of civilization in Africa and provided the content for it. Europe, however, threw the Arabic-speaking scholars out of Spain and Portugal, together with their Islamic faith, at the same moment at which, in 1492, Europeans were beginning to penetrate Africa, Asia and America in earnest. Africa, however, welcomed these refugees from capitalism in Morocco and elsewhere: Arab Jews as well as Arab Muslims and Arab pagans and agnostics from Granada, Cadiz and Catalonia — a reception that continued an 800-year-old tradition going back to 695, when Said and Solomon came to 'Zing'. Further west, the Islamic religion penetrated into the Soninka–Ghana civilization in present-day Mali, into Kano in Nigeria and then into Timbuktu, so

---

* Marx, in *Grundrisse*, derived the 'Roman' and 'German' forms of proto-class primitive communism from an *'original Indian form'*.

linking the Sudan and Niger states with those on the Mediterranean. ranean.

This link, in the form of trade across the Sahara in salt, moving south, and gold, moving north, was not new. For a long time, from western Egypt, Libya, Tunisia and the northern banks of the Nile, many of the people had come whom Islam was later to convert to Allah — the Peuls and Toucouleurs of Senegal, Mali and Guinea and the non-Bantu peoples of Uganda, Kenya and Tanzania. The tribal Arab influence had come into West and East Africa long before Islam, and had long become an integral part of what European and American 'Africanists', from the time of the slave trade down to our own times, referred to as 'Black Africa'.

The Communal-Despotic Dialectic

A scholar of the African Institute of the USSR, the late Professor Potsekhin,[52] and his follower Professor Davidson,[53] are among those who have long shown that communal land tenure could coexist with many different forms of African socio-economic organization. Communal land tenure and the collective labour that it involved did not rule out various forms of exploitation and oppression. The past in Zanj, Zaire–Angola and the Sudan–Niger–Guinea complexes has to be viewed as a combination of all these elements.

During the five centuries of European colonialism, European historians tended to emphasize the tyrannical side of pre-colonial society in Africa. During the struggles for independence in the 19th and 20th Centuries it was natural to go too far in the opposite direction, to stress the communal, collectivist and co-operative aspects of pre-colonial societies. Moreover, African nationalists, socialists and Marxists were largely educated by European and American 'African studies' centres run by liberals, missionaries, socialists and Marxists. These centres, according to an article in the *Capetown Journal*, the 50-year-old organ of the anti-racist Teachers' League of South Africa, in a (banned) special 'Soweto' number of September 1976, have a colonialist interest in the cults of 'identity' or 'personality'. Such cults, in their turn, take the communal side of pre-colonial society as one of their points of departure and reference. There were thus two potentially divergent groups both stressing the communitarian as against the oppressive side of the pre-colonial societies. After independence, around the late 1950s, a tentative effort began to focus with both eyes on the subject of the past. This stereoscopic view makes it clear that this past in Africa was simultaneously 'communist' and 'despotic'.

No Property in Land and People

On 2 June 1853 Marx wrote to Engels: 'Bernier rightly considered the basis of all phenomena in the East — he is referring to Turkey, Persia, Hindustan — to be *absence of private property in land* [emphasis in original]. This is the real key, even to the Oriental heaven.' In his reply Engels agrees:

> The absence of property in land is indeed the key to the whole of the East. Herein lies its political and religious history. But how does it come about that the Orientals did not arrive at landed property *even in its feudal form* [our emphasis]? I think it is mainly due to the climate, taken in connection with the nature of the soil, especially with the great stretches of desert which extend from the Sahara straight across Arabia, Persia, India and Tartary up to the highest Asiatic plateau. Artificial irrigation is here the first condition of agriculture and this is a matter either for the communes, the provinces or the central government. An Oriental government never had more than three departments: finance (plunder at home), war (plunder at home and abroad) and public works (provision for reproduction).

Eight days later, on 14 June, Marx returns to the subject:

> As to the question of property, this is a very controversial one among the English writers on India. In the broken hill-country south of Krishna, property in land does seem to have existed [compare the Ethiopian highlands]. In Java, on the other hand, Sir Stanford Raffles, former English Governor of Java, observes in his *History of Java* that 'the sovereign was absolute landlord' of the whole of the surface of the land where rent to any considerable amount was attainable. In any case it seems to have been the Mohamedans who first established the principle of 'no property in land' throughout the whole of Asia.

This 'principle' was a legalization of a pre-existing, non-Muslim general practice and custom. These Marx–Engels letters, together with Engels's comment on the compatability of Javanese 'state socialism' with Dutch colonialism, form a heuristic basis at least, *mutatis mutandis*, for grasping the double nature of the 'lost past' in Africa.[54]

All liberation movements, outstandingly those of Mali, Senegal, Ghana, Dahomey, Nigeria (with Benin and Kano), Zaire, Guinea, Ethiopia (in its anti-imperialistic rather than its anti-feudal struggles), Tanzania, Mozambique and Zimbabwe, have recalled the past civilizations to help to overcome the slave mentality, with the 'inferiority complex' induced by conquest, white racialism and indoctrination and

super-exploitation. The high levels of material and cultural achievement achieved by those civilizations, of agricultural and craft and
construction production, of commerce, of universities, as well as of
administration and armies, have been revealed to millions of African
toilers for the first time and given their movements and aspirations a
new sense of self-respect, dignity and organization. The people have
begun to know that they came from societies that were as rich and high
as those of their conquerors and subjugators. They have seen that those
conquerors themselves, like the Spanish of Cortez in Mexico, the British
of Clive in India, stood in awe wondering at the splendour, the
magnificence, wealth, power and culture of those they were about to
conquer and destroy for centuries to come.

Whole oppressed peoples have begun to learn that pre-colonial
Bantu-speaking peoples, like those of Zanj and the Niger–Benin, were
literate, not merely sculptors in bronze and wood, that Timbuktu in
Mali and Kano in Nigeria, were not Arab but African cities, existing
from the 9th Century onwards as part not of a Saharan but of a Niger-
Sudanese–Guinean complex. Students know that 'backward' Casa-
mance, reduced to poverty by the French in Senegambia, was once the
starting-point of the Mandingo empire of the 13th and 14th Centuries,
embracing the commercial city of Ghana in present-day Mali and the
towns of Djenne, Timbuktu and Gao and extending into the present
Cameroons. In the time of the monarch Kankou Moussa there were
some 12,000 camels in Mali being used in a considerable trade between
northern and western Africa. In Timbuktu, Kano and other towns there
were splendid mosques and semi-religious, semi-secular seats of
learning, linked with each other and with Cairo. There were palaces in
the capitals.[55] Timbuktu, according to Ibn Battuta's description of 1353,[56]
had a matriarchal system that gave women more rights than they were
to enjoy later under colonialism. In 922 El Masudi[57] told of a rich
Ethiopian city, and described the high level of gold, ivory and copper
production reached at Kilwa and Sofala, in Zanj, which were linked
with Zimbabwe, the massively walled capital of the Bantu-speaking
Mwene Mutapa (Monomatapa) tribal monarchic confederation. In
1077 El Bekri[58] described cities in the Sudan of West Africa with
markets, roads, vineyards and many-storied buildings.

In 977 Ibn Hawkal[59] wrote of the kingdom of Ghana, adding: 'The
king of Ghana is the richest king on earth' — and this at a time when
Charlemagne's Holy Roman (German) Empire regarded itself as the
apex of human achievement. The 11th Century saw the beginnings of
the powerful and wealthy Songhai kingdoms and dynasties that rose to
their height under Sunni Ali Ber, crowned in Timbuktu in 1468, the
vanquisher of the Upper Volta Mossi tribal kingdom which had broken
into the city in 1336. Sunni Ali combined pagan customs with Islamic;
Arabic was a non-Koranic language together with other African
languages. The same combination of Islam and paganism made up the

culture of the Sonni dynasty of Gao in the 15th Century. By 1591 El Saidi could say that Songhai was so powerfully organized as a state that its army contained 12,000 cavalry, 30,000 infantry and 2,000 military canoes, until this empire, with its dynasty, was laid low by Djouder from Morocco.[60] But Djouder's victory was not a triumph of Arab over African, but a consequence of European expansion: by 1441 Europe had already penetrated African trade and the slave traffic was established in Oran, Tunis and Ceuta, Agadir and Arguin. Arguin city itself became the main port from which Portuguese, Italian, Spanish, Dutch, German and French merchants shipped gold and slaves out of Africa into Europe.

Even at this early stage the colonial period overlaps with the 'lost past'. But the destructive influence of Europe on African civilization was still indirect, operating through North African kings or chiefs driven south by European pressures. The first important effect of the kind was the Almovarid's conquest of the rich commercial state of Ghana in 1076, an indirect consequence of the pressures of the European Crusades on the Arab-cultured areas of Arabia and North Africa.

Zanj

El Idrisi's descriptions of East African cities in *Kitab Rujar* (1154) recorded a trade with the interior of Mwene Mutapa and, eastwards, with China, India, Molucca and Java. Iron was the main metal in use in the commercial ports of Lamu, Kilwa, Pemba, Zanzibar, Sofala and Mombasa. There appear to have been social classes based on means of production other than land, which remained common property under both Islamic and Kiswahili law. The relative absence of any large dominant clan or tribal grouping in what is now Tanzania, where there were many weak tribes, led to an overall weakness and minimized any kind of clan-despotism. At the same time there was nothing like a Hindu caste system, with its fine division of labour. Private property in craft industry, commerce and domestic slaves became the basis on which society was divided into classes. 'Slave' revolts such as those between 853 and 880 along Zanj were violently suppressed. But the communal rural landed property, communal labour on the land, the old communal functions of chiefs and kings, customary ancestor-worship, sun-worship and Islamic, Swahili and other Bantu traditions of hospitality and mutual help made the class–caste rule patriarchal and the despotism benevolent. Despite some Iranian–Byzantine arrogance towards Azania (the deserts north of Zanj) there was no racialism in Zanj itself. Wealthy and powerful Arabs wed Bantu women and ruled together with them, laying the foundations of new dynasties. The cultures of Zanj and of Zing remain the inspiration of modern

Tanzanian and Zimbabwean liberation movements. The South African ANC and Non-European Unity Movements reject 'Azania' as remote and slavish, but it is accepted by 'Black Consciousness' movements as a name for a free South Africa.[62]

Tribal Despotisms

The 13th Century saw the beginning of centralized tribal monarchies and kingdoms in Oyo and Benin. The Benin *gens* has a common ancestor, represented in a double four-lined scarification of the forehead. The tattoo of the Benin royal ancestor is a common feature of the sculptures of the Benin kings of the 14th to the 17th Centuries, as the Ife and British Museum bronzes show. The gentile nature of the dynasties survived the dynasties themselves, symbolizing the unchanging communal lands, communal labour, customary hospitality, dignity and mutual aid, all of which lived on despite successive and evolving social formations in Benin.

The Benin found by Dapper[63] in the 17th Century had already been changed by the European slave traffic. But it was still a 'communistic despotism' with the mark of the Benin *gens'* common kingly ancestor clear. The despotic side is to be seen even today in the bronzes in the Museum of Art in the IFAN Museum, next to the National Assembly in Dakar. In the glass cases lie little 15th Century bronzes of an Ivory Coast canoe with a bound slave in it, an Ashanti canoe bearing the head of a captive or slave downstream, and another of an execution. Nearby are large bronzes, also of the 15th Century, of slave-servants bearing an ancient king of the kingdom, and similar bronzes and tapestries of like tribal-despotic kingdoms in the Cameroons. They bear testimony within Africa itself to the twin communal and despotic nature of ancient 'African socialism', eulogized one-sidedly by Europe's patronizing 'African personality' thesis. The sketches of Roussier show the existence of upper and lower ranks, if not classes, in pre-colonial Benin, although they were made after it had been corroded by European slaving. Russel's sketches in Mungo Park's *Travels* at the end of the 18th Century show remnants of an old division of labour, for example in the Ghana and other gold industries, with women employed not only in agriculture and pottery but also in gold-mining and sifting. A century later, in the German edition of Stanley's *In Darkest Africa* (1890) there is a sketch of the floating fort, made of wood, by iron tools, and the river-fleet of the 'kingdom of Uganda' (Ganda), which was able to deter Stanley from war, in spite of the ravages of Speke and the missionaries after 1860. The navy and army of the Ganda were military extensions of a divison of labour in agriculture, cattle-breeding and iron-working and other crafts, and a pre-class separation of the Kabaka and Lukiko from the commoners.

Pictures in Dapper's books illustrated the 'class' and 'despotic' social hierarchy existing in 'La Basse Ethiopie' — what European 'Africanists' would now call Black Africa or Sub-Saharan Africa. The picture of the 'emperor of Ghana' on the walls of the Slave House Museum on the island of Gorée, near the most western point of Africa, reconstructed by Sheikh Anta Diop from the descriptions of El Bekri and El Idrisi, demonstrates this social stratification in pre-colonial West Africa. Heinrich Barth, with his pictures of Timbuktu, Kano and Morzuk[64] and of 'village life', shows the high level of architecture and of civilization still to be seen in the middle of the 19th Century, when his books were written, despite four centuries of European slaving. But his pictures also show relics of the social divisions of the old pre-colonial days, of inequality within those apparently egalitarian communities of the Sudan–Niger–Guinea complex.

That this inequality was inter-tribal as well as social we can see from the painting of a Khoi-Khoin rider and his San servant, both armed for hunting or defence.[65] Painted about 1850, a very 'White South African' picture, it shows not the old relationship between the pastoral Khoi-Khoin and the socially inferior Batwa — or San — culture, based on hunting, but a relationship specifically attributable to the Europeans' conquest and expropriation of the Khoi-Khoin in Namaqualand and the dispossession and decimation of the San by Boer and Briton alike. What is relevant here, however, is that these European depredations should have been able to produce the master-and-servant relationship illustrated in the Cape Town painting. It was possible because there already existed an inequality between the two societies, at different socio-economic levels — the one 'savage', as defined by Morgan and Engels, the other 'at the lower stage of barbarism'; and there existed too as Soga, Jabavu[66] and other early Cape African writers knew — an ancient domination of one tribe by another, within both Khoi-San and Bantu-speaking tribal communities. Every tribe stood in a relationship of real or potential antagonism to other tribes, a relationship that in certain conditions became one of tribal despotism. Thus, inter-tribal tributary dependence and inequalities existed between pastoral Bunyoro and agricultural Ganda, and between Tutsi and Hutu.

In the classical Greece of Socrates, Plato and Aristotle, the 'despot' was the head of the household, a patriarch who, after the failure of Lysistrata's revolt of the women and the continued enslavement of them by men, ruled in terms of family custom and tradition, but who also had under him, in addition to the women of the family, a certain number of slaves or former slaves whom he exploited in the house, its gardens and its workshops. In the Byzantine Empire, however, the 'despot' was the prince of a province, with seigneural or sovereign powers, or even a king with absolute powers — but still ultimately the living representative of the common ancestor of the *gens*.

The Pre-Colonial 'Surplus Axis'

Under 'oriental despotism' there was no landed property, but the Asian monarch with his upper caste, including the priests, controlled the agricultural and pastoral surplus, and that enabled him to command a vast army of non-agricultural workers who built cities, palaces, temples and monuments. Yet this control of the agricultural surplus was still 'in the name of the kingdom' and based ultimately on a history of common ownership by the *gens* of the means of all production and of the whole of the surplus. The appropriation as well as the production of the surplus was 'communal'. It was not a private one, spent arbitrarily on consumption by the ruling class; it was spent on public works, productive or ornamental, necessary or extravagant — extravagant, that is, to the eye of the modern observer. For the old communities under these Asiatic 'despots' — Hindu, Mogul, Mongol, Chinese, Mahratta, Afghan, Iranian or Turkish — the palaces and temples were not extravagances any more than the pyramids and Sphinx were, but social architecture, belonging to the whole community, even though they housed the living or dead bodies only of kings and high priests.

The absence of private property in no way meant that there was no exploitation of the rural population by a city-centred hierarchy in search of a greater surplus for the use of the non-agricultural labour — exploitation of 'country' by 'city'. Nor did it signify an absence of property in the urban means of production — urban handicrafts and manufacture, private dwellings with workshops and food-producing gardens, commerce and the material means for it — shops, storehouses and the means of transport by land, river and sea. If the absence of landed property precluded a feudal class proper, it did not preclude — indeed, through the centralized urban monopolization of the surplus and its redistribution, it led to — forms of merchant's capital and the rise of a corresponding merchant class. The kings and other 'despots' acted as self-interested middlemen between the rural creators of the surplus and the merchants who disposed of what was left of it by the time it had passed through the hands of the dynastic collectors of it. But, as Karl Marx explained:[67]

> In the ancient world the effect of commerce and the development of merchant's capital always resulted in a slave economy: depending on the point of departure, only in the transformation of a patriarchal slave system devoted to the production of immediate means of subsistence into one devoted to the production of surplus value.

In the countryside of the 'communal–despotic' African countries, the combination of farming (both agricultural and pastoral) with handicrafts tended to prevent the class differentiation of the old society — a differentiation made yet more difficult by the absence of landed property.

Urban artisans and slaves were ultimately maintained by the state, which 'owned' the rural land and also drew tribute from neighbouring tribes whose land it did not own, or allowed them refuge and usufruct on the basis of such tribute. The merchants capitalized the surplus remaining after the state had taken its share on behalf of the towns, including the slaves and certain artisans and specialists, as well as the additional surplus left over by urban artisan labour after its limited consumer and productive needs had been satisfied. The merchants' capital took the form of ships, external and internal commerce, private slaves in the non-state areas of the towns, vineyards and gardens, and a slave-trade linked in the interior with gold, copper and ivory, and abroad with salt, horses and spices. Inevitably the kings and priests were involved in this slave-trade with inland and coastal tribes and with nations beyond the seas and deserts. At the height of the Songhai Empire, the rate of exchange was one horse for seven slaves.

Leo Africanus, describing the appearance of Gao in 1510, wrote that a slave was then worth six dinars.[68] In 1447, when the Genoese merchant Malfante was at Touat, a slave cost only two dinars. The difference was very largely due to the rising but over-fulfilled demand from Portugal and other European slaving centres and to the new labouring functions of the slaves. In 1591, when Djouder defeated the Sonni dynasty, he forced Songhai to pay in tribute not only 100,000 pieces of gold but also no fewer than 1,000 slaves. The gold was part of a surplus accumulated from commerce, but this commerce within Guinea–Niger–Sudan and between that region and Saharan and Mediterranean states was itself, as Leo Africanus, Dapper and Ibn Khaldoun began to grasp, fed by the agricultural and pastoral surplus. Thus the common lands, 'owned' by the state and administered by the king in the name of the tribe or comity of tribes of which he was custodian, were themselves the basis for the creation of classes in the towns, tending to spread slavery, create new class struggles and divisions and undermine the communal basis of society. However, until the Papal–French seizure of the Canaries, Cape Verde and some of the Songhai commerce about 1400, the communal system prevailed over mercantile slavery.

This fact alone partly answers the question: was the primary, dominant factor in the 'lost past' the communal or the despotic? This question is basic to an understanding of the resistance to El Hadj Omar, of Samory, Behanzin, Tippoo Tib, Mwanga, Menelik and, most recently, of Haile Selassie, to 19th and 20th Century colonialism. All these resisters were accused by their colonial conquerors of defending a system of slavery and tyranny; the same charge was brought by Faidherbe and Lyautey of France, by Stanley and Karl Peters, and by Mussolini. The question of what was the primary nature and what the secondary nature of communal despotism is thus relevant to the liberation movements even of our own times.

The element of exploitation in 'African despotism' was not small and not exceptional. For this we have the authority of R. Mauny, the French expert who worked so long at the Institute Fondamentale de l'Afrique Noire (IFAN) in Dakar, the institute founded by the colonialist French in 1936, which since independence has collected and published some of the best source material on this and other subjects. Mauny estimated that the Sudan–Niger complex of states and the 'states' of Guinea, Gambia, Ashanti, Sierra Leone and Haut Volta exported northwards to Europe and then westwards to America in the 15th and 16th Centuries no fewer than four million slaves.[69] Scholars in Haut Volta, Senegal, Ivory Coast and elsewhere consider this a reasonable count. This was in the early period of European 'primary accumulation'. It would not have been possible for the trade to have reached such vast proportions unless the pre-colonial societies themselves had been structured and functioning in a way that could generate so great an export in so short a time. The curator of the IFAN Museum in Gorée, M. Ndiaye, has told me something of the African slave-trade both before and after colonialism.

Absolute numbers such as four million in 200 years mean little unless we also know the total number of people living in the areas concerned over the whole period. Assuming that half the traffic was 'indigenous' and the other half directed to, and by Europe, directly or through African intermediaries, then some three million people were probably sold as slaves within or between African 'states' in the years 1400–1600 while their dependents numbered about 10 million. The total number of people living in Africa during those two centuries, if we take three life-spans per century and a population rising in the period from some 30 million to some 60 million would, therefore, have been about 270 million; so that some 5% of the total population were sold as slaves and dependents. We should also make a similar count, absolute and relative, for the colonial slave traffic period. If one slave in two was sold, then the slave population would have been about 10% of the total population — no small proportion, since these were mainly urban slaves. The vast majority of the remaining 90% in this calculation were communal agriculturalists and herders, living like the great mass of the people in the less differentiated, pre-class tribal societies that predominated among the Batwa, Khoi-Khoin, Arab and Bantu-speaking tribes and groups of tribes in Africa.

The 'Khaldoun' Class Struggle

What 'class relations' — if any — formed the groundwork for the 'class struggles' — if any — in pre-colonial Africa? A class does not exist in isolation, through some relationship with the natural means of production. If that were so, every tribal society owning the land and working it in common would constitute a class, in a classless society (the same would be true of a 20th-Century socialist society). A class exists only in relation to both the material means of production and an antithetical, opposite pole: another class. Like conjugate numbers, classes exist in opposite pairs. A class implies an opposite class, a conflict, a polarization, a society in division but at the same time a whole, as it were a unity of opposites. A class can be conceived only in this dialectical manner, not in a static structure or in a functional manner. Opposing classes are joined in their conflict by and on their material nexus, the land, the factories, the means of transport — the material forces and means of production. They form the poles of a total socio-economic dynamic system within a given political economy. The active or dynamic principle of 'mediation' between the poles is the division of the total labour time of the producers who actually use the means of reduction into time needed for their own reproduction as producers and time given up to support the opposite social formation. This surplus labour time may then be further divided among various other groups.

The question is not purely academic, even when applied to the study of the old purely tribal and pre-class societies of most Khoi-Khoin, San, Bantu and Arab Africans; still less in relation to the more highly developed, exploitative but still communal societies of Zanj, West Africa, and the Congo kingdoms written about by Lopez and portrayed in sketches by de Bray in 1619,[70] as well as intermediate levels such as that of Zimbabwe. The social, possibly class, nature of pre-colonial societies is an antecedent of a question important to the liberation movements and also for that matter to modern colonialism, or 'neo-colonialism' as it is rather loosely called. The question is whether peoples who live under what appears to be a system of 'subsistence economy' or 'traditional economy' are part of capitalist colonialism or whether they still constitute a pre-capitalist social formation; whether they are in fact living in a traditional way at all or, if not, what is the essential nature of their mode of life away from the plantations, cities and mines in Africa even under independence? Samir Amin and others, including myself, have tried to examine this problem[71] and it remains open-ended. It is relevant also to 'Ujamaa', 'Harambee' and to collective labour in Tanzania, Kenya, Ethiopia under the Dergue, Mozambique under FRELIMO, Angola under MPLA, in Guinea, Guinea–Bissau and other independent African socialist or African Marxist or 'scientific Marxist' states — the last-named being the term given to their political philosophy by the first leaders of Benin since the change to Benin from Dahomey in 1976–7. Indirectly, the problem of classless and class social formations in, and on the borders of, capitalism may also throw some light on social structure and struggles in non-capitalist socialist states in Eastern Europe and the Far East. It is also relevant to real struggles between African workers and 'White' workers in South Africa. Are both classes 'working classes' or only the African class, and in the latter case can there be a class struggle between an African working class and a group of 'White' workers who do not form a class (they are clearly not employers, nor on all the evidence are they creating any surplus value)? These questions do not exhaust the relevance of the problem of the social character of the 'lost past' for modern liberation movements and for independence, but they are among the more important examples of it.

Primitive Communism

We find then, broadly speaking, that there are three types of pre-colonial societies. The first is a society almost wholly 'communist', tribal, pre-class. Slavery — which, indeed, was repugnant to the Nguni Bantu in contact with the Portuguese on the east coast after the late 15th Century, to the Khoi-Khoin and certainly to the Batwa hunters and fishermen — was virtually non-existent. Here there was a close kinship, with a chieftainship or kingship sometimes with a considerable 'kingdom'. But such a tribal communism, based on low development of the instruments of labour — and so also of war — with only a small disposable surplus product, was seldom isolated. It was often accompanied by inter-tribal conflict, war, struggles for land and cattle, the capture of slaves and the levying of tribute from the defeated clan or tribe, which was however usually left in possession of its lands (unlike the tithes and corvée of feudal Europe, which implied ownership of the land). Some slaves 'belonged' to the more powerfully placed chiefs and to the king, but only in their capacity as representatives of the *gens*, clan or tribe or tribal federation. For the rest, the slaves, like almost everything else, were the common property of the dominant *gens*, clan or tribe or tribal federation.

The system was one of clan or tribal despotism, with no class system. There was exploitation, in most cases of a minority of exogamous slaves by the majority — their captors. The majority were not exploited; they were, in this sense, the exploiters. At the same time, separately from the slaves and in a different way, they were oppressed by the upper echelons of the tribal administrative structure, the chiefs and priests — who none the less remained servants of the community, albeit privileged and powerful servants, comparable perhaps to a bureaucratic caste, to use the modern term applied in some socialist states.

The surplus produced by the slaves went into the general common surplus used for social reproduction of the whole political economy of the system of 'tribal despotism'. In fact, the king was seldom (in terms of custom, never) able to act arbitrarily — in this sense, despotically — but had to conform to tribal custom and traditions as custodian of the commonwealth. But that kings and queens, and high priests too, did act despotically and arbitrarily is well known. Such tribal despotisms could be large but well-knit social organisms, able to support huge armies out of the pastoral and agricultural surplus and to conquer both lower and higher social organisms. Thus the Mandingo conquered Songhai, the Mossi of Haut Volta — a perfect example of a 'tribal despotism' — captured Timbuktu in 1336; Queen Judith seized Axum in 979 and many nomadic tribes conquered settled states in the Niger–Sudan, Nile and East African lacustrine kingdoms. Among such groups were Khoi-San, Berber, Kabyle, Maasai and Danekil pastoralists.

This process parallels the conquests of the much higher Roman civilization at the hands of the 'barbarians'. In the conquests both of the Vikings, Goths, Franks or other 'Germans' and of the Mossi, the Mandingo and, later on, the Dahomey 'Amazons', the victors had strong, well equipped armies well supplied with food. They were supported by an ample surplus product, either from farming or from plunder during the actual warfare. The defeated 'states', on the other hand, however high their material and intellectual culture, were usually found to be decadent — that is to say, they were consuming their surplus dissolutely, unproductively and rapidly. Often, faced by the barbarians, they abandoned their magnificent cities in search of a new surplus to replace that which the 'despotic state' had appropriated and disposed of non-productively, or perhaps in some other place altogether. This transference or disappearance of the surplus, usually derived from an agricultural or pastoral population living on commonly owned land as members of a tribe and not as slaves, accounted for the sudden collapse of many city-states both in Asia and in Africa and among the Mayans (whose city–country division coincided with a hand–brain work and gentile division), Aztecs and Incas of South America in their successive upheavals in pre-colonial times. The simpler structure of the 'tribal-despotic' conquerors, their mobility (especially if, like the Teutonic and Bantu tribes, they were mainly pastoral), their use of weapons as the means of production of a surplus and the rapid 'productive consumption' of that surplus in the form of a well fed and well armed military machine, ensured that no similar collapse overtook these more primitive societies. They simply moved on to new conquests or were absorbed in the social systems of their old ones. Their 'governments' had no need of monumental buildings and a cumbersome bureaucracy, they could cope very well from an army tent. The same applied to the Japanese 'bakufu' ('tent government') during the 12th to 19th Century shogunate and to the 'moving tents' to which Richard Pankhurst has drawn attention in the case of Negus–Church–Ras despotism in post-Zagwe Ethiopia. This mobility accounted for several African victories over the better armed British and French, and to the 1899–1901 Anglo–Boer war in which Kruger's Boers, with their mobile government, without offices or papers, left Kitchener's ponderous bureaucratic military machine standing, bewildered.

The 'African–European' Mixed Mode of Production in Ethiopia

The second form of pre-colonial society was that exemplified almost uniquely by the tribal–feudal mixed mode which reigned in Ethiopia after the Zagwe dynasty, when the latter was followed by the 'Solomon' dynasty which the last Negus, Haile Selassie, traced back to the story of Solomon and Sheba out of whose meeting came the first Cub of Judah. This tribal–feudal system, with its rock church monoliths at Lalibela, its Gondar architecture, its militarized landed aristocracy, its Amharic monarchy (from 1270 to 1974 only one Negus-emperor was not Amharic), its powerful Rasses (whose strong communal and even tribal surplus-producing base made them look more like the Japanese medieval 'Daimyos' than West European feudal barons or even the Kiev boyars, who exploited both serfs and obschina village communities) its oppression of Galla, Sidoma, Tigre, Somali and other tribes (as the Samurai and Shoguns oppressed and marginalized the Ainu tribes) and the policy-making land-holding Coptic Church, existed properly in the non-desert highland valleys. There 2,000 to 3,000 metres above the Red Sea and the Danekil desert, lay Lake Tana and the natural irrigation of the Blue Nile, with rich top soil, mountain slopes that could be farmed by serfs, peasants and corvee or tithe-paying labourers coming from the church parishes, the Ras lands or surrounding tribes. There were giant valleys in which villages could be divided and so multiplied and verdant lake districts — a climate and terrain naturally ideal for feudalism. There was no need for massed slave labour or for a despotism based on 'hydraulic' needs, such as had formed along the Nile, Tigris–Euphrates, Indus, Ganges, Irriwaddy, Whang-Ho or Yangtse, Niger and Zaire rivers.

This most un-European 'feudalism' combined private landed property coming via Roman–Byzantium, with a tribal system that surrounded it and existed within its interstices, in its very pores, in the desert-like Ogaden to the east, the desert to the north and the Galla, Bantu and Khoi-Khoin to the south as far as the lower Rift Valley in Kenya. The 'feudal' system appeared as a form of class despotism, a superior social order over the surrounding, interlocked tribal or clan systems. At the same time the ruling dynasty itself tended to become a *gens* dynasty, a clan dynasty, with a common *gens* ancestor traced back to the mystic legend of Solomon. This clan or *gens*, which later became the Shoan *gens*, evolved into a feudal ruling class, and at the same time the ruling class appeared in clan form. But feudalism, not tribalism, was the dominant feature.

African Communal Despotism

The third form of pre-colonial society was yet another 'unity of opposites', quite different from the feudal–tribal complex of Ethiopia; a form found in Zanj and Guinea–Niger–Sudan rather than in Zimbabwe and Angola–Zaire. The 'Congo' kingdoms of 'Sao Salvador', with the court of Mbanzangungu in Bas Zaire, were centralized confederations with a kingship at the centre. The Mwene Mutapa kingdom, with its Zimbabwean stone-built fortified settlements and its gold mines, was a similar monarchical confederation.[72] Both were Bantu-speaking societies with a communal approach to land, labour and mutual co-operation. Both were at the same time settled and pastoral, grazing cattle on a vast pasturage on which, for long periods at any rate, there was no need to move on in search of new grazing grounds. Both the central African Congolese and the south-east African Mnguni Bantu kingdoms as well as Saharan, Nile and non-Bantu Lacustrine kingdoms, were exploiting women by the 15th Century, even though matriarchal forms persisted right up to the kingship itself, borne on by the momentum of their long earlier role in Bantu society. Both kingdoms had slaves, but on a relatively small scale. The slaves were prisoners of war. They were indications, not of a slave society, but on the contrary of a tribal society of the victory and dominion of one tribe over others.

It was this very inequality, intrinsic in tribalism all over the world, that accounted for the foundation of the tribal confederations, which were rarely federations of equals but were mostly headed and dominated by the strongest tribal group and by its king or queen, personifying the common ancestor. The Zimbabwe and Congo societies, centred respectively on Zimbabwe–Mwene Mutapa and on the Mbanzangungu courts, as well as the powerful Nyoro White Nile kingdom, were in what Morgan and Engels would have called the 'middle stage' of barbarism, with a tribal domination over external tribes and slaves gathered from them, and within each tribe a domination of the 'commoners' by chiefs or kings. This society, a higher form of the tribal despotism of the first kind, evolved not into the second, Ethiopian, form, but into that of the Zanj and Niger–Sudan complexes studied by Ibn Khaldoun and Ibn Battuta in particular.

This third form is the most complex of the three; together with certain achievements in social organization, architecture and learning in Ethiopia after the 10th Century Zagwe dynasty, it is the high water mark of pre-colonial culture. In it we find a mixed civilization; a pre-class, communitarian social system is completely mixed with a class society.

Whereas in feudal Europe the class system was rurally based, in Zanj the class component was dominant in the coastal cities, because of the wealth of the Swahili-Arab merchants and the relative strength of an industry based on iron and gold working. In the hinterland, with its agricultural and pastoral tribal peasantry and its gold, copper and iron mines, including Zimbabwe and the Mwene Mutapa tribal despotism, the non-class component of this mixed civilization was dominant. The Portuguese, with their powerful, murderous attacks, were able to destroy the class–structured towns of Kilwa, Zanzibar, Malindi and Mombasa,[73] and with them to destroy much of the class structure itself and bring about a certain regression towards a proto- or pre-class society. But despite all their efforts in the two centuries following da Gama (about 1500) they never succeeded in destroying Mwene Monomatapan society, even though their ravages led to the collapse of the Zimbabwe citadel itself.

In the mixed civilization of the Niger–Sudan complex, the non-class component was permanently dominant — a tribal, communitarian, egalitarian, co-operative system without landed property — communitarian, egalitarian and co-operative, that is, within the tribal *gens* unit but not, or rarely, between tribes. The tribal system comprised both the dominant tribal communitarianism on the land and in the villages and the system of tribal despotism by which the dominant tribe exacted tribute and slaves from other tribes. The tribes' production came essentially from agriculture, fishing and the herding of cattle, sheep and camels, with a number of domestic crafts and industries — a production fundamentally for subsistence, and for the greater part consumed. The surplus product was stored and accumulated under the custodianship of the chiefs or king, or was converted into palaces, monuments, storehouses — whole cities, indeed — and, always, into armies. This surplus ensured the social reproduction of the system, often as 'enlarged' and not merely 'simple' reproduction. It came not only from the farming surplus within the dominant tribe or clan itself — generally the majority group in a given 'kingdom' or confederation — but also from tribute paid in kind by other tribes, who generally retained their own farming lands, and finally from plunder taken in war in kind, including slaves.

Nominally, and by custom, the slaves belonged to the dominant tribal group in the name of the king, who disposed of the surplus product and of the slaves on behalf of the tribe as a whole. At first the slave belonged to the conquering clan or tribe, but he may then have become a personal servant. But even this was a form of tribal usufruct — the actual productive use of a slave, not the private ownership of him. Consequently, the slave could not be sold by his 'user', as he could later, when the Europeans came, be sold by his 'owner'. When he was sold, it was by the chief or king, who bartered him for gold, horses, weapons or food. The sale was a tribal, not a private, one, and again took place on the socio-economic boundaries of the tribal system — in its contacts with other tribes or other societies. But a slave is a slave, whether he belongs to an individual or, through a king, to a tribe: he still does not possess his own body. He gives the whole of his labour time as unpaid time and he dies if his owners do not feed and clothe him; he can be sold, or killed, at any time. Slaves can thus be exploited by a non-class, a pre-class, communitarian society, and in Egypt, Carthage, Axum and Meroe, and later in Zanj and Niger–Sudan, they were so exploited. The slave was always aware of this exploitation, even though the tribal commoners enjoyed little of the product of his surplus labour time. Other tribes learned of it when the slave himself was not a prisoner-of-war but a form of tribute, as when the defeated Songhai had to hand over 1,000 slaves to the conquering Djouder.

The main form of labour, however, was not slavery but 'free' communal labour. The steles of Axum, like the Egyptian pyramids, were erected by this form of labour. The work was massive, colossal; the present-day inhabitants of the place can no longer work out how to raise such monoliths, nor indeed could many European experts since Frobenius photographed the Axum steles in the early 20th Century. Equally massive were the mosques, such as the great 1555 mosque measured by Frobenius in Timbuktu, which was a communal effort. In Axum and Meroe, in west Sudan, the dominant form of labour was Egyptian-type communal slavery under a 'state communitarianism'. Elsewhere the bulk of the surplus came, not from slaves, but from within the communal system. The slave base prevailed in the cities, the communal base in the countryside. Taken as a whole, there can be little doubt that Axum and Meroe were early forms of the later Zanj and Niger–Sudan types of society, in a state of transition from the system of tribal despotism to the mixed civilization in which the bulk of the agricultural and pastoral surplus came from free communal labour on commonly owned land.

But it was this surplus that provided the wherewithal for the great trans-Saharan trade in gold, salt, slaves, horses, camels and spices which in turn brought the wealth that gave rise to the North African Mediterranean and Saharan 'oriental despotisms', the cities of Gao, Ghana, Timbuktu, Djenne and Kano, and to a great extent, also Benin. The ancient system of 'African socialism', classless, pre-class, formed the social, economic and political basis for a system combining slavery, mercantile exploitation and dynastic despotism. The dynasty itself was the apex of a considerable caste, a ruling caste, not a class in itself any more than a bureaucracy in a socialist state is a class. It was a caste living off a communitarian society. It exploited the commoners and managed the communal surplus as the upper caste of a tribal system, not as a slave-owning or tribe-owning class. It did not own any of the means of production, but controlled the public works, especially irrigation, the building of mosques, palaces and monuments, and the army, on behalf of the whole tribal community. When it fell, the whole tribal society fell with it, and no new class rose from among the commoners to take its place. Conquerors from other lands, not new classes, replaced the fallen dynastic castes.

The tribal ruling caste comprised the king and his court, owing their existence to tribal law and custom, including the laws of Islam and ancestor-worship; the priestly sub-caste, which often threatened the power of the dynasty itself and disposed of much of the common labour and property; armies of cavalry and infantry, and often navies as well, and finally a section of the merchant class. But these last were a free, foreign factor rather than an indigenous tribal element, coming like the slaves from outside the tribe, though not of course bound like them. Many of them, as on the periphery of Zanj, Benin, Mali, Ghana, Gao and Songhai, rose from tribalism to become merchants in the ports or river trading towns. Others came from different parts of Africa, from Arabia (such as the aristocratic Mazrui resisters of East Africa), India, Iran and even China. They formed a distinct merchant class, with its own internal divisions — retailer, wholesaler, exporter, importer. Their goods came both from a tribal hinterland, which was their market as well, and from abroad, where they likewise found an export market.

The tribal upper caste, the classes of slaves and merchants, had under them the communitarian, 'egalitarian', co-operative tribal system for the reproduction of the system, for the surplus product — which financed both slavery and commerce — and also for a market, with trade conducted by barter. The communal system not only contained the majority of the population but also formed the base of the dynasty, of commerce and of slavery. It was the fundamental, dominant factor in the economy, the basis of the 'state'.

In the mixed civilizations of classless and class society in Zanj and the West African complex, the classless society was primary, and the class society secondary and derivative. It is essential to grasp the primary nature of the communal aspect and the secondary nature of the exploitative aspect for a proper understanding of the two-sided nature of resistance to colonialism; to see how colonialism reversed the order of things, making the primary factor secondary. Here is the key to an understanding of what 'African socialism' and 'African Marxism' mean within a political economy inherited from this colonial inversion of the 'lost past'.

Notes

1. B.M. Kies, 'The Contribution of the Non-Europeans to World Civilization', pubished lecture, Cape Town, 1953, p. 36.

2. El Bekri, (trans. V. Monteil), IFAN (Institute Fondamentale de l'Afrique Noire), Dakar, 1968; El Idrissi, *Description of Africa and Spain* (trans. K. Dozy, M.J. de Goede), Leiden, 1866.

3. Ibn Haouqal, *Description de l'Afrique* (trans. de Slane), Paris, 1842.

4. Ibn Khaldoun, *History of the Berbers*, 4 Vols, 1925–56; *The Maqadimmah* (trans. Rosenthal), London, 1958.

5. Ibn Battuta, *The Travels of Ibn Battuta*, London, 1929, 1962; *Voyages* (trans. Defremey, Sanguinetti), Vols. 1–4, Paris, 1848, 1893, 1914, 1922.

6. El Masudi, *The Meadows of Gold and Mines of Gems (Muraj El Dhabab, 935)*, (trans. Sprenger), London, 1841; (Paris 1861).

7. Leo Africanus (Al Hassan Ibn Mohamed el Wezas al Fasi), *Descrizione Dell' Africa*, Venice, 1556; *Delle Navigazione et Viaggi*, vol. 1 (G.B. Ramusio), Venice, 1550–9; *De Totius Africae Descriptione*, Antwerp, 1556.

8. Dapper, *Beschreibung von Afrika*, Amsterdam, 1670 (trans. London, 1968).

9. Duerte Lopez, *Relazione de Reame di Congo* (trans. Pigafetta), Rome, 1591–1601; German trans. 1619 (with illustrations by de Bry). In IFAN Library, Dakar.

10. A. Cresques, Catalonian map drawn 1375, showing Sudan, with Keita kings, in IFAN Library, Dakar.

11. Mungo Park, *Travels in the Interior Districts of Africa, 1795–7*, London, 1798, Paris, 1820.

12. H. Barth, *Travels and Discovery in North and Central Africa*, 5 vols, London, 1857 et seq.

13. Leo Frobenius, *Kulturgeschichte Afrikas*, Vienna, 1933; *History of African Civilization*, Berlin, 1909; *The Childhood of Man* (trans. Keane), 1909.

14. H.S. Wilson (ed.), *Origins of West African Nationalism*, London, 1969 (collection of original addresses and writings).

15. Kwame Nkrumah, in *Africa and the World*, April 1968; *I Speak of Freedom*, London, 1961; *Autobiography*, London, 1957; *Address to OAU*, Addis Ababa, 24 May 1963; *Consciencism-Philosophy and Ideology of Decolonisation*, London, 1964.

16. Sekou Toure, *Discours* (with de Gaulle), Conakry, 25 August 1958; 'Experience Guineenne et Unite Africaine', with foreword by Aime Cesaire, in *Presence Africaine*: in *Relazioni Internationale*, no. 1/1, January 1972.

17. Amilcar Cabral, 'Declaration of Principles', Cuba, in *La Vittoria O La Morte*, Milan, 1971; 'On Makonde Sculpture', *UNESCO Corrierre*, November 1973; *Die Theorie als Waffe*, Berlin, 1968; *Die Ekonomie der Befreing*, Frankfurt, 1969.

18. L.S. Senghor, *Selected Poems*, London, 1977; *Discours*, Dakar, 19 April 1962; *Negrita e Politica Africana*, Rome, 5 October 1962; *Theorie et Pratique du Socialisme Senegalais; Discours*, Tunis, 1–7 July 1975; *Discours*, Brazzaville, 24 February 1974; *Pour une Relecture Africaine de Marx et d'Engels*, Dakar, 1976.

19. Julius Nyerere.*The Arusha Declaration and Tanu's Policy on Socialism and Self-Reliance*, Dar es Salaam, 1967. *Discours*, Dakar Assembly, 19 April 1962.

20. Agostino Neto, 'Speeches, 1962–71', in M. Albano, *Angola*, Milan 1972; in *Vittoria o Morte, MPLA*, 1970; *Un Popolo in Rivoluzione*, Milan, 1971; *Colonialismo, Cultura e Rivoluzione*, Milan, 1972

21. Samora Machel, 'Speeches, 1969–77', in *FRELIMO Pamphlets* (Newport St., London); *Mozambique; Sowing the Seeds of Revolution*, London, 1974; *Message to the Nation*, Mozambique, 25 June 1975.

22. J. Nyerere, *Arusha Declaration*, op. cit.

23. Ibn Khaldoun (1332–1406) put forward a Marxist principle of historical materialism when he 'elaborated to explain the progression of history, a dialectical "theory" opposing the role of the egalitarian spirit of solidarity

(asibiyya) to the dictatorship of the king' and declared 'the differences in customs and institutions of the various peoples depend on the manner in which each of them provided for its subsistence.' (J. Kizerbo in *UNESCO General History of Africa*, California, 1981, vol. 1, p. 738).

24. S.A. Benson, *African Repository, XXXII*, in Wilson, *W. African Nationalism*, op. cit: Inaugural Addresses, 1856, 1858, pp. 87–91.

25. E.W. Blyden, Addresses, 1857, 1865, in Wilson, op. cit., pp. 79–86 and 94–104; *Discourse*, May 1880, in *Christianity, Islam and the Negro Race*, 1877; in *Sierra Leone Times*, 3 June 1893; *African Life and Customs*, London, 1908.

26. J.A. Horton, *West African Countries and Peoples*, London, 1868.

27. J.E. Casely Hayford, *Ethiopia Unbound: Studies in Race Emancipation*, London, 1911; *Gold Coast Native Institutions with Thoughts upon a Healthy Imperial Policy for the Gold Coast and Ashanti*, London, 1903.

28. Tippoo Tib (Ahmed Ibn Muhammed, 1838–1905), *Autobiography* (Brussels African Museum Royal Library material on 'T. Tib').

29. J. Kizerbo, *Storia del l'Africa*, Milan, 1980; in *UNESCO General History of Africa*, vols. 1 and 2.

30. S.M.Cissoko, *Tombouctou et l'Empire Songhay*, Dakar, 1975.

31. Centro Camuni, Capo di Ponte, Brescia, Document, 1984; showing 0 as start of East African Early Iron Age; B.G. Trigger, *International Journal of African History*, New York, 1969; H. De Contenson, in *UNESCO General History of Africa*, vol. 2., p. 357, on iron in early Axum; J. Hiernaux, F. Maquet, *L'Age du Fer au Kibiro* (Ouganda), in *1968 Annals du Musee Royal de l'Afrique Central*, Tervuren.

32. M. Poznansky, in *UNESCO General History*, vol. 2, p. 539.

33. T. Shaw, *Igbo Ukwu*, 2 vols, London–Ibadan, 1972; M. Poznansky, 'The Iron Age in East Africa', in W. Bishop and J. Clark, *Background to Evolution in Africa*, Chicago, 1972; on Igbo Ukwu in *Archaeology*, 25 April 1973.

34. Reports on 'Sao Bento' and 'Santo Alberto' shipwrecks in 16th Century, and 'Stavinesse' wreck, (W.M. Theal, repeated in *Oxford History of South Africa*, vol. 1, 1973), showing that Natal and Cape Nguni smelted iron; Wikar, *Journal*, Cape Town, 1935: Moffat, *Missionary Labours and Scenes in Southern Africa*, London, 1842, 1894; showing Sotho mining and smelting of iron, copper and tin as ancient crafts.

35. K. Marx, *Abstract of Morgan's Ancient Society*, Moscow, 1945; F. Engels, *The Origins of the Family, Private Property and the State*, Moscow. (1st edition: Zurich, 1884.)

36. Khartoum Museum; J. Leclant, 'The Empire of Kush', in *UN*, vol. 2, pp. 292–4; A.A. Hakem, 'The Civilization of Napata and Meroe', *UN*, vol. 2, p. 309; W. Michalowsky, *Meroe*, 1967; U. Monneret de Villard, *Nubia, Meroe*, 1935–8.

37. Y.M. Kobishanov, 'Aksum' in *UN*, vol. 2, pp. 383–95; Tekle Tsadik Mekouria, 'Christian Aksum', in *UN*, vol. 2, pp. 402–18; Abu Mabuza, 'The Ethiopian Monarchical System', in *Challenge*, New York, February 1968.

38. J. Kizerbo, in *UN*, vol. 1, pp. 739–40, p. 740.

39. J. Kizerbo, *UN*, vol. 1, p. 740: 'As for production based on slavery, did it exist in Africa? Here again, the reply must be negative.' During a Russian debate on 'Asiatic despotism', the historian, Struve, said: 'I saw as immediate producers only the peasants and craftsmen of Egypt ... I saw no slaves in Egypt, since neither Eduard Meyer nor Maspero nor Breasted had seen them.' (in S.P. Dunne, *The Fall and Rise of the Asiatic Mode of Production*, London, 1982, p. 51); J.H. Breasted, *Ancient Records of Egypt*, vol. 4, Chicago, 1906.

40. S. Pankhurst, *A Culture History of Ethiopia*, London, 1955; R. Pankhurst, *An Introduction to the Economic History of Ethiopia from Early Times to 1800*, Addis Ababa, 1966: on 'moving camp-capitals' and semi-tribal nature of 'feudalism', pp. 29–35, 52–8, 77, 107, 154, 173; Pankhurst read a paper in Addis Ababa in 1982 on the 'moving tent' capitals, which hindered any urban private property or capitalism. Marx had dealt with this in *Theories of Surplus Value*, letters, and *Tribune* articles. (H. Jaffe, *Marx e Colonialismo*, Milan, 1977).

41. For the privatization of land and people (slaves, serfs, wage-workers) by the Ptolemies (323 BC to 30 BC) see A.E. Samuel, *Ptolemaic Egypt*, and *Encyclopaedia Britannica*, 15th edition, vol. 6, p. 484; and T.G.H. James, ibid, p. 468–70 on communal interests, by contrast, of Pharaonic Egypt. The privatization was developed by Roman colonialism in Egypt (30 BC to AD 642).

42. Engels wrote

> When Athens was at the height of prosperity the total number of free Athenian citizens, women and children included, amounted to about 90,000. The slaves of both sexes numbered 365,000 and the dependents — immigrants and freed slaves — 45,000. Thus for every adult male citizen there were at least 18 slaves and more than 2 dependents. In Corinth, at the city's zenith, its (number of slaves) was 460,000 and in Aegina 470,000. Rome had 40,000 mine-slaves in Carthage; Cicero's Rome had 2,000 slave-owners — in both 10 times the number of free burghers. (*Origin of Family*, chapters 5 and 9.)

43. T.G.H. James op. cit; E.F. Wonte, *Late Kandy-side Papers*; A. de Book, *The Egyptian Coffin Texts* (trans. O. Faulkner), London 1935–61; Ipuwer, in *UN2*, on 'Intermediate Periods' when nomads and tribes failed to change the property(less) relations.

44. *Encyclopaedia Britannica*, 15th edition, vol. 11, p. 492: 'In the Old Babylonian period slave labour was never an economically relevant factor.' Ur documents contain few references to private property. Hammurabi law made land inalienable, except under special royal-sanctioned conditions. R. Meissner, *Babylonia and Assyria*, vol. 2, 1925; L.M. Diakanoff (ed.), *Ancient Mesopotamia*, 1969; J. Oates, *Babylon*, 1979; B. Boumaza, *Ne Ayatollah, Ne Emiri*, Milan, 1981 (on Iran).

45. Private property as ownership (as distinct from possession or usufruct — a distinction on which Marx insisted, *Capital*, vol. 3; *Grundrisse*, London, 1973, pp. 475, 477) was absent from primitive communist as well as Olmec, Mayan, Toltec, Aztec and Inca tribal or communal despotisms. See Engels, op. cit. on pre-class societies in America, based on H. Morgan, *Systems of Consanguinity and Affinity of the Human Society*, Washington, 1871; B. de Sahagun, *Historia General de las Cassas de Nueva Espana* (in Mexico after 1529), 5 vols, 1938; B. Diaz del Castillo (1519–21), *The True History of the Conquest of New Spain* (trans. A.P. Maudslay), 5 vols, 1908–16; I. Bernal, *The Olmec World*, 1969; G.C. Vaillant, *The Aztecs of Mexico*, 1966; G. de la Vega, *Royal Commentaries* (1609) (trans. A. Gheerbrandt), 1961; P. de Cieza de Leon (1553), *La Chronica del Peru* (trans. V.W. von Hagen), 1959; S.F. Moore, *Power and Poverty in Inca Peru*, 1958; A. Metraux, *The Incas*, 1963; B.C. Brundage, *Lords of Cuzco*, 1967; B. Cobo, *Historia del Nuovo Mondo* (17th Century), 4 vols. 1890–5; G.P. de Ayola (1534), 1200-page letter to King Charles V in Copenhagen Royal Library (trans. A. Poznansky, 1944); and W.H. Prescott, *History of the Conquest of Peru*, 1847 (first

English history of Incas); Pedro Sarmiento de Bamboa, *History of Incas*, based on oral accounts (42), sent to King Philip, 1572; F. Garrido, *Historia de las Clases Trabajadoras*, Madrid, 1970 (first published 1871).

46. K. Marx, letters to Engels; articles to *New York Tribune*, in *Marx on Colonialism*, New York, 1972, with sources (T. Macaulay, F. Bernier, H. Jones, T.S. Raffles, and other colonial officials; plus others in pp. 366–82.)

47. K.A. Wittvogel, *Oriental Despotism*, Newhaven, Mass., 1957; J. Needham, *History of Chinese Civilization and Science*, 1956; Kuo Mo Jo (1950), 'La Societé Esclavagiste Chinoise', in *Recherches Inter-nationales à la lumière de Marxisme*, May–June, 1957; on China, Hegel wrote: 'there is no hereditary aristocracy in China, no feudal situation ... In China we have the reality of absolute equality and all the differences that exist are possible only in connection with administration ... Since equality prevails in China, but without any freedom, despotism is necessarily the mode of government.' *Philosophy of History*, vol. 2, p. 124 (trans. J. Sibrec Willey) New York, 1944.

48. J. Kizerbo, in *UN*, vol. 2: 'in primitive societies, contrary to European experience (ancient and Germanic) where the private ownership of land developed from its communal ownership, in Africa there is no sign of private ownership. There was no private ownership or assignment of land, hence no fief. The land was an inalienable community asset.'; J. Suret Canale: 'There is no private ownership of land, in the sense of Roman law of the Civil Code' (of France) in *Les Sociétés Traditionelles en Afrique Tropicale et le Concept de Mode de Production Asiatique*, Paris, 1964, p. 108.

49. The Stalin 'Short Course' which dogmatized historical materialism into an obligatory sequence: primitive communism–slavery–feudalism–capitalism–socialism, was rejected by Trotsky, E.S. Varga (later Stalin's economist), and others (see S.P. Dunne, op. cit.), and, separately, by Suret-Canale, Godelier, S. Amin, G. Frank, I. Wallerstein, but E. Mandel, *The Formation of the Economic Thought of Karl Marx*, London, 1971, ch. 8, confines Marx's 'Asiatic mode' to Asia only. J. Kizerbo, op. cit., thinks it little applicable to Africa. H. Jaffe, *Africa*, Milan, 1978, applies it to certain class-forms in East, West and North Africa.

50. L.S. Senghor, op. cit.

51. K. Marx, *Marx on Colonialism*, op. cit.

52. Potekhin, 'Land Relations in African Countries', in *Peoples of Asia and Africa*, no. 3, Moscow, 1962.

53. Prof. Davidson, Leningrad, USSR Academy of Sciences Africa Institute, in discussions with author, February, 1966.

54. J. Suret-Canale, op. cit.; and *Afrique Noire, Geographie, Civilizations, Histoire*, Paris, 1962. On 'despotism', he wrote: 'In this system, in fact, the sharpening of class exploitation, far from destroying the structures founded on collective ownership of the land, strengthened them: they constituted the framework within which the surpluses were drawn off, the very prerequisite of exploitation.'

55. El Idrisi, Leo Africanus, Ibn Khaldoun, op. cit.; E. Lopez, op. cit.; D. de Bry, *Beschreibung des Konigsreiches Kongo in Afrika*, Frankfurt, 1597.

56. Ibn Battuta, op. cit.

57. El Masudi, op. cit.

58. El Bekri, op. cit.

59. Ibn Haqal, op. cit.

60. Cissoko, op. cit.

61. El Idrisi, op. cit.

62. *African National Congress (South Africa)*, in 'Sechaba' map showing 'Azania' to be remote from S. Africa (reproduced in H. Jaffe, *Africa*, op. cit., p. 105).

63. F. Alvarez, *Travels*, 1540, (trans. London, 1890); O. Dapper, op. cit.; Russell's and Paul Rossier, in IFAN Library, Dakar.

64. H. Barth, op. cit., sketches of Timbuktu, Kano, Morzuk life.

65. T. Baines, painting (c.1850) of Khoi-Khoin with San 'client', W. Fehr collection, Cape Town.

66. J.H. Soga, *Amaxhosa Life and Customs*, Lovedale, Cape (undated) and *South-East Bantu*, Lovedale, 1930; D.D.T. Jabavu, *The Black Problem*, Lovedale, 1920; 'Bantu Grievances', in *Western Civilization and the Natives of South Africa* (ed. I. Schapera), London, 1934.

67. K. Marx, *Capital*, vol. 3 (on 'merchant's capital'), Moscow, 1959.

68. Leo Africanus, op. cit.

69. R. Mauny, *Tableau Geographique de l'Ouest Africain au Moyen Age, d'Apres les Ouvres Ecrites, la Tradition et l'Archeologie*, Dakar, 1961.

70. E. Lopez and D. de Brey, op. cit.

71. S. Amin, A.G. Frank, H. Jaffe, *Quale*, 1984, Milan, 1975, Madrid 1976.

72. G. Caton Thompson, *The Zimbabwe Culture*, Oxford, 1931; B. Davidson, *Old Africa Rediscovered*, London, 1959; *Guide to African History*, London, 1963; *The Africans, a Cultural and Social History*, London, 1973; Hailey, *African Survey*, 1938–57; J. Kizerbo, *Histoire de l'Afrique*, Paris, 1971, Turin 1977; R. Michelet, *African Empires and Civilizations*, Paris, 1933; B.A. Ogot, J.A. Kierman, *Zamani*, Dar-es-Salaam, 1969; M. Shinnie, *Ancient African Kingdoms*, London, 1965; Summers, R. (ed.), *Zimbabwe: A Rhodesian Mystery*, London, 1963; H. Jaffe, *Zimbabwe Memo*, Luxembourg, 1980 (for sources).

73. E.G. Ravenstein, *A Journal of the First Voyage of Vasco da Gama*, 1898; D. Barbosa, *Descriptions, 1500*, 1517–8, Hakluyt Society, London, 1918; Jao de Barros, *Descriptions* and *Romerugte Scheepstogt van Francisco d'Almeida na Oost-Indien*, Leyden, 1706; Diogode Alcancora to Emmanuel I, King of Portugal, 20 November, 1506; J.H. Van Linschoten, *Descriptio Totius Guineae Tractus Congi Angolae et Monomotapae* (trans. C.P. Burger), The Hague, 1934 (original, 1599); J. de Barros, 1552 — in 4 vols. in Portuguese, Lisbon, 1944–6.

PART TWO

European Colonialism — Resistance and Collaboration

European Colonialism — Resistance and Collaboration

Europe was driven outwards not by wealth but by poverty. A millennium after the Crusades, Japan which, like Europe, was rich agriculturally, but poor by nature in industrial potential, renounced her old despotic, shogunate past in favour of capitalist-colonialism. Africa, like Asia and America, was not poor in mineral and industrial potential and was able to survive and develop without extra-continental expansion on the basis of enlarged reproduction within communist or communal despotic societies. The 'surplus axis' had long been communal at both ends outside Europe, where, on the contrary, it had long become privatized at both its poles. The latter system, a product of the geo-economic conditions of Europe, found Europe inadequate to its purposes. Whereas in Africa, America and Asia — as for a very long time also in Europe — use-value was the ruling principle of production and distribution, in Europe, from about the time of the Crusades (late 11th Century to 12th Century), exchange value slowly but surely became the driving force of society. This force had an impulsive effect on the Atlantic and Mediterranean ports of Europe.

The first recorded commercial explorations by Genoese merchants in Africa were as early as 1291, in Dante's lifetime. In 1341 Portuguese merchants were going to the Canaries with the Italians, and three years later the Vatican ordered the French admiral de la Cerda to seize the Canaries. By 1364 Normans from France were trading and raiding along the Cape Verde coast; by 1375 the Spanish in Majorca knew enough to enable Cresques to show Timbuktu and Gao on a map, with other Mali and Niger towns. In 1402 merchants from Toulouse were settling in Timbuktu and Gao, and in the same year de Bethencourt seized the Canaries. Thus the 14th Century saw considerable penetration of West and North Africa by Italian, Portuguese, French and Spanish colonialists.[1] This period of primitive primary accumulation prepared the 'take-off' of capitalism, which Marx put at the year 1500.

The Portuguese seized the Azores in 1431, and Pope Martin V legalized an already established European slave-trade. In 1445 the Portuguese began slaving from Gorée, off Senegal; by 1447 they had reached the Gambia river, and the first marked African resistance was reported when they tried to extend the slave traffic in Guinea. By 1460 missionaries were slaving in the Congo, using Ngola, the Kumbundu king. In 1462 the Portuguese were in Sierra Leone, in 1469 Gomez was threatening the civilization of Ghana; in 1471 Fernando Po penetrated the Cameroons coast; in 1482 the Portuguese were erecting their fortified slaving posts at Da Mina and São Miguel in Guinea and Luanda; in 1482–5 Diego Cão slaved up the Congo river and down as far as Namibia; in 1484 de Alveira came armed into the Benin court and Namibian Khoi-Khoin fought off Cão's conquistadores. Financing the Portuguese, and accompanying them on some of their voyages, were Germans from the old Hanseatic League, particularly from Antwerp, Frankfurt and Hamburg: 'hidden German colonialism' was beginning.[2] In 1487 Khoi-Khoin tribalists resisted Bartholomew Diaz's armed bands, but Diaz succeeded in rounding the Cape of Good Hope. In 1488 the Portuguese missionary du Covilha tried to undermine the feudal regime of Eskender in Ethiopia. By 1490 Arguin was shipping a thousand slaves a year to Portugal and its fortress town of Da Mina. A plantation economy was started in Santiago, Cape Verde.

By about 1500 Portugal alone had taken some 700 tons of gold out of Africa, a massive 'primary accumulation' for nascent, still weak capitalism, worth in today's money 8 billion US dollars — the first instalment of some 13,500 tonnes of gold (worth about 160 billion US dollars) estimated by Mauny, of Dakar and Paris Universities, to have come out of the Niger–Sudan complex alone during the whole colonial period.[3]

By 1490 São Tomé was a slave port, and slaving and sugar plantations worked by slave labour had reached Benin itself, where the king was corrupted by missionaries. In the same year the missionaries were baptizing those chiefs who collaborated, while Wolof and other peoples were opposing armed resistance to the slavers. The capture of Granada, the last Arab stronghold in Spain, by Spanish mercantile-feudalism in 1492 paved the way for an even more rapid escalation of European colonialism in Africa. By 1500 Vasco da Gama began the Portuguese destruction of the civilization of Zanj, and, to a lesser degree, of 'Monomatapa', and from then on all three types of African despotism began to oppose mass resistance to the Europeans.

By 1503 Lisbon was already exporting African slaves to the Spanish slave-owners in the West Indies, and Portugal had surrounded almost the whole of Africa with its armies of slavers. In 1493 Pope Alexander VI had divided the world into Spanish and Portuguese spheres of interest, in effect pronouncing for the first time that Europe was to rule the world.

Colonialism as Genesis of Europe

The 15th Century, then, saw the multiplication of the primary accumulation of European capitalism; and Africa played the most important part in the process as the principal arena of European colonialism, the very genesis and foundation of the capitalist system. From the turn of the 16th Century the Americas and Asia were added to this foundation, and out of this totality arose capitalism and modern Europe itself. Before capitalist colonialism there was no Europe,[4] only a collection of feudal, mercantile and tribal towns, farms, villages, discrete states and kingdoms vying and warring with each other, just as in Africa, but on a different property basis — that of private property in the land. Europe then was neither a concept nor a reality, at most a vague idea that Arabs — but not 'Europeans' — had had long ago of some place north-west of Greece. As long as Europe remained isolated from the world, there was no Europe. When it became connected with, and dependent on, first Africa, then the Americas and finally Asia, it began to become a reality and an idea. Only when Portuguese, Spanish, French, Italian, Dutch, English, German, Danish and Swedish confronted and clashed with Africa, America and Asia did the need arise for them to consider themselves as a set, a whole, different from, hostile to and, eventually, superior to Africans, Americans and Asians. Colonialism gave them a common interest.

This common interest — slaving, plantations, the world market, looting, precious metals, spices and territory, markets and sources of wealth — was also the source of their conflicts among themselves. From 1500 on they had already started to quarrel and fight over the colonial booty. In these intra-European conflicts Portugal and Spain had in time to give way to Holland and France, and these in the 18th Century to Britain, while German 'hidden colonialists', Calvinists, Catholics and Jews alike, steadily garnered what they could of the booty without shedding their blood or losing their own property in the process. The 'scramble for Africa' that led to the 1884–5 Berlin Conference had its roots in four centuries of struggles between the European powers for the division of Africa. Colonialism, the basis of European unity, was the basis also of its disunity.

Europe was born out of colonialism, as the exploiting, oppressing, negating pole that tried always to destroy and assimilate its opposite pole: the rest of the world. Europe was 'the emergence of novelty out of the conflict of opposites' — capitalism and those pre-capitalist systems of oriental, American and African despotisms* which this capitalism

---

* The American, Asian and African modes of production may be defined in terms of their 'surplus axis' which was communal at the producing end, and also, via the despots, at the distribution end as well (of the form C—C, where C = 'communal'). The 'European modes of production', after 'primitive communism', were based on privately employed labour and privately owned land at the producer end and private consumers or redistributors at the distribution end of the surplus axis (i.e. of form P—P).

destructively assimilated. This assimilation was its first life-blood. This conflict was the first content of colonialism; after the destruction and assimilation the content of it changed. The first form was that of 'primary accumulation', from the 14th Century to the 19th; the next was that of regular accumulation, with an inertial momentum carried forward from the primary accumulation.

With capitalism arose Europe, and with Europe the myth of 'European civilization' — a civilization based on African slavery, American plantations, Asian spices, precious metals from all three 'non-European' continents — based, too, on Indian numerals, Arab algebra, astronomy and navigation (an Arab–Indian took da Gama to India from Mombasa) and Chinese gunpowder, paper and compasses. This non-European European civilization was the narcissus-like admiration of its own conquests. The sword, gunfire, murder, rape, robbery and slavery formed the real material basis for the idea of European superiority.

It was out of this process that the very idea of a European man arose, an idea that did not exist even in etymology before the 17th Century. Before the slave-trade in Africa there was neither a Europe nor a European. Finally, with the European arose the myth of European superiority and separate existence as a special species or 'race'; there arose indeed the myth of race in general, unknown to mankind before — even the word did not exist before the lingua franca of the Crusades — the particular myth that there was a creature called a European, which implied, from the beginning, a 'white man'. Colonialism, especially in Africa, created the concept and ideology of race.[5] Before capitalist-colonialism there were no races; but now, suddenly and increasingly, there were races: once born, the myth grew into a 'reality'.

Mankind's ignorance about the existence of that European invention, race, was so deep that even as late as 1619, after two centuries of slaving, the Portuguese writer López could portray the European and the non-European, not as such, but as equal men, dignified and altruistic.[6]

But López's view was exceptional: long before his time, racialism had become an instrument for mass expropriation, slaving and decimation in Africa, as in Asia and America. Colonialism was always racialist, from soldier to missionary, king to trader, and — from the 19th Century — from capitalist to 'socialist'.

The chronology of the expansion of colonialism in the 16th, 17th, 18th and 19th Centuries is also the chronology of racialism. But it is at the same time a history of struggles between capitalist colonialism and the 'lost past'. Colonialism won this war clearly and thoroughly everywhere. But it could not win by merely destroying the lost past: it had to transform it, to assimilate its exploitative non-communal features into capitalism itself and reshape the communal features to make them part of the same capitalism. The process of transforming the enemy into a part of the victor was long and difficult for Europe: the resistance was never-ending. Many African peoples still say they were conquered and dispossessed, but never defeated and subjected in spirit. Nor was this resistance even and simple, and it is with the complexity of it that we are now concerned.

The Resistance–Collaboration Contradiction

There are many questions: was resistance general or exceptional? Did Africa 'crumble before the European invasion', as some have implied from the work of Basil Davidson, who, after André Gide,[7] is the most important exposer of European atrocities in 20th-Century Africa and is, with Sartre, the grand architect of the 'African personality'[8] and historian of the 'lost past'? Or was there a grand resistance, as the Russian Davidson and others[9] have implied? If there was, what was its motivation? Was it to conserve what is now the 'lost past'? Did the African kings who resisted do so in defence of the old system of slavery and slaving and 'African despotism'? Why did some kings decide: 'If we can't beat them, join them'? What was the weight of this collaboration with colonialism? That it existed can be seen in the West African cannon preserved at Gorée, used by African kings to secure or subject African slaves, and from a thousand and one pieces of evidence. Was resistance to an inevitably victorious higher order of society reactionary or progressive, humanitarian considerations apart? What is the link between resistance to 'primary accumulation' and the modern class struggle and liberation struggle in Africa? The evidence for the existence of mass resistance is vast and impressive. More and more of the mountain of facts will become known as the mists over Africa are dispersed. Our own chronology will be found to be fragmentary and wanting; research continues in Dar es Salaam and elsewhere.

Resistance in the 14th and 15th Centuries was as sporadic as were the colonialist incursions of those centuries. In the 16th Century the slave traffic and expropriations, physical and spiritual, by force exerted on the peoples' bodies by slavers and soldiers and on their minds by missionaries, produced an equal and opposite reaction of resistance. But it also produced a growing, and proportional, collaboration. Each reaction, resistance and collaboration, reflected a different aspect of the pre-colonial societies: the one their communal, the other their despotic nature. But there were despots who also led mass resistance. There was a definite social cause for this: in brief, the greater relative weight of the communal over the class components of the old societies now being torn asunder by European colonialism.

There is architectural evidence of resistance in the numerous forts built along the coasts and rivers by all colonial countries. The fort of Elmina in Ghana, the Luanda fort, the Dutch Castle in Cape Town, the

Portuguese Fort Jesus in Mombasa, the fort of Gorée, the fort in Zanzibar, the later French forts in Senegal, in Guinea, in Mali, the Foreign Legion fortresses in West and North Africa and the numerous British, Danish, Italian, Portuguese, Dutch, Belgian, Spanish and German forts were not built for comfort, but for two main purposes: one, the slave traffic and slavery; the other, to contain the tribes. One, then, was to contain slave rebellions, the other to contain rebellions of the free, non-slave peoples. The Cape Town Castle was built to hold down the slaves and to ward off Khoi-Khoin attacks. Robben Island, like Gorée, was used to imprison rebellious slaves. But Gorée was used also, and indeed mainly, for the mass export of slaves: according to a French count, M. Ndiaye informed me, 20 million of them passed through the little tragic door in the slave house to the Atlantic outside, while a Dutch count puts the figure at 40 million. One third of those who were dragged over the rocks into the little boats that took them to the big slave ships at anchor in Dakar bay died on the middle passage to the Americas.

The Gorée curator and Leopld Senghor put the total number murdered by European slavers at 200 million (more than my estimate of 150 million in a work on Africa of 1971).[10] How many more would have been killed had they gone meekly to slavery can only be imagined. The death toll was about one in every three of the 600 million Africans who lived during those centuries of Dark Europe in Africa. The death toll was created by the mode of the slave traffic, the long journey to the coast, the violent seizure of slaves from tribes and societies by chiefs collaborating with the Europeans, the lack of food and the long voyage. Resistance saved whole villages, untold millions of lives, engineered many escapes, frightened off many slaving expeditions, thus raising the cost of a slave and of slaving, making it more difficult to finance and execute. (Captain Newton, the slaver and abolitionist, complained in 1752 that French competition threatened to drive British slavers out of the market.)[11] The capital outlay to prevent the frequent rebellions of slaves at Gorée and other slave ports, on the ships, en route to the coast and at the slave-marts under the cannon of the forts was in proportion to the scale of resistance. Resistance by unenslaved farmers and artisans, intellectuals and congregations, pagans and Moslems, had a double effect, protecting those not yet enslaved and fortifying the slaves and aiding their rebellions. Just as the old pre-colonial societies had a communal basis for their largely domestic slavery, so the tribal, and tribally based, despotic societies set up a resistance to slaving which formed the basis for the rebellions of the slaves themselves. Before they were slaves they had been members of those very societies (and were to perpetuate them in many cultural ways under slavery in America and the West Indies). When communal resistance destroyed the forts, it clearly destroyed the very means for slave trading until the slavers could rebuild them. Every mission razed served that same purpose of reducing and postponing enslavement and its death toll.

Resistance arose everywhere — against the collaborator King Alphonso I in Mbanza, Congo, against Çao and da Gama, against the Portuguese Viceroy of the East Indies, D'Almeida, who was killed in 1509 by Khoi-Khoin herders,[12] against the sacking of Kilwe and other Zanj towns. Portuguese forts were destroyed at Kilwe and Mombasa, there was a popular urban uprising in Mombasa in 1529, a mass rebellion in Mbanza after 1534, a mass armed Islamic rising under Granye against the Portuguese in Ethiopia in 1540 and popular rebellions that drove the Portuguese out of Ethiopia for ever and humbled the dynastic collaborators and the Catholic converts. There were attacks on British slave-traders in Guinea in 1556; de Silveira was slain, and his Portuguese army defeated, by the Mwene Mutapa resisters in 1560; a popular slave rebellion killed many Europeans on São Tomé; tribes used 'poisoned arrows' against John Hawkins of Plymouth in 1567; Jagas resisters besieged the Portuguese at Mbanza court. There were the Manicongo rebellion against Portugal in 1570, the 1573–4 Mwene Mutapa defeats of Barreto and Vasco Fernandez; the 1576 and 1589 defeats of Diaz's powerful army by Ngoa; the Zimba rising against the Portuguese on the Zambezi; resistance to the Augustinian missionaries on Pemba in 1597. All these were high points of 16-Century resistance.

Resistance continued in the 17th Century despite the development and consolidation of the slave-trade, forts, missions, commerce and plantations. The people of Mozambique resisted the re-entry of the Jesuits in 1607; in Tete the Portuguese had to use an armed guard of 2,000 collaborator-troops against massive resistance; in 1612 the Angolan bishop complained of mass resistance to baptism; in 1613–16 Madagascar peasants rejected Portuguese colonists from Goa; in 1616 a Ducala river revolt in Angola was crushed; in 1628 the new Mwene Mutapa king attacked the Portuguese. In 1631 the Mombasa sultan led a revolt against the Portuguese at Fort Jesus and in 1644 the Malagasy wiped out would-be British colonists. The year 1652 saw not only the landing of the Dutch at the Cape, but also the beginning of two and a half centuries of tribal resistance there. Rebellions along the Swahili coast in the same year broke the power of Portugal north of Mozambique. In 1659 Autshumao led a war against the Dutch and was sent to Robben Island, which has remained a political concentration camp for over 300 years. In 1660 Capuchins told of African hostility to them, and a slave revolt broke out at the Cape. In 1668 the Makalanga revolt in Mozambique crippled Portugal there for decades. In 1672 the Cochoqua Khoi-Khoin revolted against Holland at the Cape and Ngouenema led a war which only ended with his death in 1682.[13] Not until 1685 did the Portuguese defeat Matamba. The next year saw another slave rising in Cape Town. In 1693 the Danish fort in the Akwamu kingdom was seized. in 1693 Omani-led Africans besieged Fort Jesus. In 1701 the Senegalese Damel of Cayor seized Brue, Director of the French Royal Company.[14] Three hundred years of colonialism had gone by, and 300 years of resistance. The inability of the European soldiers and men of God to break Africa's spirit is depicted in the satirical bas-relief by Dahomey craftsmen in the courtyard of the Gorée slave museum, showing a Christian on a stranded ship.[15]

The 16th Century saw a massive increase in slaving and dis-possession, but an increase also in resistance, though there were a number of chiefs who collaborated. Slaves in Cape Town rose in 1707, 1713 and 1719; Khoi-Khoin fed them and fought to the death by their side. Resistance thwarted the growing system of 'treaties', illegal by tribal law and custom, concluded with chiefs by France. In 1729 the Oman-led Africans retook Fort Jesus, and Portugal was forced to flee from Kenya, the second lasting defeat of their empire in Africa. The African victory also led to Mombasa's independence from Oman in 1741. In 1745 the 'Cape coloured' people, derived from enserfed Khoi-Khoin and ex-slaves, forced the collapse of the German Moravian mission at Genadendal, Cape Province. In Cape Town early working class resistance began among artisans, the very first struggles of their kind in Africa. The San hunters fought numerous unchronicled battles against the Boers (Dutch farmers) and Dutch troops until they were decimated. The Khoi-Khoin fought the Boers and Dutch every kilometre of their way eastwards and northwards from the Cape and in 1773 the first grand Xhosa Bantu resistance began in joint actions with the Khoi-Khoin.[16] On the other hand, in 1773 the Ashanti, led by their Asantehene, became involved in slaving and gold trading as vassals of Danish and Dutch slavers. In Ghana the old tribal despotism took a step towards integration in the European slave trade, which the despotic upper caste of the old 'empire' served for another century. But in 1779–92 Ndlambe rose to lead a united Batwa, Khoi-Khoin and Bantu resistance to Dutch land-robbery, while in the Cape Malay police joined forces with a popular semi-rising of slaves and 'free' labourers. Far away, towards Timbuktu, Africans ended the life of the 'explorer' Houghton, and later of Mungo Park. In Sierra Leone there were by now 24 forts for protection against slaves and free resisters, and the century came to an end with a great Cape uprising of slaves, serfs, wage-workers and Khoi-Khoin and Xhosa tribal resisters. Already the resistance of the tribes was paving the way for a modern proletarian class struggle. Herein lay its progressive nature.

The opening of the 20th Century saw a new danger: the increasing use of 'treaties' and a policy of 'divide and rule', in both of which the missionaries, Protestant and Catholic, played an essential role. Khoi-Khoin and Xhosa resistance in the Cape was gradually worn down, particularly by the London Missionary Society.[17] In Ghana the British were already playing Fanti and Ashanti chiefs and their 'kingdoms' against each other by 1805, using as their basic means British-made products including alcohol and guns, slaving and private landed property. But in 1811 the Khoi-Khoin destroyed the first German mission in Namibia. In 1807–16 the Ashanti renewed their resistance to the British, who, after the abolition of the slave traffic in 1807, justified their land-seizure and wars by accusations of slaving against the king, the Asantehene. But it was not slavery that the Ashanti were defending, it was their land. Further south there were popular rebellions in 1818–9, and Makanda, Ndlambe's general, led a famous victory over Britain's collaborator Ngqika and the Theopolis mission-fortress before being defeated by a vast British army supported by Ngqika. Incarcerated on Robben Island, he escaped but was drowned in 1819, and his 'coloured' co-fighter Stuurman was exiled to Australia. Another Ashanti revolt in 1824 led to the defeat of the British and their Fanti allies; the British Governor was killed and the British were forced to withdraw, but two years later, exhausted by war and impoverishment, the Ashanti were defeated. On the East coast, in 1826, Said's army forced Britain to leave Fort Jesus for a year. Xhosa resistance resumed under Maqomo and Zulu resistance began simultaneously with British attempts at dispossession in 1829. Tens of thousands died in Algeria resisting French annexation in 1830, and Abd al Kadir led another rising in 1832. The Xhosa under Hintsa united to resist the British in the eastern Cape in 1834.

It was fear of this Xhosa resistance rather than the abolition of slavery in the Empire in 1834 that led to the so-called Boer treks to Transvaal, Natal and the Free State, in the course of which the Matabele defeated the Boers at Vechtkop in 1836. But Boer massacres forced Mzilikazi to take his moving 'kingdom' towards Zimbabwe. In Kenya the Sultan retook Fort Jesus, Mombasa, in 1837. In 1838 Dingane, who had succeeded Tshaka as Zulu king, defeated the Boers under Retief, but was defeated and overthrown by a combined Anglo-Boer force later in the year; puppet chiefs took his place, and through them missionaries began to formulate a clear policy of 'indirect rule' in segregated cheap-labour reserves.[18] In 1843 Britain violently put down a new mass rising. In Algeria, though Abd al Kadir had been banished in 1847, resistance continued until 1879 and cost France the lives of 150,000 soldiers. The middle of the century, following the 1848 revolutions in Europe, saw the greatest combined wars of resistace of the Xhosa and Khoi-Khoin together now with the Sotho under their king Moshoeshoe, and mass resistance by Nigerian and Dahomey kingdoms, already permeated by European slaving and commerce, to the British armies that razed Lagos on the pretext of abolishing slavery and 'barbarism' — a charge that was repeated in the British House of Commons and from pulpits in Britain when the Dahomey kingdom was dispossessed. Eighty years later, Mussolini was to use this pretext, of freeing Ethiopia from slavery, in Italy's genocidal war.[19]

The mid-century saw the liberatory jihad of El Hadj Omar, who rallied millions in West Africa against France until his death in 1864. In

1854 the Transvaal Sotho rose under Makapan against the Boers. In 1856 the Damel of Cayor led another Senegalese rising, and resistance continued until his death in 1886, a year before the treacherous slaying of his co-resister Mamadou Lamine.[20] A new Ashanti rising in 1863 closed the internal trade routes in Ghana, and in Namibia the Nama again destroyed the German missions; but the Germans began to use the Herero against the Nama, though they later decimated them. In 1864 Tippoo Tib led a large-scale East African resistance against Britain, allied with the Zanzibar Sultanate[21] and the Royal Navy was called in. In the same year Lagos and Gold Coast rebellions shook London's finance houses, parliament and churches amidst renewed British charges of barbarism and slavery against the Behanzin tribal-despotic dynasty in Dahomey.

The Tswana tribalists and serfs of the Boers rose in 1865, the Xhosa in the same year. Ahmadu, son of El Hadj Omar, carried on resistance against the French conquistador Faidherbe and captured him for a while. In 1867 the Ethiopian King Theodore committed suicide after Napier's British invaders had scaled his Magdala stronghold. But in that year came the writing on the wall for all resistance with the opening of the Kimberley diamond mines and the Suez canal (the latter by the French utopian socialist, de Lesseps). Moshoeshoe rallied his people again in 1867, and in 1868 Bismarck had to ask Britain to protect the Germans from the Africans in South West Africa. In 1873 Samoy raised the standard of united revolt in Haut Volta and led a vast resistance for a quarter of a century.[22] The same year the Xhosa rose, for the penultimate time, under Sareli, followed by a Zulu peasant rising under Langalibalele, supported by miners at Kimberley. This resistance blends with the rise of early 'African nationalism' and 'African socialism' in Southern and West Africa. In 1874 the Freetown dockers struck. In 1875 there were already the beginnings of modern-style political movements in the Cape, while in Mombasa the Sultan's troops rose in revolt and had to be crushed by British warships. Rhodes was already in the Cape, Stanley was marching along the Congo river and the atrocities of King Leopold were round the corner as the Duke of Brabant called for a Belgian colony. Goldie was founding the Unilever empire in Nigeria, and 'explorations' were the order of the day. The resisters were fighting a losing war, but still they fought on. In 1876 the Gabon peoples resisted, in 1877 Sareli raised a final Xhosa army and Sekukuni called his Transvaal warriors together and routed Kruger's Boers. In 1879 Suleiman Zubair stood out against the British General Gordon along the Nile, and in the same year the Sotho launched a guerrilla struggle against the Boers and British (traitors helped the British to murder Sekukuni in his cave stronghold). Also in 1879 Cetswayo won a celebrated victory over the British at Isandhlwana before being defeated at Ulundi, whence he went via Cape Town to London, where Queen Victoria had to treat him as a defeated king. In 1880 Ahmadu and

Samory defied Ferry and only then could France subject Algeria and ensure the safety of the vast number of *colons* there.

In 1882 the old 'hidden' colonialism of the Germans, with its slave-forts, came out into the open in Namibia and the Cameroons and at once met a heroic and prolonged resistance, put down with the greatest brutality under the personal direction of the Kaiser and Bismarck with the participation of the Krupp family, Hamburg merchants, the banks and 'pioneers' like Herr Goering, a forebear of the Nazi Hermann Goering, and the support of the pro-imperial Lassalle socialists. In 1882 Moses Witbooi led a Namu resistance, but was assassinated. He was followed by Hendrik Witbooi, the resistance hero of the present SWAPO liberation movement. In the same year the Amazons of Dahomey rose again under the great resister-despot Behanzin. Samory rallied a new rising at Keniera, and Somalis and the Tigre people died opposing the Italian invaders, whose colonialism was later, in the era after Garibaldi and Mazzini, endorsed by Labriola's socialists. In 1883 the Mahdists trounced the British at Shaykan. In 1884 Lock Priso led a rebellion against Germany in the Cameroons, and Dinizulu, son of Cetswayo, was exiled after an insurrection. In Europe the great powers at Berlin prepared to carve up Africa among themselves.

Resistance continued into the imperialist epoch after the 1884–5 Treaty of Berlin. After Kabaka Mutesa's death in Uganda in 1885, Mwanga united resistance against the invading Catholics and Pro-testants. In the Cape, Tile was gaoled for fighting British taxes; Samory's men occupied Fakab, a rising of the Huambe slaves of Portugal in Angola began that was to last until 1910, and although the redoubtable Tippoo Tib became a provincial governor in E. Zaire, he resisted the massacres of Stanley and King Leopold during the reign of terror that accompanied the building of a new Manchester–Amsterdam–Antwerp–Brussels empire. Despite a temporizing 'treaty' of 1887 Samory continued an empire-wide war of the half-conquered tribes against the French; the Pangani tribes resisted Germany, while in the Cape the first modern African political organizations were being formed by Jabavu[23] and peasant revolts and workers' strikes of the modern type were worrying Rhodes's government in the 'Xhosa' Reserves, the first 'Bantustans'. In 1888 the Abushir and Macemba revolted against the German colonialists — the real fathers of Nazism. In 1889 the Germans were resisted by Witbooi, while oppressed tribes in the Cameroons ambushed a party of Germans. In 1890 Malawi rose up in arms, and so did the Kikuyu in Kenya, the Nyamwezi and Tabora in Tanganyika and the Sobas in Portuguese Bié. In 1890 the Belgians at last defeated Tippoo Tib, and in 1891 they slew his ally, the Nyamwezi Shaba resister Msiri, who had also organized commercial resistance against Belgium and Britain. In 1891 the Hehe rose up against their German oppressors in Tanganyika. The Wobgho, king of Haut Volta, refused to allow any more Europeans to enter his powerful, million-strong 'tribal despotism' for fear of losing the lands of the Mossi.[24] In 1892 the French invading Somalia from Djibouti met with resistance. In 1893 the people of ancient Timbuktu launched a new struggle against France, but Ahmadu had to flee to Sokoto. Dahomey rebels, including the famed women troops, the 'Amazons', seized the German palace, the Cameroons kingdoms rose in a final resistance, Dahomey was overcome and King Behanzin, the despotic resistance hero, husband of a thousand wives and master of a great army of soldiers and slaves, was exiled, first to Martinique, then to Algeria, after an epic resistance to the dispossession of the common lands of Dahomey by European capitalist private property. The German conquest in the Cameroons was made possible by the collaboration of Mebenga m'Ebono (Martin Samba), an officer in the Schutztruppe, who became a resister after 1902 and in 1914 was executed by his former masters.[25]

In 1894 Lobengula, a hero of modern Zimbabwean liberation, fell defending the common lands of his kingdom. In 1895 the Chagga in Tanganyika rose again and in Haut Volta the Wobgho Bokari continued a Mossi resistance until he died in exile in Ghana, in 1904. In 1895 the oppressed Batatela, Luluabourg and Kasai peoples revolted against Leopold in the Congo; Samory tried to regroup his forces from North Ghana and Prempeh, the Ashanti king, attempted a final resistance to the dispossession and impoverishment of his people by the British, but was seized and exiled, while Kumasi was plundered by the British. In 1896 the Mazrui nobles caste again rose along ancient Zanj, but the British quelled the rising, using Indian troops. In that same year Menelik and Ras Makonnen inflicted a historic thrashing on Italy at Adowa in a feudal-tribal resistance; Madagascar was taken only after long resistance; the Matabele and Mashona joined hands in a great united rising, bloodily quelled by Rhodes, while in France the Second International, led by Jaurès, applauded the crushing of Sudanese resistance by Marchand, though at Bebel's insistence Peters was mildly indicted for atrocities in 'German Africa'.[26] In 1897, while Britain occupied one region after another, reaping the fruits of a long and well established period of accumulation, the king of Benin wiped out a British delegation; the Tswana attempted an armed insurrection, Sudanese troops mutinied and joined the resistance led by Mwanga and Kabarega of the Buganda and Bunyoro kingdoms respectively.

In 1898 Samory was captured and exiled. In 1899 Rabah Zubair organized a new resistance over the whole of central Africa against the French and British. In 1900 he finally fell to the French, but his followers carried on his activities. In the Gold Coast there was renewed resistance; in East Africa the Barue rose against Lisbon's racial despotism; Samory died in Gabon. Today he is an official hero in Sekou Touré's Guinea. In 1902 Bié revolted again. In 1903 the emirates aroused new resistance in Northern Nigeria, and the Nama and Herero united in a new resistance against a Germany supported by the full weight of

Krupps' monopoly capitalism — the most 'primitive' society against the most modern. The Namibian resistance was not quelled until 1908. In 1905 the Maji Maji peasant rebellion threatened the German empire in East Africa, while Tippoo Tib, bereft of his sword, put down his pen as well, and died. In 1905 there was a revolt among tribes in Kenya, and in 1906 the Bambatta peasant revolt shook the British in Natal and provoked the pro-British, anti-African Gandhi into his political philosophy of Satyagraha; the Zulu workers' leaders were executed in the Anglo-German style.[27] In 1908 the Cameroon tribes, now half-integrated into German capitalism, were crushed in a revolt in which Martin Samba took part, and massive anti-Portuguese revolts ran through Portuguese Africa. 'Tribal' resistance was no longer really tribal, but was merging with the modern struggle of exploited conquered peoples against their exploiters. The period from the death of Tippoo Tib, Samory, Zubair, Lobengula, Bokari and Witbooi and the exile of Behanzin, Prempeh and Kabarega, from about the turn of the 20th Century, is already part of the imperialist period. The 'lost past' and its resistance is gone, or fast going. New social formations, new resistances, new modes of accumulation and oppression are coming into being. The Nigerian novelist, Chinua Achebe (born 1930), illustrates this simultaneous process in his *Things Fall Apart* (1956) and *The Arrow of God* (1964), as it affected the Ibo clan society in Eastern Nigeria.

The pre-colonial resistance continued deep into colonial times[28] and into imperialism;* in Morocco in 1908, in Libya against the Italians in 1911, in Turkey, in Egypt and in Ethiopia in 1935–40.

Long before the arrival of imperialism, at the end of the major conquests in Africa and Asia and of slavery in America, the struggles between tribalism and capitalism had blended into the class struggle within victorious capitalism in Africa. Slavery itself was the first form of exploitation of capital in Africa and America. With it went private landed property, involving not only slaving and slavery but also serfdom, as practised in Angola and Mozambique under the *Prazeros* and the missions, on many Cape farms and in conquered West and East Africa. Finally, with the advent of free wage labour, the ex-slaves and ex-tribalists raised workers' struggles alongside the struggles of slaves and serfs. All three were intertwined with the dying, but never-ceasing, resistance of pure and mixed tribal kingdoms.

A capitalist social formation had existed for a long time in the Cape, on the island of Gorée, in Mombasa, Luanda, Lourenço Marques and elsewhere. In Gorée freed slaves and former 'kingdom' people formed both an artisan and a petit bourgeois class. Chevalier de Boufflers, the French governor on the eve of the French revolution, had Gorée 'hetaerae' who, in Gorée, stood equal with his Parisian mistresses.[29]

---

* Which V.I. Lenin dated as '*not before 1900*' in his *Imperialism* classic.

At the head and in control of the exploiting classes everywhere were the colonialists and their settlers. All other exploiting layers were subject to them, secondary and minor. This relationship within the 'ruling class' became a permanent, fundamental feature in the opinion of many writers in the cause of freedom, enduring into our present epoch of independence not in Africa alone but also in Asia.

African resistance to enslavement, conquest and dispossession was specifically against these elements of capitalist primary accumulation and not in defence of any slaving or caste privileges which the 'despots' in pre-colonial Africa unquestionably enjoyed, either from the past or from colonialism itself. Colonialism multiplied the slaving of the old days a thousand times and transformed its character from domestic to chattel slavery, gold and ivory slave trading, and a vast commerce in its own right; slaving became the major commerce inside Africa itself, involving more people and money than all other commerce put together. For three centuries it was the major means, form and vehicle of the primary accumulation that raised Europe to that wealth and power which thereafter enabled it to engulf the world in the imperialist system of regular accumulation through colonial super-exploitation yielding super-surplus value.

Colonialism as Genesis of Race

Accompanying and energizing the two major changes wrought by colonialism — slavery and private landed property — was the ideology, the means of conquest and subjugation, known as racialism. The resistance struggles of five centuries have always had, besides their anti-slavery, communal content, an anti-racial element. The fight to be treated as a human being, not as a mere, soulless thing that could be thrown into the Atlantic Ocean without arousing protests from Catholics or Protestants, was an important and growing element in African resistance, not simply ideological but a matter of life and death.

Racialism was not simply a rationale to justify conquest and domination, but far more — a means of conquest, domination and rule. It was a means to unite the conquerors and demoralize the resisters:to enslave by inducing the slave-mentality that ensures docility; to segregate slaves from masters territorially in the towns, as well as socially and politically; to drive the dispossessed into reservations or reserves in the non-producing countryside and into locations and compounds on the plantations and mines and in the towns; to deny social cohesion and political rights and powers to the dispossessed and exploited; to use physical means — in particular the reserve, the compound and the location — to operate the growing mechanics of cheap labour exploitation by a unified 'White' settler and foreign class or complex of classes.

Racialism was an integral cog in the machine of colonialism, forged by the process and making it work. It was there in the Crusades, in the slave traffic and slavery, in conquests and dispossession, finally in exploitation and oppression. It was in the Americas, Africa and Asia. It was practised equally by Catholic conquistadores — Columbus, Cortez, Pizzaro, da Gama, Crispi and Leopold — by Protestant land-robbers and murderers — Van Riebeeck, Kruger, Rhodes, Peters — and by their Jewish cohorts and peers in slaving, shipping and mining. It was at once the creature and creator of Europe. Throughout Europe racialism was common to all countries and all classes — the landed nobility which owed much of its post-medieval wealth not to European but to colonial lands; the Church, the greatest single colonial power next to the state; the rising, then triumphant, bourgeoisie, which drew the strength to overthrow feudalism less from any internal process inside England or France or Germany than from the vast colonial possessions already in its hands by the time of the bourgeois revolutions — the Renaissance in Italy, the Reformation in Germany and Holland, the rise of a landed, colonial bourgeoisie in England and Scotland under Elizabeth I, Cromwell's revolution in 1648, the French revolution in 1789, the revolutions in Europe in 1848. Symbolic of the colonial aspect of the bourgeoisie is Napoleon's decree retaining Senegal as a slave colony.[30] The revolutionaries in France crushed slave rebellions in Haiti and other French territories. There was rapid expansion of slaving by Britain during the Commonwealth. Colonial conquests and trafficking in slaves provided the precious metals and general wealth that permeated the ages of Leonardo, Galileo, Newton and Beethoven. Abolitionist movements were headed by such racialists as Wilberforce, John Philip and Abraham Lincoln, against slavery but not in favour of equality.[31] The serfs, the unemployed, peasants, demobilized soldiers, workers and criminals who went out to settle in the colonies were racialists already before they set sail, and became more so as they slaved, plundered and lived on the shoulders of African, Asian and American cheap labour.

The entire working class of Europe, in its birth and rise, its growth through Chartism, trade unions and anarchism, socialism and communism, was saturated with the ideology of racialism and took part in the racialist process of colonialism.[32] The 'colonial question' that lay behind every bourgeois revolution, that gave the bourgeoisie of France, Britain and Holland parts of America, Africa and Asia before they even had the means to win power inside their own countries — this question was a minor one in the European revolutions, even the proletarian revolution of the Paris Commune.

Only Rosa Luxemburg,[33] Liebknecht and a small handful among German social democrats between the 1890s and the First World War had anything to say against German colonialism. British labour and socialism, like that of Holland, sent to the Cape and the South African mining cities racialists who joined hands with British and German mine-owners in the world's worst totalitarian system. The first mass rallies of British labour demanded the retention of the colonies by Palmerston. The 'social formation' of European labour in Africa was itself a physical racialist factor. Racialism was a social force, not simply an ideology.

Types of Racial Colonies

The inter-continental and inter-modal clash between colonialism and the old societies gave rise to various kinds of racialist colony. Where the overthrown society was one (following Engels's definition) of 'savagery', occupied mainly in hunting, fishing and food-gathering, it was wiped out physically, enclosed within reservations, and the 'colony' became a 'dominion' or independent 'White' state, as happened in Australia, Canada and the United States; the ex-colony became itself a colonial power. In the United States, which, unlike Brazil and Mexico, was linked to a rising and not a declining colonial power, New England became a 'metropolis' on the basis of the slave trade and slavery. There was not simply a 'triangle' in the British slave-trade — Liverpool–Guinea–West Indies — there was a quadrilateral, with New England and above all New York as a fourth corner, between the West Indies and England, the fourth vertex being Gorée–Guinea–Angola. Colonial slavery and slaving metropolitanized the eastern United States and launched the transformation of the country from a colony into a colonial power, growing up inside the world-powerful British Empire, which it was to rival and overtake in the 20th Century. This process could not materialize in the case of the settler-colonies of declining capitalist-colonial powers, like Portugal and Spain. The soil in which this took place was that of the hunting Amerindians; much the same happened in Canada and Australia. Their states were racial — Indians and negroes were excluded from Washington's and Benjamin Franklin's Declaration of Rights — and exclusive; Australia and Canada banned non-European immigrants. Colonies of this type did not arise in Africa or Asia.

A second racial form of colony was formed where there was also large-scale European immigration of settlers of *colons* on former 'savage' or 'lower barbarism' soil, together with mass importation of slaves, as in Brazil, the Southern States of the USA, and the Cape. There an institutionalized system of racialism developed as a result of the special combination of tribalism, settlers and slaves. This form was found in Africa mainly in South Africa, Namibia, Angola, Mozambique, Rhodesia, Kenya, the Belgian Congo and Algeria.

The racial states in Rhodesia, Namibia and Algeria did not have a chattel slavery basis, but arose out of the domination of European settlers over African ex-tribalists. The form did not arise where the tribal system had developed into a mixed system of tribal-despotism. In Asia, Mexico and West Africa the smallness of European immigration was due, not to the climate, which was and is as good or bad then as now for 'Whites' or 'Blacks'; it was not so much a good climate or even a good top-soil that drew millions of European settlers to Southern Africa and South America; it was the social vacuum left by the pre-class societies before colonialism. These societies provided no potential local ruling class to sub-serve colonialism. The settlers filled this social gap. In India, Java, Malaya, Burma, Mexico and West and most of North Africa, however, there were already in existence classes or powerfully developed castes in mixed-civilization pre-colonial societies, and these became the intermediaries and sub-agents of the colonialists — moguls, maharajahs, sultans, emirs, sheikhs, kings. European immigration *en masse* would have challenged these ruling layers and precipitated a social convulsion which would have made the exploitation of the 'natives' impossible. It was not the heat, or the mosquito or the tsetse fly that kept the Europeans out of these colonial areas, but the pre-existing class or caste despotisms from the transmuted 'lost past'.

But these societies retained the cult of European racialism until independence, in this third form of colony — that which emerged from the conflict between European colonial despotism and oriental, Aztec or African communal despotism. In Africa particularly it was in this third form that the policy of indirect rule took its purest form. In the non-settler 'Bantu' or Luo or Moslem 'reserves', where there were no Europeans, with chiefs and with common lands converted into Crown land, it developed in a lower form, that of direct rule by Europeans through indirect rule by chiefs. This variant is found also in South African reserves and 'Bantustans'.

Liberatory Despots or Despotic Liberators?

The resistance struggles from the 14th to the 19th Centuries were against this racial, slaving, private landed property system of colonialism, in defence of their opposites — the non-racial co-operative humanitarian Ujamaa aspect of pre-colonial society, the absence of chattel slavery, the communal lands and 'Harambee' collective labour. The chiefs and kings, as custodians and representatives of these three elements of 'African despotism', could not but resist for these reasons, especially in defence of the economic basis of their own despotic caste, the common land and its surplus. This was the dominant element of the old society and the primary element in African resistance to Europe. The Africans defended their independence on this basis. The resistance of the emperors Samory in Guinea and Behanzin in Dahomey–Benin, of the sultanates in the east who resisted Portugal and Britain, of the

Toucouleur emperors in the west, the religious resisters El Hadj Omar and his son, Ahmadu Lamine, the Mazrui aristocratic resistance in post-Zanj, the military commercial 'empires' of Zubair and Tippoo Tib, the resistance of despotic tribal kings like Bokari, Moshoeshoe, Cetswayo, Lobengula, Kabarega and Mwanga, of the Islamic Ethiopian Granye, of the communal-feudal emperors Theodore, Menelik and — near our own time — the utterly despotic Haile Selassie, of Mohamed Ali, Hussein and Idris — all were 'just' anti-colonialist resistances in defence of the common lands and tribal or 'national' territory and unity. In particular, even in Ethiopia, the communal lands and customs were at the core of all resistance, whether it was military and open or temporizing as with some of the treaties of Moshoeshoe, Lobengula, Samory and Bokari. They provided the underlying motivation too for vain and counter-productive attempts to conserve the old society by collaboration with the colonialists,[34] seeking European allies for Ashanti against Fanti, for Ashanti against Holland, Xhosa against Boers, Mossi against France, Cameroons against Germany. Once the tribal partitioning of the old society fell into European hands, the old society was doomed. It had within itself the seed of its own destruction by an enemy applying the old Roman maxim, 'divide and rule'.

Capitalist Retribalization

The tribalization of the pre-colonial societies was both external and internal; 'clan' despotism of one tribe over others as well as the dominance of one clan-caste within a given tribe. European expansion forced the formation of new tribal groupings. The Nguni of Natal, caught between the British coming in from the sea, the Boers from the Cape and the Portuguese in Mozambique, gave birth to the Zulu kingdom of Dingiswayo, Tshaka, Dingane, Cetswayo and Dinizulu. This kingdom was itself a dominion of a small Zulu clan over other tribal groups, an admixture of these, a consolidation of a military unitary tribal kingdom, not simply a confederation,[35] an expulsion or withdrawal of groups like those of Mzilikazi who became the Matabele. The Sotho kingdom was unified under Moshoeshoe in the early 1820s under the northward thrust of Boers, Britons and Germans. It arose as a confluence on the highlands of Lesotho of many scattered tribes, their admixture and the formation of a new unity which had not existed before, the Sotho kingdom, around which lay Baralong and other chieftaincies which the missionaries used to break into the kingdom of Moshoeshoe. A similar tribal unification process occurred elsewhere, in the Congo under Portuguese pressure and in West Africa under French and British pressure. The newly formed kingdoms became nuclei of anti-colonial resistance under kings and even 'emperors' — Sekou Touré gave the title of emperor to Samory, whose fall in 1898 put an end to Guinea's independence until 60 years later.

Colonialism also had the opposite effect, that of dividing tribes and setting them against each other. The Mossi of Mogo Naba Wobgho in 1889 was still head of a dominant clan-caste with 300 'vassal-cantons', to use the term used by French observers such as Crozat. But by 1895 Destenaves used the Yatanga tribal group against the Wobgho, and the Mossi kingdom was sub-tribalized. The Wesleyans similarly divided the Sotho and Baralong and the London Missionary Society the Xhosas and the Fingos, who became a collaborator tribe when the English, German and Dutch settlers and missions blamed the Zulu for a European 'Mfiqane' (destruction of the people).[36] In the Gold Coast the British created a long-lasting schism, which was made possible by the already existing tribal partitioning of the Fanti and Ashanti. At the end of the 18th Century the French used the Cereres against the Wolofs to divide the Cayor kingdom. In Nigeria the British used the under-developed Ibo tribal formation, with its weak chief structure easily penetrated by Christian missions, against the Islamic Hausa emirates and their resistance around Kano; the weakness of Ibo despotism lowered its resistance to British subversion, as did its less coherent communalism. The strategy of 'divide and conquer', followed by 'divide and rule', deepened pre-colonial divisions and antagonisms between tribes. The division of Africa at and after the Berlin Conference further divided even single tribes and initiated a new breaking-up, a Balkanization, of tribalism.

This redivision of tribalism was however only a boundary change, a small part of the overall restructuring of tribalism and the transformation of its inner mechanism brought about by European colonialism. Firstly, the whole basis of tribalism was removed when the common lands were seized and occupied by the European conquerors and dispossessors. The preservation of the outward form of common property in the 'native reserves' throughout Africa was not a preservation but a destruction of tribalism. These reserves were, without exception, cheap labour reservoirs of landless, unemployed, dispossessed, conquered people. Even as property they belonged to the Belgian, British, French or Portuguese governments and not to their ostensible African occupiers. The reserves, with their apparent 'subsistence' or 'traditional' economy were part not of the communal, tribal society but of capitalist colonialism. European colonialism was the first to bring private landed property to Africa outside Ethiopia and a few exceptions in isolated Zanj and West African sultanates. It was the same in the Americas, where the Spanish and Portuguese introduced private property in land as a new socio-economic form. Old patriarchs in a Hindu-dominated Moslem village near Goa (India) told me that neither in their old pre-Moslem Hindu society, which was converted to Islam, nor in the Mogul-ruled society, was there private property. It came, said their 500-year-old *memoria*, from the Portuguese da Gama.

The overthrow of communal property by private landed property was the major social-economic change brought by capitalism in Africa. The transformation of domestic into chattel slavery and the subjection of most of Africa to the European slave traffic was the second. This slave traffic itself created the so-called Arab slave traffic which Livingstone, Stanley, Burton, Mungo Park[37] and other conquistadores gave as the reason for their 'civilizing' missions. The Saharan and East African 'Arab' traffic was entirely and increasingly inside and under the European slave trade, from the late 14th Century until late in the 19th. The 'Arab' label was a divide-and-rule device, a racialist device, for the bulk of the 'Arab' trade was carried on by African chiefs, kings and merchants who might be Arab, Bantu, Khoi-San or Luo speaking, animists, Moslems or Christians. This slave traffic turned the old societies inside out; chiefs and their followers became slave-hunters, kidnappers of slaves, slave-porters, slave-drivers, slave-sellers. The despotism of clan over clan, tribe over tribe, was increased tenfold. Whole tribes were broken up, especially in the Congo and Angola, where the Portuguese, Dutch and British decimated the population with the traffic. Mwene Mutapa in east-central Africa was broken down into ivory and slave-hunting 'kingdoms', with chiefs and their *gens* followers either victims or slavers, and often each in turn as the Europeans changed from one chief or king to another to speed or increase the traffic in people. The commoners belonging to a *gens* now became merchandise, commodities. Reification and alienation pervaded the lower and higher orders of African despotism and communalism. Communal collective labour and mutual help changed into commercialized body-hunting and murder at the behest of European slavers, including soft-handed missionaries waiting at the coastal and river slave ports, trading stations and even missions.

The slave traffic implied an exchange of goods for men. Guns, brandy, commodities came in from Bordeaux, Lisbon, Liverpool, Antwerp, Hamburg to Rufisque, Cape Coast, Lagos, Luanda and up the Senegal, Gambia, Niger and Congo rivers: along the Zambezi too, from the east coast. One section of the old society was converted into slave-porters of these goods, another into slave-drivers, another into traders. The chiefs and kings were drawn into the commerce. Gold Coast gold began to pour out of Africa towards Europe in exchange for the wares of European handcrafts and small industry. Whole towns in Europe began to live off the slave traffic alone. Under Henry VIII and Elizabeth I, the Hawkins family, based in Plymouth, became the richest family in England, on the strength of the slave trade, which itself rested on American slave-labour capitalist plantations for the European productive and consumer market. Dieppe, Bordeaux, Antwerp, Amsterdam, Hamburg, Plymouth, Bristol and Liverpool owed their rise and prosperity to this trade.

The slave traffic, private landed property and racialist exploitation and humiliating oppression met everywhere with resistance, as we have seen. But resistance needed weapons and the old ones no longer sufficed against the cannons and muskets of the Europeans, Resistance itself created a trade, gold and slaves being exchanged for weapons. The resistance of Ashanti and Fanti implied the mutual slaving of each by the other so that the victor could buy weapons. Tribalism was not an altruistic society, but a divisive, externally exclusive, even destructive one. The European-aroused and developed slave traffic induced a resistance along the coasts and rivers which in turn furthered the slave traffic in a desperate, defensive search for guns, gunpowder and ammunition. To that extent certain resistance leaders became involved in the slave trade for the sake of a tribal resistance, internally communal but externally indifferent.

On the other hand, as individual tribal resistance proved more and more unequal to the task of halting the insatiable European plunder of people and gold. Kings, emperors and merchants like Samory, El Hadj Omar, Zubair, Tippoo Tib, Paul Martin Samba and Moshoeshoe formed multi-tribal alliances, even confederations and new 'empires', to halt the European massacre and rapine. This in turn tended to end the trade of slaves in exchange for weapons.

The destruction of the old communal-despotism by colonialism took place not only during the long conquest but also in the subsequent period of exploitation. With the fundament of the old society, the common lands removed, the conquerors not only converted its other prop, the chief, king or emperor, into a slaver working for the European slavers, or a gun-buyer or a trader, but also into a recruiter of labour, a tax-collector and a policeman. These changes in the role of the old communal leaders or rulers began as soon as conquest turned into domination. The change properly belongs to the period of regular rather than that of primary accumulation. Suffice it to say here that the chiefs who came out of the process of conquest and dispossession were already no longer the chiefs of old. Those that came out of the next process, that of 'indirect rule' and European settlement, bore even less resemblance to their ancestors. For all practical purposes it was not only the common lands but also the chiefs resting on this communal basis and on the communal co-operative labour that were destroyed by colonialism. Their place was taken by non-communal lands belonging to the conquerors and by policemen, tax-collectors and regimenters of labour employed by and paid by those conquerors. With these two trans-formations, nothing material was left of the old society.

But the *memoria* died hard. And colonialism understood this well, not least the missionaries and policy-framing colonial administrators such as Venn and Grey[38] in West Africa, Philip and Shepstone[39] in South Africa, Faidherbe and Lyautey in 'French' Africa and, later, Lugard[40] and Curzon in West and North 'British' Africa. The kernel — common lands, communal labour, the chiefs as custodians of the commonweal

— was cut out by conquest and subjugation, but the colonialists kept the shell of the old order — the old names, the old titles, the old ceremonies, the old rites — and paid lip service to the more obsequious kings (an old Lagos paper speaks of one as 'His Majesty the Awujale of Ijebu'). The people were classified according to 'tribe', and their chiefs — no longer chiefs — fostered the myth. Poverty, common suffering, the survival of millions only thanks to the 'enlarged family' whose members kept each other alive amidst mass unemployment, with the momentum of the past customs, traditional beliefs and forms — as in every closed family or religious society — all gave further credence to the colonial legend of tribalism. This *memoria* in its turn began to play its part from the very beginning in the writings, speeches and thought of the post-conquest African political movements and in the literary works of such as Sol Plaatje, Achebe, Ngugi, Soyinka, p'Bitek and others from South, West and East Africa.

Africa, detribalized by colonialist primary accumulation, was retribalized by colonialist regular accumulation. The change, which had already begun during the conquest period, developing unevenly as it was applied throughout Africa, was of major importance both to European colonialism and to African anti-colonialism. In its total movement the change from tribalism to a detribalized society and from that to a retribalized society forms the 'negation of the negation' cycle of the last 500 years of African history.

Notes

1. R. Mauny, *Tableau Geographique*, Dakar 1961; IFAN Map of Tombouctou, 23 May 1948, showing trade links between city and River Niger; F. Braudel, 'Monnais et Civilizations', in *Annals, Economies, Societies, Civilizations*, Paris, 1969, part 1; V.M. Godinho, *L'Economie de L'Empire Portugueseaux XV et XVI Siècles*, Paris, 1969, part 1; D.P. Pereira, *Esmeraldo de Situ Orbis* (R. Mauny, Journal 19, in Bissau, 1956).

2. K. Marx on Hansa League, Welsers, Fuggers and other German–Rhine-to-Antwerp banker-merchants who financed colonialism; H. Jaffe, *Germania*, Milan, 1979 (for sources), p. 31; J.A. Goris, *Etude sur les Colonies Merchandes Meridionales à Anvers de 1488 à 1567*, Paris 1925; V. Von Klarwill (ed.), *The Fugger Newsletters, 1568–1605* (trans. P. de Chary), 1924; Ludolphus, *Ethiopia*, Frankfurt, 1631 (in English 1684) belonged to the ever-powerful German 'Africanist' school, still active (Kaufmann, von der Ropp, Natorp et al) in South Africa, from Hamburg, Frankfurt and Munich academic centres linked, inter alia, with a partition plan for South Africa, and government-backed firms making the A-bomb there — and in Brazil — since 1972 (H. Jaffe, *Germania* and *Storia Dell Sud-Africa*, Milan, 1980, for details.)

3. R. Mauny, D.P. Pereira, F. Braudel, op. cit.

4. H. Jaffe, *Pyramid of Nations*, chapter on Formation of Europe, Luxembourg, 1980.

5. S.J. Gould, *The Mismeasurement of Man*, Harvard, 1980, on the racism of Agazzis, Franco-American biologist, Cyril Burt, who faked IQ tests in England; and of US Presidents from 1776. In a letter to the author, 20 October 1983, Gould wrote:

> I agree that the concept of race can be rejected on social grounds, as you do, but I thought it would be interesting to point out that it also has no biological rationale any more in the light of current work on the continuity of geographic variation and the different patterns of geographic variation shown inevitably by different characters of the same organisms — hence my essay in *Ever Since Darwin*.

A. Lincoln, *Addresses*, New York, 1914, pp. 67 and 96 show the South African type racialism of Lincoln. Jefferson, Washington and Benjamin Franklin were among 'democrats' who believed in 'races' and their inequality and who drafted the anti-African and anti-'Indian' racist clauses of the United States Constitution. The European settlers in the Americas were as racialistic and genocidal as those in southern Africa, Kenya, Tanganyika and Algeria.

6. E. Lopez, op. cit. (illustrated in H. Jaffe, *Africa*, op. cit., p. 201). The illustrated and German text show signs of pre-colonial non-racialism and humanism.

7. B. Davidson, op. cit; A. Gide, *Voyage au Congo*, Paris, 1927; *Le Retour du Tchad*, Paris, 1928; *Travels in the Congo*, 1929; *La Nouvelle Revue Francaise*, 1927 (on West Africa).

8. F. Fanon, *Toward the African Revolution*, Paris, 1964, London, 1970; *Black Skins, White Masks*, New York, 1967, ch. 1–3, 5, 8; *A Dying Colonialism*, London, 1965; *The Wretched of the Earth*, London, 1961.

9. Sekou Touré traces Guinean independence back to Samory, in *Relazione Internationale*, No. 1, January 1972, op. cit.; A. Mahjoubi, 'The Romans and the Resistance of the Indigenous Populations' in *UN 2*, pp. 466–8; A.B. Davidson, 'African Resistance and Rebellion Against the Imposition of Colonial Rule', in T.O. Ranger (ed.), *Emerging Themes in African History*, Nairobi, 1968, pp. 177–88; T.O. Ranger, 'African Reaction to the Imposition of Colonial Rule in East and Central Africa' in *Problems in the History of Colonial Africa, 1860–1960* (ed. R.O. Collins), New Jersey, 1970, pp. 68–82; H. Jaffe, *Africa dal Tribalismo a Socialismo*, Milan, 1971, Mexico, 1976, chapters 8–11; J. Homer, *Repression and Revolt in Portuguese Africa*, New York, 1960.

10. H. Jaffe, ibid., ch. 6; Senghor's estimates 'From 15 to 20 millions deported to the Americas, and from 150 to 200 millions killed' (Speech, Brazzaville, 24 February 1974); W. Blommaert, 'Het Invoeren de Slavernij', *Cape Records*; B. Davidson, *Black Mother, Africa*, London, 1961, Turin, 1966; V. de Kock, *Those in Bondage*, Cape Town, 1950; A. Falconbridge, *An Account of the Slave Traffic on the Coast of Africa*, London, 1788; V. Fernandez, *Description de la Côte Occidentale Afrique, 1506–1510* (ed. R. Mauny, Monod, da Mota), Bissau, 1951; A. de Galvao, *Tratado dos Descubrimentos*, (1563), Oporto, 1944; R. Hakluyt, *The Principal Navigations, Voyages, Traffiques and Discoveries of the English Nations*, London, 1598; W. Howitt, *Colonialism and Christianity*, London, 1838; Rinchen, Dieudonne, *Les Esclavage des Congolais par les Europeans — Histoire de le Deportation de 13 Million Noire*, Brussels, 1929; W. Smith, *A New Voyage to Guinea*, London, 1744; E. Williams, *Capitalism and Slavery*, London, 1944; H.A. Wyndham, *The Atlantic and Slavery*, London, 1935.

11. J. Newton, *Diary from the Duke of Argyle, 1750–5* (ed. B. Martin and

M. Spurrel, Epworth Press, private). The diary includes an entry of 11 December 1752 of a slave revolt aboard. Newton was a slaver who became a Wilberforce abolitionist.

12. J. de Barros, sketch of battle in which Khoi Khoin herders killed Portuguese Viceroy, D'Almeida at Saldanha Bay, 1509, in *Romerugte Scheepstogt van F. D'Almeida*, op. cit., 1706.

13. Mnguni, *300 Years*, vol. 1, Cape Town, 1952, based on Journal of Riebeeck, and Dutch East India Company Journals in Cape Archives.

14. Sketch, 1701, of arrest of Andre Brue, Gorée Museum, Dakar.

15. 16th Century bas-relief by Dahomey artists, showing a Christian captain on an anchored, stranded, ship, Gorée.

16. Mnguni, *300 Years*, vol. 1, op. cit.

17. N. Majeke (Dora Taylor), *The Role of the Missionaries in Conquest*, Johannesburg, 1952.

18. G.W. Eybers, *Documents Illustrating South African History*, London, 1918; J. Philip, *Researches in South Africa*, 2 vols., London, 1828; J.W.D. Moodie, *Ten Years in South Africa*, 2 vols, London, 1835.

19. S. Pankhurst, *Ex-Italian Somaliland*, London, 1951; A. del Boca, *The Ethiopian War, 1935–41*, Chicago, 1970.

20. Aba Diame, Mage, *Voyage dans le Soudan Occidentale, 1863–6*, Paris, 1868, p. 370 (with sketch of S.M. Ahmadou, king of Segu, and Toucolour resister); Cheick Moussa Kamara, *La Vie d'el Hadj Omar* (trans. Amar Samb, IFAN Director) with sketch of El Hadj Omar, IFAN, Dakar; Brosselard, *Report on the Insurrection of Mamadou Lamine, and Abdul Bokar*, Lille, 1888; Pictures of the display by the French of Lamine's head to the resisting populace, Gorée Museum, Dakar.

21. Tippoo Tib, op. cit.

22. Yves Person, *Samori*, 2 vols, IFAN, Dakar, 1971–5.

23. T. Jabavu, op. cit.

24. F. Bretout, *Mogho Naba Wobgho*, Dakar, 1976.

25. M.M. Samba Azan, *Martin Samba*, Dakar, 1976.

26. K. Peters, *New Light on Darkest Africa; Die Grunding von Deutsch Ostafrika*, Berlin, 1906; *Das Deutsch-Ostafrikanische Schutzgebiet*, Munich, 1895.

27. The *Graphic*, 12 May 1906 and 7 April 1896 (*Radio Times* Picture Library, London) shows execution of Zulu revolutionaries by British firing squads.

28. On Abd El Krim, whom Ho Chi Minh called the 'pre-cursor of the armed struggle for independence', see: D.S. Woolman, *Abd El Krim and the Rif Rebellion*, 1968; R. Furneaux, *Abdel Krim, Emir of the Rif*, 1967; *Encyclopaedia Britannica*, 1981, vol. 17, p. 440.

29. Chevalier de Boufflers, *Memoirs*, Gorée Museum and IFAN, Dakar (pictures of the Governor and his 'Coloured' mistress, Anne Pepin, 1786, in the collection).

30. Napoleon decree, copy, Gorée Museum, Dakar.

31. J. Philip, A. Lincoln, op. cit. for their racial policies: also Autobiography for Library of Congress, June 1858; Washington racist relics: Mt. Vernon slave farm, Virginia.

32. F. Engels to K. Marx, 7 October 1858 (on 'bourgeois proletariat'); Marx to Meyer and Vogt, 9 April 1870; Engels to Kautsky, 12 September 1882; V.I. Lenin, in *Imperialism*, 1916, Moscow; 'Socialism and War', from *Collected Works*,

vol. 21, Moscow; 'Imperialism and the Split in Socialism', from *Collected Works*, vol. 23, Moscow (Progress Publishers).

33. R. Luxembourg, *The Accumulation of Capital* (1913), chapter 27 on Algeria, chapter 29 on South Africa.

34. Oliver and Fage, 'Collaboration as a Form of Resistance', in *Problems in the History of Colonial Africa, 1860–1960*, New Jersey, 1970, p. 49; Ranger, pp. 68–80; B.A. Davidson, pp. 50–58.

35. F. Engels saw the Zulus as 'what mankind and human society were like before class divisions arose' (*Origin of Family*, chapter 3), but Suret-Canale ('Tribes, Classes, Nations', in *La Nouvelle Revue Internationale*, 130, 1969) and I. Wallerstein (in *The Capitalist World Economy*, New York, 1980, p. 167) saw Zulu society as class-divided.

36. The missionaries cultivated the legend of a 'Mfiqane' or 'destruction of the people' by Tshaka's Zulus, to cover up the colonial Mfiqane (whence the term 'Fingo') of Boers, British and Portuguese, between whom the Zulus were trapped (Article on 'Mfiqane', *Journal of the Teachers League of South Africa*, September 1983.)

37. R.F. Burton, *The Lake Regions of Central Africa*, 2 vols, London, 1860; *First Footsteps in Africa*, London, 1910; *Land of Cazembe*, London, 1873; D. Denham and J. Clapperton, *Narrative of Travels and Discoveries in Northern and Central Africa*, London, 1826; H.H. Johnston, *England's Work in Central Africa*, London, 1897; J.L. Krapf, *Travels in East Africa*, London, 1860; M. Kurtze, *The German East Africa Company*, Jena, 1913; D. Livingstone, *Missionary Correspondence* (ed. I. Schapera), London, 1961; *Missionary Travels and Researches*, London, 1857; *Private Journals* (ed. I. Schapera), Berkeley, 1960; G. Nachtigal, *Sahara und Sudan*, 3 vols., Berlin, 1879–89; G. Rohlfs, *Quer Durch Afrika. Reise vom Mittelmeer dem Tscadsee und zum Golf von Guinea*, 2 vols., Leipzig, 1874–5; J.H. Speke, *Journal of the Discovery of the Source of the White Nile*, London, 1863; H. Stanley, *In Darkest Africa*, London, 1886, New York, 1890 (including description of military river-boats of the Baganda, and other African resistance to his massacres); Address to Anti-Slavery Society, Manchester, 23 October 1884; Address to Manchester Chamber of Commerce, 21 October 1884; Letters to King Leopold, 1881–2 (published only in 1957); *The Congo and the Founding of its Free State*, 2 vols., New York, 1885.

38. Earl Grey (1802–94), *The Colonial Policy of Lord John Russell's Administration*, London, 1853; H. Venn, in W. Knight, *The Missionary Secretariat of Henry Venn*, 1880; and *Papers*, July 1861 and 8 January 1866; British House of Commons Select Committee Report, 26 June 1865, in *Parliamentary Papers*, 1865, vol. 412, iii (approving the missionary proposals for 'Indirect Rule').

39. Theo. Shepstone, *Memoranda*, November 1864, 1874, Durban.

40. F.D. Lugard, *Dual Mandate in British Tropical Africa*, Edinburgh, 1922; *The Rise of our East African Empire*, London, 1893; D. Cameron, *My Tanganyika Service*, London, 1939; M. Crowder, 'Indirect Rule — French and British Style', in *Africa*, XXIV, 1964, Oxford; L. Curtis, *With Milner in Africa*, Oxford, 1951 (on 'Direct Rule'); L. Delafosse, *Maurice Delafosse le Berrichon Conquis par L'Afrique*, (private letters), Paris, 1976; S.O. Biobaku, *Lugard Lectures*, Lagos, 1955; H. Deschamps, *Les Methodes et les Doctrines Coloniales de la France* (de XVIeme Siècle a nos Jours), Paris, 1953; L.H. Lyautey, *Choix de Lettres, 1882–1919*, Paris, 1947; Pierre Lyautey, *Le Politique du Protectorate en Afrique Marocain, 1905–18*; 'Convegno Volta', 4–11 October 1938, by Royal Academy of Italy.

PART THREE

Africa in the Inter-National Class Struggle

Africa in the Inter-National Class Struggle

The clash of opposite modes and nations, the history-making conflict between the 'European' sequence of antagonistic modes of production — slavery–feudalism–capitalism — and the African, Asian and American sequence — ancient communist–communal despotism — was the genesis of the capitalist world system of international exploitation and oppression of most of the nations and workers of the world by a 'handful of rich nations'. Europe — and later Japan — was constructed on the ruins of American, Asian and African social formations. What happened to Africa, taken as a whole and in every corner of the continent, was part of a global process of modal revolution: from feudalism in Europe and from ancient communism and communal despotism outside of Europe, to one single, unified world-capitalist system. But this unity was one of opposites and Africa was at the base of the pyramid of nations constructed by the most traumatic nation–class struggles of all history: the struggle from the Crusades onwards between Europe and the rest of the world.

The European partition of Africa, the European-owned plantations and mines, railways and harbours, the European chartered companies, the European banks and, from the 1880s, even a stock exchange in Johannesburg, the European multinationals of Rhodes, Barnato and Beit — of British and German finance capital, in particular — and of the Anglo–Dutch Unilever commercial and plantation empire in Nigeria and the Congo, European shipping lines and telegraph and electric light companies, stores, commerce and mass colonization — all came close in the wake of conquest and dispossession This was the 'next stage of capitalism', its highest stage according to Lenin, imperialism itself. It came swiftly and with totalitarian power in the last quarter of the 19th Century, transforming the previously unconquered parts; the major conquests occurred in this period, of the rest of the Cape, of Transvaal, Sotholand, Swaziland, Zululand, Tswanaland, Rhodesia, South West Africa, Tanganyika, Kenya, Uganda, the Congo, Northern

Nigeria, the Sudan, Egypt, Somalia, the Red Sea and desert parts of Ethiopia and parts of the Ethiopian highlands as well, most of French West Africa, Morocco, Tunisia and Libya — all fell between the Berlin Conference and the First World War.

Imperialism, with its banking capital and Krupps machine guns, was not only the major means of conquest, but also the means for a retribalization and total reordering of African social formations and political economy. Capitalist slavery at the Cape and slaving elsewhere were replaced, after 1807, 1834 or 1848 (depending on which European power was the new land and labour proprietor), by 'free' wage labour, by the sale and purchase of African labour power. Serf forms were really variations of this form of labour. The 'reserves' with their tribal, 'traditional' economy were cheap labour reservoirs in disguise and forms of continent-wide mass unemployment.

In the period of this new system between 1885 and 1914 the old kind of tribal and 'civilization' resistance was mixed with new and different kinds of struggles, social struggles of class against class, of African exploited classes against European exploiting classes.

The African class struggle was a struggle against national exploitation and oppression, against exploitation and oppression by capitalists from Europe and by European capitalist settlers in Africa — a struggle against exploitation and oppression by whole European states and nations: the class struggle was between nations. The world, as Lenin wrote in his *Imperialism*, was now divided into oppressed and oppressor nations. The class struggles in Africa were, ipso facto, anti-imperialist struggles. The struggle against capitalism became indistinguishable from, and one with, the struggle against imperialism. The anti-imperialist struggle was not nationalist or bourgeois but working-class, against capital itself, in its most modern form, imperialism. This African struggle was part of an international struggle in which the super-exploited classes in the Americas — mainly Negroes and Indians — and the toilers of all Asia formed the remaining mass components. The rest of the 'international struggle' was composed of an ambiguous, equivocal, dependent class struggle between plebeian workers and patrician capitalists struggling on the backs of their colonial slaves for a redistribution of the colonial loot. This world model, which Europeans and Americans will find simplistic, and which Stalinism has replaced, after Lenin, by an East–West model, has increasingly become the model of African internationalists, who naturally look at the world from where they are, believing that their view is that which would be seen by a socio-political observer from outer space. In this view, the 'socialist' countries tended to become new semi-dependencies of dominant capitalism.

The world knows a great deal about American and European class struggles, but little of the class struggles in Africa. The rising of the Bambatta Zulus in 1906, the Freetown dock strikes; the protests of Chinese dragged into the Johannesburg mines in 1905; the

Langalibalele revolt, linked with diamond miners in Kimberley; peasant resistance after the 1894 Glen Grey law of Cecil Rhodes, then prime minister of the Cape Colony; peasant risings in British-settled Uganda and Kenya and German-settled Namibia; Tanganyika — the Maji Maji rising — and Cameroons before the First World War; anti-Portuguese risings by Mozambique workers and Congo peasants after 1906 and by the Vile Lusa peasants in Angola in 1913; the anti-pass campaign of African women in Bloemfontein in 1913; the strike of Indian coal miners (betrayed by Gandhi) in the same year — these were among the early anti-imperialist class struggles in conquered Africa.

Economic struggles in Africa were rare, almost impossible. The capitalist class was almost wholly imperialist — foreign and settler. Every strike became an anti-imperialist protest and, at least until independence, was usually put down by force by the European state concerned; so every strike involved the foreign state and was political. Moreover the system of racial discrimination and racialist cheap labour policies made it impossible to fight, as workers fought in Europe, for a fair wage or better living conditions without tearing the fabric of the system of European racial despotism, of 'White domination', throughout Africa. Yet 'Socialists' and 'Communists', from the 2nd through to the 4th Internationals, were economistic, and put 'class' above 'colour', reform above non-racial anti-imperialism.

The peasant struggle against land-hunger was one that immediately confronted the imperialist plantation multinationals or the national monopolies; it became political everywhere, a struggle for national liberation. When miners went on strike, it was on the property of the world's biggest concentrations of monopoly capital, and this foreign capital, whether British, French, German, Italian, Spanish or Portuguese, did not hesitate to resort to arms, even to war.

Imperialism as Fascism

Imperialism and capitalism were indivisible, and it was a totalitarian imperialism — in Nigerian and Zairois plantations belonging to Anglo-Dutch monopolies or the Belgian monarchy, in Anglo-German diamond and gold mines in South Africa, on Portuguese, Italian, Spanish, German, British, French farms, mines, railways and ports.

The rise of Nazism was new for Europe, but something indistinguishable from it had long existed in many parts of Africa, the absolute totalitarian dictatorship of monopoly capital, fused with the state; a dictatorship of the combination of monopoly capital and the state that is an essential part of Nazism and Fascism. This dictatorship shared another essential factor with the later European dictatorships: a mass social base in the middle class such as was found in Germany, Italy and Spain. In Africa this 'popular' base was found internally among the *colons* and settlers of all classes, farmers, traders and workers. But besides this settler aggregate of classes, such as was found in Southern Africa, Kenya and Algeria, colonial Nazism had another popular base, the alliance of the workers and capitalists in the dominant foreign countries. Real Nazism existed in South Africa in particular,[2] where all its three essential elements, economic, social and political, and the fusion of them, existed from about the time of the Berlin Conference itself. In a real sense it was at that conference in 1884–5 and not in the flames of the Reichstag half a century later that Nazism was created. Its advent in Germany was a reimport of an old European, and not just German, export, the totalitarian type of imperialism. After 1957 another united Europe, the European Economic Community, itself a product of the European unity that divided Africa in 1884, was to attempt a different *modus dominandi* over Africa. The first absolutely modern Nazi state in the world arose not in Europe but in Africa. It was against this Nazi system that the class struggle was directed. That this struggle arose at all under such conditions is in itself a tribute to the working class of Africa as a proper working class in the Marxist sense.

The political-economic struggles of workers and peasants were linked with the rise and work of political movements, including breakaway church movements, and with trade unions and peasant unions. The chronology will be seen to become increasingly dense in strikes, peasant rebellions, trade unionism, political organization and struggles as we move from the First to the Second World War, and thence to independence in the 1950s and 1960s and on to the liberation struggles of the 1970s in Southern Africa. The events speak for themselves: they constitute a rich history of class struggle which belongs fully to the international history of the world proletariat.

These proletarian class struggles are continuations, under new conditions, of the resistance struggles of the preceding five centuries. Those had been progressive, not because they opposed some rationalized, reified, alienating capitalist system or its artificial enlightenment and utilitarian science, as Catholic and other 'identity cult' European charlatans of their colonialist church believe, but because they opposed capital in such a way as to condition and pre-organize the future colonial slaves to struggle permanently against their new masters. The former tribalists became slaves, and formed the new proletariat. Had they not struggled before the change they would have had a history only of docility and acceptance, of disorganization and division, of collaboration and submission. Instead, their centuries-long wars of resistance gave them a history and tradition of struggle not only proud but also useful, of non-acceptance, of non-collaboration, of liberation itself. Further, knowledge of how they were divided and conquered entered the arsenal of their new, modern struggles, for the enemy had changed, yet was still the same European capital and its nation-states. The progressive nature of communal, tribal-despotic resistance lay not in the conservation of a dying and slaughtered past, not in the resurrection of pre-colonial society, but in the seeds sown for the creation of a post-colonial society. Those seeds were part of the communal *memoria*, but more relevant and more important was the tradition of resistance, of non-acceptance, scepticism, of non-collaborationist struggle without and with arms.

Whereas the old struggles had taken place under the old communal political forms of chief, king or emperor and his caste, the new ones forged new political organizations, with new political ideas cemented into those carried forward from the old 'socialist' past. The struggles and the organizations form an ever-developing whole, each coming out of the other, rising and falling together, dying and being born or re-born together. The chronology itself is a mere summary and we can do no more here than make a synopsis of that summary.

Early South African Anti-Racist Class Struggles

During the First World War there were strikes by Cape and Transkei anti-war workers and peasants, protests, even a rebellion led by the Ethiopian Church nationalist Chilembwe, in Malawi. His church had roots in 19th Century Cape and American separatist anti-segregationist churches. The South African protests were made against official policy by the already established African Peoples Organization of Dr Abdurahman at the Cape, by the African National Congress, formed in 1912 by followers of Jabavu but without Jabavu himself, and Gandhi's Indian Congress. The first of these, the APO, was reformist, reflecting the 'Coloured', ex-Khoi-Khoin and ex-slave artisan and a very small professional group, and was under British liberal and socialist influence from London and Cape Town. The ANC was also liberal-patronized and had in it the forms of retribalization already encrusted since the implementation of the Shepstone policy of indirect racialist rule through chiefs in cheap labour reserves. The Indian Congress reflected the dominant role in the Indian community of an India-oriented, wealthy but oppressed merchant and property-owning Moslem, Tamil and Hindu bourgeoisie. This last was an exception to the rule noted by Senghor in a speech made in Brazzaville in February 1974, namely: the absence of an African bourgeoisie and the general proletarianization of the former slaves and tribalists. But the re-tribalized chiefs, sultans, sheikhs, emirs and kings persisted in form, though without their traditional functions or powers, endowed with new authority by a racialist 'Native Law' made in Europe. This retribalization was the particular form of indirect rule developed particularly in French and British colonies. It exploited for capital the distorted relics of 'African socialism', in a manner rather different from that adopted by the Dutch in Java, as described by Engels in a letter of 18 January 1984 to

August Bebel. In Java, he wrote, 'on the basis of the old communistic village communities the Dutch Government has organized all production in so 'socialistic' a fashion, and has so nicely taken all sales of the products into its own hands, that aside from about 100 million marks in salaries for officials and the army it receives a net income of some 70 million marks a year to pay interest to the luckless states which are creditors of the Dutch.' But in South and West Africa the ancient system of 'communism' was perverted into a non-commercial 'subsistence economy' inside non-producing cheap labour reserves.

In the south, during the First World War, apart from the non-European, anti-racist organizations mentioned above, there were also racist, anti-African unions that operated a colour bar, a Labour Party formed by 'white labour' and an International Socialist League, all of whose members were white workers and lower middle class, forerunner of the Communist Party, defender of the industrial colour bar and a policy favouring the reserves (to save the Africans from capitalism, they argued, it was best that they should remain in their 'traditional economy' — in the racialist reserves).[3] Their 'socialism' was of the Jack London white-racist type — a contradiction which really existed.

The 20th Century independence movements grew up in a hothouse of proletarian class struggles in town and country, by miners, railway workers, dockers, plantation labourers, municipal and factory workers and teachers. The urban proletariat was massacred in thousands, their rural brothers were killed in hundreds of thousands, unhonoured by international socialism and trade unionism as were the 'white' Haymarket, Communard and other workers in North America and Westeern Europe. Just as, to the colonialist, Africans, indigenous Americans and Asians were cheap labour, with cheap lives, whose lands, and the produce of their toil, were then without payment, so did the socialist flank of colonialism look down on the growing proletariat and its struggles in the three colonial continents. But there were epic class struggles there which still need to enter the annals of internationalism. These struggles were nearly always political and gave birth not only to unions and socialist parties but also to the independence movement itself. This was especially true in Africa, where colonial policy inhibited, indeed virtually prevented, the rise of a national bourgeoisie. The liberation movements were forged by the class struggles of a *sans-culotte* proletariat, without land or possessions, starving, half naked, unshod, unhoused, illiterate, unarmed, with no trade unions or civic or political rights, with nothing but their children and only their chains to lose, toiling under conditions worse than those in the factories and slums of the European Industrial Revolution, with lower wages, surrounded by an uncountable reserve army of unemployed. This last, combined with a system of European totalitarianism, with army, police, concentration camps, executions and torture ever present, kept wages below their value and thus generated the super-surplus value characteristic of imperialistic capital. While Europeans debated whether these were really proletarians, in Africa the discussion centred on the nature, not the existence, of this proletariat, mainly found in mining and plantations and non-industrial production.

The first fact to be established is the very existence of the class struggle as a significant and essential historical moment. The chronology suggests that there was indeed such a set of struggles, which can be divided into those of urban and non-urban workers. But it must be remembered that the division into 'town' and 'country' made by colonialism is also one of racial, retribalized oppression, in which the non-plantation, non-mining and non-railway workers are not peasants but unemployed potential or former workers. Africa cannot be seen correctly through 'European' eyes, however Marxist the spectacles used.

Political Strikes in Africa

From the First World War to the eve of independence in the 1950s, the city and mining workers waged struggles that included many strikes, including several nation-wide general strikes. There were major strikes in the Rand mines in 1917, 1918, 1920 (when there were 70,000 strikers), 1922, 1926 and 1946. In Cape Town the Russian revolution and racial discrimination combined to generate the greatest single industrial union in African history, the Industrial and Commercial Workers Union, led by Clement Kadalie. This ICU called anti-racialist strikes from 1919 to 1928, until it was 'organized out of existence' by British trade union 'socialists' and British liberals.[4] In 1928 the ICU's 100,000 members were refused admission by Labour and Communist Party white racist trade unions fearful of being swamped by the African proletariat.[5] With the APO and ANC, the ICU fought the 1922 'white' workers' strike against the right of African miners to do skilled work, a strike which included pogroms into the locations and barracks, which the Communist Party, still a hundred per cent white in membership, hailed as 'the most glorious event in the history of white civilization in South Africa' (S.P. Bunting, Ivor Jones), which it helped to lead against the Africans under the banner: 'For a White Socialist South Africa'.[6] This left for decades a racist image of European 'socialism' in all non-European liberation movements and parties, including the CPSA anti-racists; but it was 50 years before the CPSA officially admitted its 1922 'error'.

African strikers died in Port Elizabeth in 1920, led by Masabalala of the ICU, again in Bulhoek, Cape Province, in 1921 and in Bondelswartz, South West Africa, in 1922. There were anti-pass rallies in Durban in 1930. There were strikes in the Cape in 1938 and 1939 during giant antisegregation struggles organized by the National Liberation League and the Non-European United Front; and in 1943 the Cape workers backed the anti-Coloured Affairs Department struggle of the newly rising Non-European Unity Movement. Nation-wide 'defiance campaign' or 'day of mourning' strikes by the ANC brought Nazi-like police arrests and killings in their wake. These South African strikes have continued to the present day, with mass general strikes during the 1960 Sharpville uprisings in the Transvaal and Cape, the strikes of industrial workers in Durban in the 1970s, strikes during the Soweto rebellion of students and workers in June–November 1976 and repeated strikes in the mines and in the racial colony of South West Africa in 1959, 1970 and 1973–5.

Town and plantation workers struck in Malawi in 1915 and 1959; there were strikes in the Anglo-South African copper mines in Zambia in 1935, in the 1940s, in 1959, 1960 and 1962; in Kenya there was a strike in 1920, a general strike in 1930, strikes in 1939, 1942, 1944, another general strike in 1949, again in 1950, and strikes in 1952, 1955, 1958, 1962 and 1963–4, right up to and after Uhuru and Jamhuri. Ugandan workers struck against Kasanvu forced labour, 'indirect rule' and racialism in 1920, 1921, 1938, 1945 and 1949. In Tanganyika the strikes of 1959–60 continued a previous history during which three quarters of a million workers were unionized. In the Congo the town, mining and plantation workers struck in 1921 when religious Kimbanguist workers were arrested and tortured *en masse* by the Belgians, and in 1953, 1956 and 1959 there were strikes in support of the demand for non-racial schools. The 1978 Lumumbaist Kolwezi revolt, bloodily suppressed by the EEC, continued the Zaire tradition of miners' struggles, against racism. Workers in Khartoum and elsewhere struck in 1934, 1946, 1947 (general strike) and 1961. Workers in Mozambique came out in 1947 and 1953; Angolans in each decade and in 1961–2; Guinea-Bissau workers in 1957, 1959 and 1961; Somali workers in 1948 and 1958; Zanzibari workers in 1963–4 during the anti-feudal and anti-British revolt; Nigerian workers came out in 1921, 1925, 1940, 1942, 1950 and 1963, and backed the war against 'Biafra'. Togo workers struck in 1960 after a long struggle; Dahomey workers in 1957–8 and 1960 (a general strike, directed against the 'French Union'); Cameroon workers, after long anti-German and anti-French strikes, came out again in 1955, 1958 and 1960; Mali workers in 1946, 1953 and 1957; Tunisians in 1946–7 (a general strike which was met with a massacre); Guineans in 1935, 1946, 1953 and 1955, when Sekou Touré broke with French trade union colonialism. In the former Ubangi–Shari (Central African Republic) Bokassa faced a strike crushed by French troops in 1960; Ethiopian workers struck against the British military occupation in 1946–7. Ghanaian workers on cocoa plantations and mines came out in 1915, 1930, 1948, 1950 and 1961; Sierra Leone workers in 1919, 1926, 1955, 1957 and 1961, led among others by Siaka Stevens, now the president; Senegalese workers demonstrated against conscription in

1914 and struck in 1935 and 1953; Ivory Coast workers struck in 1935, 1944, 1946, 1949, 1950 and 1959;[7] Algerian workers struck repeatedly and stood with the FLN against France in the war of liberation in 1954–62. Tunisian, Moroccan, Egyptian and Libyan workers have a proud record of economic-political struggles against France, Britain or Israel and against their own neo-despots, the servants of imperialism. In January of 1984 hundreds of Moroccan and Tunisian workers were killed during bread and school strikes.

Urban and peri-urban struggles of workers were joined with agrarian struggles of closely-family-linked workers, for in Africa the city worker has the country racial 'reserve' as his place of unemployment. The location and the compound are the urban outposts of these reserves, and farm workers have stable links with the reserves. Farm workers struck or revolted in Mozambique in 1917 and repeatedly during FRELIMO's victorious war of liberation in the sixties and seventies; in Angola before and during 1961 and throughout the MPLA's victorious war; in Guinea-Bissau in 1956 and during the PAIGC war. The serfs and labourers of the Belgians rose up in the Congo in 1962, 1963 and 1964 during the Belgian counter-revolution against Lumumba. The Kimbanguist church movement was part of the agrarian struggle, as were the separatist church movements in Rhodesia, Kenya, Malawi and the 'Israelites' massacred by Smuts in 1921 at Bulhoek, Cape.[8] Madagascar workers rose up together in 1947 when the French Popular Front–Gaullist–Socialist–Communist government, still at war with Vietnam, massacred 140,000 people. Libyan peasants and workers lost 10,000 lives in their revolt against Italy in 1934. Over two million Ethiopians (at a most conservative figure) perished during the 1935–41 Italian war, but their resistance and national war ultimately brought the Italian empire down. Italy was toppled not by Smuts or Montgomery but by Ethiopian resistance and the mutiny of 140,000 Eritrean and Somali conscripts in 1941.[9] The Italian surrender was a racist one, too, to save themselves by alliance with the British and South Africans from the vengeance of the Ethiopians and Somalis.

Sudan cotton-serfs of Britain struck in 1946. Somali workers were bombed during a 1919 strike, and 1946 saw another strike. There were peasant strikes in Ghana and Nigeria, in the foreign-controlled cocoa plantations on which 'independent' peasants did, and still do, piecework for European multinationals. Kenya farm and reserve toilers rose in 1919, 1921, 1939, 1947 and 1948 before their grand agrarian rebellion of 1952–9 known as the Mau Mau.[10] After Uhuru, in 1964–5, the peasant rising began again and was repressed by a British-officered military and police force under the nominal control of Kenyatta.[11] In 1942 the Galla rose in Ethiopia; their revolt was crushed by RAF Blenheims. Zambian farm workers around a mainly mining economy struck in 1919, Ugandans in 1921, 1925, 1945, 1946 and 1953 in highly political anti-Lukiko, anti-British struggles. Cameroon rural toilers saw their leaders executed by Germans in 1914 after a heroic struggle; but they rose again in 1955 and 1960. Malawi farm serfs on British plantations revolted in 1956 and 1959. The workers of European plantations and dock companies in Eastern Nigeria, virtually slaves, struck in 1920 and again on the eve of the Biafra civil war. In South Africa the peasants of Witzieshoek, Zeerust and Transkei carried on land struggles mixed with armed uprisings against Bantustanization, in which chiefs were killed, in 1948, 1958, 1959, 1960, 1961, 1962 and 1976.[12] In South West Africa Ovambo workers struck amidst rural anti-South African unrest in the early 1970s.

Between 1954 and 1962 the Algerian toilers rose to a man against French racist colonialism in a war of liberation. This long uprising of a whole oppressed people constitutes one of the great liberating wars of 20th Century Africa, together with the Ethiopian liberation war against Italy and the Mau Mau peasant rebellion. To these nation-wide armed wars should be added the just national struggles of Egypt against Israel in 1948, 1956, 1967 and the 1970s; the victorious wars of the workers of Mozambique, Angola and Guinea-Bissau, which also freed Portugal from Salazar; the Zimbabwean struggle up to the 1980 Lancaster House agreement; and Namibia's continuing struggle.

Liberation movements were not formed by a few individuals making plans but were forged in the flames of these mass struggles of the 20th Century. They all had proletarian bases, urban and rural. They were formed and led by workers with, at most, an aspiring petit bourgeois intelligentsia, as distinct from an existing national bourgeoisie. Unlike India, China, Java, Malaya, Burma, Iran, Turkey and similar colonies and quasi-colonies, Africa had, broadly speaking, no equivalent of the *zamindars*, *compradores*, merchants and landowners. As for industrialists, this sub-set of the bourgeoisie was totally absent, except in Egypt, long after independence and then only partially. The Indian merchant class that bedevilled liberatory politics in South and East Africa was without any roots in industry or mining or even in plantations. It was based on commerce and property, and to a certain extent on usury. In Uganda it seemed to be strong on the land and in banking, but it always had the City of London looking over its shoulder. As for an African, non-Asian, bourgeoisie, such a class was simply not able to form properly under the mechanics of imperialism in Africa. So thorough was this inhibiting process that to this day such a bourgeoisie cannot be said to exist except in Egypt, Liberia and Tunisia. There may be a bourgeois ideology, but it is without a bourgeoisie. It was the proletariat that had to, and did, carry out the independence element of the 'bourgeois democratic revolution'. Its unions and political organizations became basic to the KANU, TANU, FRELIMO, MPLA, PAIGC, CPP (Ghana), RDA (French Africa), SWAPO, ZANU and ZAPU, ANC and Lumumbaist independence organizations and the comparable movements in Sierra Leone, Nigeria, the Sudan and Tunisia.

The Pan-African conferences of Du Bois, Blaise Diagne and others in Paris, Lisbon and elsewhere had little or no effect on these struggles;[13] nor had Marcus Garveyism and the 'Negro' movement. But the Russian revolution in 1917 encouraged the formation of the giant ICU in South Africa and the spread of Marxism in southern and northern Africa. But it was part of the crisis-stricken, African-fearing racist white middle class and labour intellectuals in South Africa who took up Marxism most enthusiastically, forming a 'Communist' party which, like the International Socialist League, its main forerunner (founded in 1915 during the First World War) took a stand based on the idea that the European workers were a revolutionary class.

The Racist European Semi-Proletariat

The British and French trade unions and socialist and communist parties had a likewise racist-colonialist influence in Africa, for which European Marxism has been an unmitigated disaster ever since the formation of what Engels called a 'bourgeois proletariat' — a very real contradiction in terms — in the imperialist and racialist countries. The colonialist stance of French socialists, of German social democracy, Italian socialism, Spanish anarchism (except for an anti-conscription struggle that was ended by a massacre) and British socialism during the 'scramble for Africa' in the late 19th Century, was everywhere continued. All wanted socialism at home and empire abroad. Marx and Engels had applauded the Algerian national war in 1853, the resistance of the Zulus in the 1870s, as they had the anti-colonial struggles of the Turks, Irish, Indians, Javanese, Afghans, Chinese and West Indians. Lenin had raised this banner, and anti-imperialism was the logical outcome of his famous study of the work of Hobson and others. But the view of Bernstein, Kautsky and Plekhanov that the European proletariat was the preordained leader of the world proletariat became more and more prevalent, and did its due damage in Africa. This view is the socialist variant of the racist concept that the 'white race' of Europeans has the civilizing mission of leading the children of Ham to the promised land. Coming from a mechanistic, undialectical interpretation of Marx and Engels, it saw socialism as a creation of an advanced proletariat, resulting from the 'contradictions of capitalism' in 'advanced countries'. It did not even recognize the colonial base of those contradictions. Out of self-interest, it combined 'socialism' with imperialism and hence also with racialism.

European Marxists extracted what suited their paternalistic civilizing mission from a letter that Friedrich Engels wrote on 12 September 1882 to Karl Kautsky:

In my opinion the colonies proper, i.e. the countries occupied by a

European population — Canada, the Cape, Australia — will all become independent; on the other hand, the countries inhabited by a native population, which are simply subjugated — India, Algeria, the Dutch, Portuguese and Spanish possessions — must be taken over for the time being by the proletariat and led as rapidly as possible towards independence. How this process will develop is difficult to say. India will perhaps, indeed very probably, make a revolution, and as a proletariat in process of self-emancipation cannot conduct any colonial wars, it would have to be allowed to run its course; it would not pass off without all sorts of destruction, of course, but that sort of thing is inseparable from all revolutions. The same might take place elsewhere, e.g. in Algeria and Egypt, and would certainly be the best thing *for us* [Engels' emphasis].

But this passage was immediately followed by Engels' evaluation of the revolutionary capacity and role of the European proletariat and of the colonial revolution:

You ask me what the English workers think about colonial policy. Well, exactly the same as they think about politics in general: the same as the bourgeois think . . . the workers gaily share in the feast of England's monopoly of the world market and the colonies.

The Cape, with its wines, wool and diamonds, was, with India, already a major source of surplus value for Britain and of the corruption of the British worker. The racist Canadian, Cape and Australian settlers did become independent, as Engels predicted, but the course prognosticated for India was unhistorical, would be regarded as at least paternalistic, unthinkable in the 20th Century, and would be rejected by every real — that is, anti-imperialist — internationalist. Engels was assuming that the 'bourgeois proletariat' corrupted by imperialism would make a social revolution as a result of some internal class struggle in an imperialist country. At the end of the First International, before the modern anti-colonial struggles in 'India, Algeria, the Dutch and Spanish possessions' and before the corruption *en masse* of the imperialist proletariat, when the vast majority of workers were still materially poor, whatever their ideology, Engels could still write as he did. But nearly 100 years later, after socialist revolutions in China, Korea, Vietnam and Cuba, all previously colonies, after the achievement of political independence not only by the 'white' colonies but in the whole of Asia and Africa, and after the material as well as the ideological corruption of the North American and West European proletariat by modern colonialism, the illusory hopes of Engels in 1882 were still being repeated three internationals later.

The point here is that the British and other European workers also at this stage formed part of the racial-colonial process against Africa, Asia and the Americas. They exported their imperialist and racist parties and unions. Exactly at the time at which Engels wrote his letter, masses of English, Dutch, German and other European workers were coming with 'socialist' ideas to join with the British and German-Jewish capitalists in the mining industry in oppressing the Southern African proletariat with a system of racialist totalitarianism. The British trade unions and Labour Party, and the Communist Party too, place 'trade unionism' above non-racialism (as did the CPSA when it worked the Industrial Conciliation Act). This priority colonialized the African unions in all zones of Africa. The 'we are your Marx-given leaders' racist attitude of the French CGT and Socialist and Communist Parties was a major issue in the development of the trade union and independence organizations in Senegal, Ivory Coast, Mali, Guinea and Tunisia into anti-colonialist organs of struggle.[14] The Portuguese Left tried to 'guide' FRELIMO, MPLA and PAIGC, but after the FRELIMO workers had freed Portugal from Salazar in 1974 the Socialist and Communist Parties in Lisbon kept the gold from the colonies to raise Portuguese wages and permitted the return of 800,000 racist, mainly working-class settlers who, in turn, put paid to the Portuguese revolution.[15] Since 1974 the Eurocommunist parties are dragging Angola and Mozambique into the EEC 'Lomé' Convention. The Italian Socialists and Communists called for the reoccupation of Eritrea and Somalia, and also for a time of Libya, during the United Nations discussions after the war. The argument put by Togliatti's and Nenni's men was: we have a Popular Front government now, not an imperialist one, so let us have our old colonies 'taken over for the time being by the proletariat and led as rapidly as possible towards independence'. After 1960 all Italian parties backed 'Eritrea' against the national unity of Ethiopia. 'Biafra' was the same ploy. Engels' heavily qualified idea was thus converted into colonialistic, racialistic arrogance. In the field of post-independence planning, Euro-Marxists like Emmanuel and Bettelheim gave neo-colonialist advice to Zaire and Mali. European Marxism clearly played its part in the pre-independence struggles chronicled above. Among the difficulties in combating this Europeanism is the inevitable accusation of the heresy of 'revisionism' by this European Marxism itself.

The slaving and conquering companies of the primary accumulation period, side by side with the churches, first the Catholic, then also the Protestant, and the monarchies of Europe, laid the foundations during feudalism for the wealth and power of the European bourgeoisie, for its revolutions, its Industrial Revolution, later for its Free Trade expansion and the rise of industrial capital and finally of finance banking capital. This last development coincided with the rise of imperialism as the stage of colonialism under which regular enlarged reproduction or capital accumulation occurred. This required the export of investment capital, not for slaving or conquest, but for the reproductive process itself in what was becoming one world economy. The export, even when Lenin wrote his *Imperialism*, was small compared with the total accumulated capital invested annually out of the total surplus value made by the system. But it was this small portion that yielded the greatest return and became the life-blood of the capitalist system for making profit. With the change from direct colonialism to other methods, known loosely as neo-colonialism, the contribution made by the colonial surplus value to the global profit increased rapidly.

This increase manifested itself in a general tendency in Western Europe, North America, Australia, 'white' South Africa and Israel for the proletariat to identify themselves with the bourgeoisie. In the two last countries, not only for economic but also for political reasons, the process became so marked that the working class became a part of the system of colonialism, an enemy of the colonial workers, fascist and racist. The process had become irreversible. In certain imperialist countries, notably West Germany, the same irreversible trend occurred after the Second World War. As we can see from East Germany, it cannot be excluded that such working classes can never come to socialism except through the undesirable means of a 'foreign blessing'. This process of the irreversible corruption of a part of the workers became of major political importance in South Africa. Already in the early 1940s myself and others had pointed out that this group earned more than it produced in value, lived off surplus value made by Africans, and was the Nazi-type social bulwark, the political ally of the imperialist Anglo-Boer ruling class in the super-exploitation and super-oppression of the non-Europeans. During the fifties this analysis was extended, *mutatis mutandis*, to the 'imperialist bourgeoisie' as an entirety. It was confirmed by the experiences of the liberation movements in Africa and the occurrence of socialist revolutions, for the time being, only in colonial and semi-colonial countries (China, Cuba, Korea, Vietnam and Eastern Europe) and the most undeveloped imperialist-cum-colonial country, Russia itself.

As late as 1977 a conference in Dar es Salaam, debated whether the South African 'white' workers were part of the proletariat or not. The majority said 'No', but a Communist Party minority (against the ANC and some CPSA members who put non-racialism above 'class') held to the racist viewpoint of the old CPSA and ISL of 1916–26,[16] an attitude which could sacrifice the liberation struggle in South Africa to the phantom of 'class unity'. Similar racist illusions prevailed among Portuguese leftists behind Soares and Cunhal regarding the 'white' workers in Angola and Mozambique, even after these had joined the racist flood back 'home' after the African revolutions of 1974–6. The Algerian 'white' workers similarly fled as a racist whole after the victory of Ben Bella and Boumedienne, despite the neo-colonialist Evian accord with France. The same efflux, however, did not follow the 1980 Lancaster House–Zimbabwe racist and neo-colonial deal. The European illusion exists among Communists, ex-Stalinists and ex-Trotskyists alike, that the anti-Arab Israeli worker-settlers can make, even lead, a socialist transformation of a country which they have always refused to recognize as the national home of the Palestinians of all creeds. The growing Marxist attitude in Africa itself to these specific groups of workers is a result of considering a real historical development — the irreversible absorption of a part of the proletariat into the imperialist system. All the hope in the world cannot reverse an irreversible chemical, or social, reaction.

This factor of 'bourgeoisification' played a role, to a lesser degree, in French West African trade unionism and socialism, forcing Senghor, Touré and Keita to leave the European-controlled bodies to which they had belonged and leading to more independence for the African unions, for example in Tunisia.

In certain countries — Algeria, Angola, Mozambique, South Africa, Rhodesia and, later, Zambia — the 'white' workers became a massive physical obstacle to liberation, an obstacle that still remains in South Africa and continues to baulk Zimbabwe even though the 'white' population there is a mere 250,000 compared with some five million in South Africa in 1984.

Racist Liberalism

The second 'European' obstacle to liberation, which also arose out of the economic processes of imperialism, was liberalism and the concept of benevolent rule by a mother country. The economic basis of this political element, which penetrated deeply into every national movement, was monopoly capitalist chartered and Crown companies, followed by the great financial houses of today. Monopolistic capital had its roots, not in European craft guilds, but in the great European colonial mercantile 'guild' companies, which fixed a rate of profit which no member of such a company might exceed except at the risk of expulsion and ruin.[17] The capitalist 'motor' of a general rate of profit was, in fact, as Engels showed, born in the colonial system long before the bourgeois political and industrial revolutions. Among the early European companies operating in Africa were commercial bands of French Normans from Dieppe and Rouen, from 1364; Toulouse merchant groups, from 1400; Royal Portuguese companies set up in the 15th and 16th Centuries; Venetian and Genoese groups, by 1450; Gomez's Royal Chartered Company of 1469; a Florentine company selling cloth in Timbuktu by 1470; German companies from before 1485; King João's royal monopoly over Guinea from 1480 to 1500; Portuguese 'contractors' in Angola; the German company backing da Gama's murderous expedition around 1500; 16th Century Flemish slaving companies; the Elizabethan slaving companies of England, with royal charters; the English Barbary Company, 1585; 16th and 17th Century Jesuit slaving companies of missionaries; the French Company of Senegal and Gambia, 1624; the French West Africa Company, 1626; the Chartered Company authorized by Charles I to slave in Africa, 1631; the 1633 Dieppe and Rouen Senegal Company, with a ten-year slaving monopoly from Richelieu; the 1638 Cape Verde Company of Lambert; the Dutch East India Company, formed in the 17th Century; the British East India Company; the Dominican Company in Mozambique, 1650; the Mozambican Jesuit company, with its own fleet of slave-ships; the 1657 Swedish slaving company; the St Louis slaving company of Louis XIV, 1659; the British Royal African Company of Charles II, 1672; the Prussian slaving company of Friedrich Wilhelm in 1677; the Danish slaving company of the 17th Century; Brue's Royal Senegal Company, round 1700, later part of the French Company of India; private slave companies from England after 1698 (in the next decade the private slavers' ships carried 72,000 Africans to Jamaica, Barbados and Antigua, compared with the 18,000 shipped by the Royal Company, as 'free trade' follows the rising bourgeoisie); the purchase by the British monarchy in 1713 of the Spanish 'Asiento' slaving monopoly; 18th Century Birmingham and Liverpool slaving companies; private French slaving companies that succeeded to the Royal Company's monopoly when that was abolished in 1791 during the Revolution; the 1795 African Association exploration company which backed Mungo Park and his successors; the 19th Century 'exploration' companies from Britain, France, Germany, Italy and Portugal, and the American Colonization Society of 1821, which used ex-slaves to found US colonies in Liberia.

These companies increasingly used the politics of free trade and liberalism as the slave-trade became redundant to capitalism before being abolished by the British in 1808, and as slavery became a burden, with its slave revolts, sabotage and the requirement of feeding and clothing the slaves. Free ex-slave labour in the colonies was cheap; slavery was unsuited to the European metropolises growing up in the colonies, and in the cold climates of the northern regions into which capitalism was spreading, slavery could not function. The new liberalism of the colonial companies rapidly entered into the consciousness and activities of the West African intelligentsia after the British, American and French occupation of Ghana, Sierra Leone, Lagos, Liberia, St Louis, Dakar and Abidjan. It was combined with a form of 'African socialism' in the works and the actions of Blyden, Benson, Horton and — much later — Aggrey and Hayford. In the Cape it at once influenced the sons of African chiefs who had been educated in England or at mission segregated schools in the conquered Western Cape; the first Xhosa and Sotho dictionaries appeared long before conquest was completed even in the Cape. Missionaries and 'liberal' governors and newspapers educated Tiyo Soga, translator of the

English classics, and 'Tengo' Jabavu, the first African political leader, together with the priests of the Ethiopian Church. But already, by the second half of the century, the content and form of capital in Africa were changing.

Capital had got the land it needed, with access to all the wealth of the land — mineral and vegetable — for the cost of wars which were paid for many times over by the conquered themselves, each tribe or kingdom paying with toil and taxes for the conquest of the rest, like a row of dominoes felling each other. Capital now had at its disposal not only the land, the basic 'fixed capital', but also potential labour, the 'variable capital'. It had conquered both at low cost, and in the course of the conquest had built up an outlook and system of racialism which undervalued everything that was not European, not 'white'. Africa, and Africans, became cheap, and this was to have an important effect in the next period, producing a vast hidden surplus value which consisted of the difference between the sub-value cost of exports from Africa and their true value when sold as finished goods or ingredients in manufactures. This hidden surplus value, however, could not emerge without a simultaneous colonial super-surplus value obtained through regular super-exploitation by the capital invested in colonial production to create the exports of raw materials.

The greater part of Africa was taken over by this imperialist form of capital on the base of its previous conquests. The need to unite land and labour under capital, to expropriate the resisters and subject them to capital, was felt all the more keenly with the capitalization of the Suez Canal (one of the fruits of the revolutions of 1848), the sugar plantations in Natal of the 1860s, the Kimberley diamond mines in the 1870s and the gold mines of Johannesburg and the Reef in the 1880s. The new empire built up by Manchester manufacturers and by Leopold of the Belgians was officially blessed by the Manchester Chamber of Commerce and the abolitionist and missionary societies in October 1884 — even before the Berlin Conference.[18] Capital rolled ruthlessly over the dead bodies and expropriated lands of West, Central, East, North and South Africa, from the coastal conquests inwards to the remotest recesses. Rhodes,[19] and the German financiers who shared his financial empire, the Scottish landed aristocracy, the Krupps industrialists, the Unilever monopoly, French and Italian finance and industrial houses, all hastened the conquest, sending out explorers and missionaries to pave the way for the Maxim guns, the cannons, the executions and mass hangings and finally the expropriators themselves, the respectable European financial bourgeoisie. Alongside this respectability arose the Reform Laws and social democracy, votes for men, then votes for women, civil liberties, Habeas Corpus and all the democratic rights taken away from or denied to the conquered Africans, Asians and Americans. Property and democracy in Europe was born from dispossession and dictatorship in Africa. The foundations of the present ever-widening gap, economic and political, between the developed and underdeveloped countries were laid in this late 19th Century period and reinforced systematically throughout the 20th Century by ever more effective methods of disguised economic and political totalitarianism.

This totalitarianism, with its armed might in the colonies and its all-class social alliance at home, accounts for the Nazi-like fierceness, and thoroughness with which workers' strikes and peasant revolts were quelled. The economic purpose of this permanent dictatorship was to keep wages down to the barest minimum by forced labour, intensified labour and longer working hours, piece work (the basis of the cocoa, coffee and similar trades which enriched giant companies and powerful families in Europe), educational starvation, the system of compounds, locations and reserves, retribalization, pass laws and racial discrimination on all planes. Integral to this dictatorial political economy was the so-called 'traditional' or 'subsistence' economy on the fringes of the plantations and in the 'native reserves'; for this traditional or subsistence economy was — and still is — a euphemism for enforced unemployment on a colossal scale. Whereas not more than 10% of the 'imperialist proletariat' is unemployed, not more than 10% of the colonial proletariat is regularly employed. This camouflaged mass unemployment is a factor working together with direct force to preserve the cheap labour structure and dynamics of the imperialist mode of the colonial system.

The scale on which lives were taken during the class struggles in Africa far exceeds anything known in the more classic European and American class struggle. The massacres, both during strikes and land rebellions, and during the decimation and genocide against the Mau Mau, and in Ethiopia and Algeria, and the massacres by Europeans in Madagascar, Angola and Mozambique — this physical assault on the toilers had also an ideological aim: to wipe out for ever the living *memoria* in the toilers of their lost lands. For this *memoria*, like that of the Palestinians for their homes expropriated by Israel, is a living factor of resistance and liberation. Its elimination, the expropriation of the mind, was necessary for the expropriation of the lands and their divorce and alienation from the means of production.

Every class struggle was accompanied by loss of life or mass arrests, executions and fresh control laws. This was the work of monopoly capital, centred in some of the world's biggest concentrations and centralizations of finance capital in London, Paris, Berlin, Hamburg, Rome, Milan, Lisbon, Madrid, Brussels, Amsterdam, Stockholm and Zurich. But the same monopoly capitalist combinations appeared as philanthropists, with foundations, trusts and race relations institutes alongside the missionaries and their churches, which likewise had European centres in Rome, London and Canterbury, Berlin and the Rhineland, the Hague and Amsterdam. The Cape liberals in the South

African Parliament who helped Rhodes and Smuts to dispossess and disfranchise the Africans and to lead every African political organization up a collaborationist garden path — the Merrimans, Roselanes, Moltenos and their mid 20th Century offspring, with their French equivalents around Dakar, all of them had near, close or the most intimate family relations with this monopoly capital. From De Beers to Anglo-American, from Leopold's Company to the Société Générale and Union Minière, from the Rothschilds to the Boussacs and the Frenchified Aga Khan, the Krupps of old to the Krupps of the EEC, from the Lombardy companies to the Piedmont–Milanese ones, the story was the same: the most ruthless monopoly capital was presided over by the most liberal family 'governments' and national statesmen in every country of Western Europe, of every faith and every political creed. The 'essence' was masked and turned into its opposite by its 'phenomenon'. But the economic content of South African liberalism was not so much industry as the racialist Chamber of Mines. Nor was it different in French Africa. As for the Belgians and Germans, they, like the Spanish, Italians and Portuguese, did not trouble even to make such pretences; it was the mailed fist to the end in Africa, with liberalism for home consumption only. There was no room for such liberal manoeuvres for powers which had come into Africa too early or too late.

The Imperialist Missionaries

'The role of the missionaries in conquest' is the subject of several African histories. The success of this role may be measured by the paucity of works on the role of the missionaries after conquest, which is in fact more pertinent to the liberation movements. The missionaries were land and labour seizing organizations of feudal-capitalist European churches. They converted tribal usufruct into illegal private property for their missions, often for themselves (on a grand scale, in the Portuguese African empire), and for European companies and settlers. They broke down tribal loyalties to chiefs by means of commerce, the Bible and deception. They divided tribes internally, exploiting inter-tribal divisions or creating new ones, to the point of war. Nearly all were linked with the Crown or with governors and conquistadores. Their missions served as military bastions, which accounts for their frequently strategic situations. They functioned as 'divide and rule' recruiting stations. During and after conquest they became cheap labour training depots. They founded the entire segregationist educational system of South Africa and Rhodesia, which still has not changed. They dominated the minds of the conquered peoples through their churches and suppressed breakaway movements like the Ethiopian Church. They raised fratricidal 'divide and rule' conflicts between Christians and Muslims in Uganda, the Sudan, 'Iboland' and Senegal. But they never struck deep roots in Africa's soil, nor did they become a part of Africa as Islam did, on account of their colonialist and racialist character, manifested not only during conquest but in almost every strike, peasant rebellion and liberation war described above or in the chronology of the 20th Century. They tried always to divide, break, confuse and diffuse every organization that they could infiltrate, frequently by the creation of rival bodies. For the missionaries, playing 'liberation' is an old colonialist game. They played it, and still do, in Southern Africa, Angola, Mozambique, Sudanese Azania, Uganda, Namibia and Zimbabwe. In particular, they 'educated' many of the leaders of liberation movements and through 'aid' exploit famines and droughts caused by imperialistic underdevelopment. They appoint African bishops as collaborators. The structure of the Anglican and Catholic churches, in particular, is imperialistic, with theocratic governments in Canterbury and Rome respectively. In the case of the Vatican, this theocracy is a ruling class and state at the same time, with 250 million 'citizens' in Europe, North America and among the *colons* of Central and South America, and with 500 million 'subjects' in the Americas, Africa and Asia. The Vatican state-class owns capital property on a vast international scale, and is the apex of a secular and spiritual empire.

One of the most important, but most hidden, forms of resistance to primary accumulation was the anti-missionary and anti-Christian stand of the chiefs, kings, merchants, slaves and commoners in the old tribes or kingdoms. Fadiouth, in Senegal, was the very first properly organized Christian mission in Africa. Christianity there is about 500 years old, as old as the slave traffic with which it arrived in the 15th Century. Today it is a 'Christian village', and there are other 'Christian villages' near by, all built round a missionary enclave. The enclave has had many functions: it recruited slaves, sold them, put them to work, divided tribes and kingdoms, taught the conquered to dress for the benefit of the cloth-merchants of Lyons, Antwerp or Manchester, trained a handful of clerks to run the 'administration' for the French, restricted the majority to manual education, blessed them when they obeyed, excommunicated them when they revolted, prayed as their leaders were hanged in public and when they buried their dead warriors. It usually prospered in trade, with a cattle ranch or plantation near by, sometimes even a gold or other mine. After slaves they sold ivory abroad, and locally anything they could induce the people to buy with their small wages — Europe's surplus cutlery, old pianos, sewing machines, even clothes collected for nothing by European 'charities'. Fadiouth was a typical colonialist 'enclave', and such nuclei of colonialist exploitation are still common in Zaire. Around them there grew up a protoplasm of cheap labour and a reserve army of unemployed for the Belgian racists — compounds, manioc farms, huts, some stores and smaller villages petering out into nothingness until the next 'cell' of a European nucleus surrounded by African protoplasm. Such was the historical-economic nature of the mission stations throughout Africa. Time after time they were attacked, burnt or destroyed by major uprisings, because the people grasped their nature from experience. But Fadiouth seems different: it remains Christian, but, whereas Islam mixed easily and freely with paganism and entered into the spirit of Africa, the Christians of Fadiouth and neighbouring villages first have an animistic sacrifice or celebration before every Christian burial, wedding or other major occasion. Their animistic or ancestor-worship priest attends the ceremonies and the Christian 'father' is called in only afterwards to say the last words. Sacrifices and fetish ceremonies take place in nearby woods or 'sacred places'; the fetish comes before Jesus, the ancestor before the Holy Trinity, the old *gens* beliefs and rituals before the Catholic worshipping of idols, ritual drinking of blood and eating of bread and other practices that the people see as fetishistic.

Christianity here has become a thin, artificial skin grafted on to the old animism, ancestor and sun-worship. Where it did strike deep roots, in the Congo, the Cape, Rhodesia, Malawi, Uganda, Zambia and Kenya, it did so as an anti-colonial 'Ethiopian' or 'Messianic' church, away from and opposed to, and by, the missionaries, who had failed to bring the promised land, which had therefore to be sought by other means. Hence the trend to go back to the the Old Testament, with its vision of a lost land to be re-won and re-entered, and the Judaic aspect of much 'Christian' liberatory religion. There were also non-European orthodox priests and congregations who remained only formally connected with the European-dominated church, fighting its hierarchy and entering the freedom movements. Such were in the ANC, APO, NEUF, the All African Convention of 1936 and the 1944 Non European Unity Movement in South Africa. Meanwhile the Anglican and Catholic missions, as seen by non-collaborators, led the Namibians and Zimbabweans into the United Nations, the International Court, the 'dialogue', the World Council of Churches which provided the founders of the 1983 UDF and NUF, and EEC aid — any one of which could only end up in collaboration with neo-colonialism. This role of the missions is a perpetuation of the traditional colonialistic role of the missionaries both during and after conquest — a role that always had an economic base in the dominant mode of capital, slaving, mercantile or imperialistic. The old Christian missionaries were supplemented after World War II by Western 'aid'-givers, trade unionists and 'advisers'.

These, then, from monopoly imperialist to 'white' worker, liberal institutions and Christian missions, comprised the socio-political bloc against which the African toilers had to wage their 20th Century class struggles. Until independence, there was no significant 'colonial bourgeoisie' to fight as a class standing with imperialism. Whether independence changed this relationship of class forces is a matter not only for debate but also for active struggle today. But before independence such a bourgeois national class did not exist as an economic-social reality. But the future sun of independence certainly cast some shadow of a future bourgeoisie on the path of the liberation movements. There were chiefs, professional men, intellectuals, trade union leaders with long and numerous connections with European liberalism, missionaries and socialism. This proto-class, pre-class, not-yet-a-class, perhaps-never-a-class, played a major role in many liberation movements to an extent depending on its relative weight in the colony and the organizations of the toilers.

It is the role played by this social layer in the liberation movements that makes its social-economic origins of prime significance. These origins are likewise responsible for the inevitably dictatorial and non-democratic nature of semi-colonial independent states. For the economic roots of the non-bourgeois 'bourgeoisie' in the independence movements were formed in a soil of mass poverty and a monopolization of great wealth — a combination fatal to democracy, especially in the absence of a stable, self-assured bourgeoisie able to dispose without coercion of a sizable surplus. When this surplus goes abroad, the means for democracy emigrate with it, and the foreign surplus dominates instead over its own source in Africa, Asia or colonial America.

Indirect Rule: No National Bourgeoisie

The relative absence of an African bourgeoisie goes back to the nature of pre-colonial society, which from far back in time has influenced the liberation movements. The predominantly communal nature of pre-colonial society did not provide the material means or the social forms for the adequate formation of classes which colonialism could take over during and after conquest to mediate its own domination, as it could and did in India, Ceylon and Java. The castes of royal courts, priests and military echelons were too tribal, too closely related to the communal land and labour base of the old society to be able to function in the new colonial system. In particular, they were not adapted to private landed property or chattel slavery; they could not serve the Europeans on the new basis of chattel slaving and slavery and private landed property. Their expropriation in terms of property as well as forms of labour at the same time expropriated them politically. They were rendered landless, their labour-base was removed, and they lost their power. As dominant ruling castes, let alone classes, they could not survive under colonial slaving, private property and labour relations. Nor could they, in their old form, maintain their power, which rested on their being communal custodians, when they had over their heads a foreign power with local European governors, generals, missionaries, laws, police, traders, soldiers and advisers. Their power evaporated as soon as it came from above and not from below. All these factors, together with the inertia of ancestor-worship and the momentum of Islam, both with strong communal tenets, and with the long tradition by which they were looked on as leaders of the *gens,* confederation of tribes or communal kingdom, each with its internal cohesion as a people — all these combined to make the despotic ruling castes and classes of the communal kingdoms into leaders of the resistance movements. A minority collaborated, but most led the wars against slavery and dispossession and even, later, the modern class struggles that arose after Berlin, as was the case with Samory, Tippoo Tib, Zubair, with Dinizulu during the Zulu rebellion, with Witbooi during the war against the Germans in Namibia, with the Maji Maji insurgents and the late Algerian leaders.

The old communal system did not readily lend itself to the transformation of the old dominant castes and classes into a class sub-serving colonialism. On the contrary it lent itself to the conversion of those castes and classes into anti-colonialist resisters. This was true of Haile Selassie's war of liberation against Italy, of the 'Mad Mullah' who opposed Britain and of Abd el Krim's struggle against France and of many chiefs who fought against Boers and Britons in South Africa, Rhodesia, Namibia and East Africa.

But the old pre-colonial system was not useless to colonialism. It provided the raw material for a transmutation into forms of 'indirect rule' through retribalization, the conversion of chiefs into puppets and the replacement of hereditary chiefs by paid ones; and for the employment of the tradition of communal labour to preserve a vast army of unemployed. The outward, apparent form of tribalism, even the old kingdoms, were preserved, but the kernel was excised. The cheap labour reservoirs were known as 'native reserves' or 'tribal lands'. Customary law became 'native law' and was used to regiment and control the conquered peoples, for cheap labour and to contain their rebellions. The communal lands became Crown lands, which seemed still to belong to the tribes and kingdoms but actually did not. Certain features of tribalism, such as the enlarged family and cooperative labour, gave rise to 'Ujamaa' and 'Harambee' respectively. These became post-independence methods of collecting and stimulating cheap labour working for foreign imperialist companies and interests. In South Africa, tribalism became the actual form of 'independence' in the Bantustans, and in Swaziland the independent government has recently become overtly tribal. British Boer and other European settlers and investors exploit the land and labour, but the government is 'communal', a tribal kingdom under an old-style monarchy. In 'Bophuthutswana', a bureaucracy manages the world's foremost platinum mine, 'Impala', the 'non-racial' 'Sun City' weekend casino, golf-links, pools for 'White' South Africans, and daily labour from Ga Runkwa Reserve for Rosslyn's 100 'White'-owned industries over the 'border'.

Before independence the system of retribalization, of continuing the pre-colonial society in a colonial form into which it had been changed by colonialism, became so general that the colonial form was often taken as the old form. When tribalism was studied, it was not real tribalism but the 'indirect rule', retribalized colonial form.

But the retribalized, colonial form of tribalism itself made impossible the emergence of a national bourgeoisie, even of a merchant class. The more prosperous Africans tended to be the offspring of the privileged, retribalized collaborators or mission-favoured protégés inside the reserves or locations. The political economy of the system of indirect rule, begun by Faidherbe from Senegalese bases, Shepstone from Natal and Venn and Grey from Ghana, Sierra Leone and Nigeria between 1850 and 1870, was completed by Lyautey, Lugard, Curzon and Milner in the early 20th Century. Under this system the European foreign companies owned the cities, mines and plantations; the settlers owned their farms, sometimes as foreign-linked planters, and the rest of the land was Crown land or native reserves. In these reserves there were no proper farms, no towns other than European commercial and mission 'enclaves', no railways, industry or viable economy of any kind.

'Pre-Capitalist Economy' or Capitalist Labour Reserves

They had chiefs and councils, but these were puppets of the Europeans, often under 'White' magistrates in the region. Their production seemed to be communal, but in some reserves — Bas Zaire, Transkei, Lesotho, Botswana, Zululand, Kikuyu, Luo, Upper Senegal, near-coastal Nigeria — nearly all able-bodied men were drained off, so that any efficient, let alone communal labour, was impossible. When the European companies and settlers had satisfied their labour demands, only the aged and the young were left. Other reserves, in contrast, were not of this 'empty' type, but were over-full to the point at which the soil was exhausted and eroded, not by over-population or over-stocking of cattle, but as a result of land-starvation. Yet others are of the Bophuthutswana form.

Land-starvation went hand in hand with industrial and educational starvation in a primary industry economy designed for the export of minerals and raw materials destined to be productively consumed, mainly in Western Europe. Land-starvation was accompanied by taxation to force the cheap labour out of the reserves on to the European estates and mines, by cattle-culling to prevent any independence and self-support, by forced labour and by recruitment through chiefs and Native Labour Recruiting Corporations linked to Nazistic Native Affairs Departments — 'states within states', powers unto themselves, totalitarian unifiers of the state and monopoly capital. The Bantu Affairs Department of South Africa today, the old, British-created

Native Affairs Department of Rhodesia, the Native Affairs Departments in the German, Belgian and British territories before independence, were all such 'states within states', complete models of Nazism before Hitler, in notable contrast to the Tory, Liberal, Catholic and Social Democratic governments in the 'home countries'. Pastoral and agricultural activities in the reserves were auxiliary to production in the European nuclei, the cities, mines, plantations and missions, not production by independent self-supporting producers consuming their produce and disposing of the surplus. The lands left for nominal occupation in the reserves, qualitatively and quantitatively small, could not produce enough for subsistence; a surplus was unthinkable, and never part of the economy. This was not subsistence economy in the pre-colonial sense, but an economy of desperate survival, to supplement — and, paradoxically, thereby to lower further — the low wages paid by the European masters. In such conditions there was no room, no chance, for a rural national bourgeoisie, peasant, capitalist farmer or merchant.

Those who overcame these difficulties, in a bourgeois sense of the term, did so as exceptions — one or two rich Africans in a vast reserve area, even in a whole country. Kenyatta and Koinange in Kenya, the Quisling satrap of apartheid, Buthulezi in Zululand, Matanzima in Transkei, Ojukwe in eastern Nigeria (Biafra)[20] — these were the exceptions that proved the rule, and most of them owed their success to family links with the puppet chiefs appointed by the Europeans, the retribalized 'Native' or 'Bantu' authorities, especially in British Africa. The Belgians, Germans, Portuguese and Italians relied more on direct rule by Europeans than on indirect rule, and did not encourage the development of such links between commerce and the tribal authorities. The Portuguese *assimilado* system was a threadbare mask for naked racialism. In Ethiopia the Italians lived in a permanent state of siege by the resistance movement, but they did develop a system of indirect rule in Eritrea and Somalia, where puppet chiefs and a small urban trading sub-class emerged which was to become the later leadership of secessionist or independence movements. The Belgians allowed no scope for any such development until after the Second World War, but they did apply the system of indirect rule extensively in their cheap labour reserves which fed the Katanga copper mines, diamond mines, oil, sugar and other plantations, railways and harbours and domestic servant requirements. This last was one of the major employment areas throughout the pre-independence period. The reserves were simply reservoirs of the unemployed for all these labour requirements of the Europeans. In such unemployment zones there was no scope for the old type of communal society despite deliberate appearance to the contrary, let alone for a modern type of bourgeoisie.

Associated with the reserve system and the plantation enclaves in West, Central and East Africa was the so-called *économie de traite*,

95

under which what looked like peasant labour grew cocoa, coffee and similar products which could be grown individually for sale to powerful overseas buying, exporting and manufacturing companies. This was not in fact an independent peasantry which could form its own rural bourgeoisie; it was a class of piece-work labourers producing indirect super-profits for imperialists who bought cheap and sold at the full value.

The Proletarian Peasantry

The cocoa and other *économie de traite* producers in Ghana, Ivory Coast, Nigeria, Niger and the Congo were the poorest labourers, unemployed during the off-season and when there were slumps in world prices, living in an economic limbo between reserve and plantation. But on the periphery of this limbo-land there developed a group of middlemen operating between the overseas buying companies and the producers. These intermediaries became totally dependent on the monopoly capitalists, who dominated their dealings with the producers, and in the end their function as middlemen became nationalized, as in the Ghana Cocoa Marketing Board, which became a state middleman for giant European multinationals. From these commission-taking groups of middlemen there grew up groups of peri-urban and urban traders and 'native markets' in Abidjan, Accra, Dakar, Léopoldville and every big African city. While these markets and their stall-holders were economically trivial, despite their extensive appearance, and were subservient to the European buyers and exporters, some small trading bourgeois elements did come out of them and enter into the national movements, inevitably with the effect of making them more and more into means for bargaining with the imperial masters of farming and commerce, into a machinery for winning property and trading concessions and for 'negotiations'. Outstanding examples of these trends were the Indian Congresses of Natal, Transvaal and Kenya, the French West African Traders and Farmers Associations and the Nigerian and Ghanaian Market societies. These were not all products of the *économie de traite*, but often of more urban colonialist complexes.

The system of indirect rule and re-tribalization was racialist. The rural reserves implied a racial segregation and discrimination in land holding. This was one side of an entire system whose other components were to be found in the locations and compounds on European-owned farms and in the towns. These locations accommodated the labour force, with their families, in segregated areas off the main parts of the European estate or of the town or city, often far from the place of work itself — a cause of the long walking or travelling time that results in so much inefficiency today. In the locations there were generally a Native Affairs Officer, a mission station, some small shops, perhaps a cinema, a bus-station, a primary school or two, perhaps even a secondary school. The compound was for bachelors and imprisoned farm and mine workers for the period of their labour contracts, cutting them off totally from all urbanization and social life other than that planned for them by the mining companies and planters. In these compounds there was absolutely no room for the development of a bourgeoisie.

The Location Sub-Bourgeoisie

In the urban location — the biggest of them is Soweto, scene of the rising of June 1976 — there was more room for such development. But the vast majority of the inhabitants were temporary, under the pass laws and labour control laws of the British, French, Belgians and Portuguese, and 'agitators' were sent either to gaol, or as forced labour to a farm, or back to die in the reserves. It was difficult for such a migrant working class, moving between mine and reserve, industry and reserve, to settle down into a 'city' proletariat. The city was probably 20 kilometres or more away, or was a prohibited curfew zone; its facilities were taboo, or could not be afforded. Trade unions and political parties were not permitted until well into the 20th Century, and strikers were shot down. The locations were strategically built so as to contain strikes and uprisings. The white-controlled police were always about; the missions were never far away. The factories, shops and European housing estates were far away, but had to be reached for the sake of survival. There were hardly any big stores, factories or production units in the locations. At most a small trading petit bourgeoisie or property-dealing group was allowed in the locations, and of course bus-owners to bridge the necessarily great distance to the European city. A small, divided, scattered, unco-ordinated 'location bourgeoisie' arose, with a location mentality — often indeed a tribal mentality, for the locations were divided into tribal sections ('divide and rule' again). In this atmosphere of racial locations and nearby racial compounds, both separated from the city but connected with the reserves, a certain 'black consciousness', supra-tribal or otherwise, began to develop from the creation of the first of such locations in the Cape and West Africa in the middle of the 19th Century.

Forms of Wage-Labour

The bourgeoisie itself was neither an industrial nor a financial one. It had no base in production; it was peripheral, dependent, semi-commercial, and only a few reached real wealth. They can be counted on the fingers of two hands for the whole of West, Central, East and South Africa. To this day they lack a productive base except through state nationalization of primary production. The colonialist process of industrial starvation supplemented the location system, and the two together inhibited the formation of a proper national bourgeoisie. But both gave a specific character to the proletariat. The proletarian remained linked to the reserve, where his family was often forced to remain. He was unfree to move, unfree to sell his labour power as an unbound commodity. Outside South Africa and Rhodesia there was little or no industry. He belonged to a mining, plantation, railway and harbour, commercial and domestic service proletariat. He was not allowed in the city, could not form free unions to bargain collectively, could not raise his wages except by risking his life and that of his fellows. He was a social pariah and a political outcast, with no fixed home, no fixed place of work, no education, no franchise. He earned a tenth or less of the 'White' worker policing his work or of the European or American worker, yet he produced a surplus value which was part of the world surplus value on which capital lived and out of which it subsidized the wages and democracy of European and American labour.

The bulk of the location proletariat worked more and more in such industry as there was and in non-primary production. the bulk of the compounded proletariat was migrant, on contract often from other colonies and, later, other independent states. Most labour in Africa was migrant before independence and migrant labour remains a major field of reality and study under independence itself.

Migrant, compounded labour formed a proletariat which had strong connexions with the retribalized reserves and with *économie du traite* producers. The labourer, even in mining, was half-rural, unsettled, non-urban. But mining was, and remains, the very hub of African economy. In particular the gold mines in Transvaal and Orange Free State, employing a half-rural, unsettled, contracted migrant proletariat, operates the financial fulcrum of the world capitalist system at its crucial point: the point of production. This very un-classical worker with the air of a peasant stands at the centre of modern world capitalist economy and is, in fact, the essence of 'universal human labour'. His labour time is the basis of all value. He produces in one hour, on an average, one gram of gold — the universal measure of value all over the world, currently worth some ten US dollars. His productivity is measured not only technologically (it is the highest in his field in the world) but in its production of super-surplus value. His wages form less than one-tenth of the value he creates with his labour. His rate of surplus value, or degree of exploitation, is 10:1, over a hundred times more than the 1:10 ratio in imperialist countries,[21] where most labour produces negative surplus value, the labour day being less than the necessary labour time. The difference is subsidized by colonial or semi-colonial super-surplus value. This gold-mining worker is a true proletarian. He may and does aspire to land, he does starve to save for some cattle to save his family from death by starvation on a distant Bantustan or reserve or in a foreign country. But he is not a peasant any more than he is a European-type proletarian. In Africa the European kind of peasant and proletarian does not exist, except as a rarity, and nowhere did he live or work or have political rights and activities as in Europe. As Marx, quoted by Senghor, explained, the European development is not a universal pattern, nor is the Euramerican privileged proletariat a world model. Indeed, the proletariat is mainly to be found in Africa, Asia and semi-colonial America. The number working directly for imperialism is some 150 million, at full strength, half of the European, North American, Japanese and 'White Commonwealth' proletariat, but there are a further 1,000 million who are peasants, unemployed or under-employed, despite toiling desperately to survive. They are members of this proletariat. This ratio of unemployed to employed is almost the inverse of the proportion in Europe and North America. It is not 'classical' — nothing really is — but it is real; and it has played a decisive role in the development of liberation movements in Africa.

This class is by socio-economic nature a class not interested in anything but emancipation and liberation. Its opposite pole is monopoly imperialist capital, with its colonial and semi-colonial cohorts and states, its international blocs of the kind that have evolved into NATO and the EEC. Its aims are inevitably anti-capitalistic in the long term, because it is super-exploited by capitalism through various labour-forms.

Capitalism has always been an economic system whose essence is the production of surplus value by accumulated capital. The form of this capital has changed during its reign of half a millennium, from usurious and mercantile to industrial and finally to banking (Africa, Asia and Latin America owe the European and American banks 1,000 billion dollars at the time of writing). The form of the labour exploited by these changing modes of capital has likewise changed, from slave to indentured semi-slave, semi-serf labour, to forced labour, to 'free migrant' labour, to 'free' chronically unemployable 'settled' labour regimented by totalitarian methods of direct colonialism, to 'free' wage labour, still cheap and producing ever-increasing super-profits, but exploited by monopoly capital indirectly through certain state-property forms under independence and through certain conventions, such as the Lomé Convention, which is the fulcrum of EEC imperialism.

With each change in the form of capitalism and labour in Africa the struggle itself underwent changes. It fell heavily under the influence of the colonialist abolitionist and emancipation movement of mission-aries and liberals up to and beyond the 1850s, which marked its approximate significant starting point in the Cape, the Senegal ports, Monrovia, Libreville and Sierra Leone. The liberal–missionary move-ment at the time of the Industrial Revolution in Europe laid a firm paternalistic, segregationist, race-conscious hand — an 'Africanist identity-cult' hand — on the shoulder of those early movements which stirred in the first formations of coastal and other urban working classes in 19th-Century Africa. The liberalism of imperialism, of monopoly finance capitalism, took a hold on the young intellectuals emerging from the new social formations in the European-controlled urban enclaves and their rural mission-station schools. And the new liberalism had a fellow: Chartism, trade unionism, Fabianism and later Labour socialism from the British middle and working classes, 'enlightenment', rationalism and socialism from the French middle class and workers, came to British and French Africa respectively. Liberalism and socialism quickly entered into the early nationalist ideas and organizations at the Cape and in British and French West Africa. Spanish and Italian anarchism had some slight influence in North Africa, but remained a 'White' affair. German social democracy, the later Spartacists apart, stood shoulder to shoulder with Bismarck and the Kaiser and stuck to national problems, leaving colonial problems to the jackboot of Von Trotha, Goering and Von Lettow. Finally, in the 20th Century forms of European capital and African labour, liberals, missionaries and socialists from Europe developed new influences upon and means of control for the fast unfolding and expanding liberation movements. Appearing more African than the Africans, they were in reality Europeanizing the mind of these movements as deeply as their capital was taking over the whole of the physical continent and its labour power.

Notes

1 . Hobson, *Imperialism* (on Rhodes); V.I. Lenin, *Imperialism*, 1916; R. Luxemburg, *The Accumulation of Capital*, 1913; H. Grossmann (1929), *Il Crollo del Capitalismo*, Milan, 1977 (Frankfurt, 1967).

2. H. Jaffe, *Pyramid of Nations*, Luxembourg, 1980; article, 1946; 'Fascism in South Africa', Fascism and Imperialism', in *Workers Voice*, July 1944, Cape Town.

3. The 1915 Founding Conference and the 1916 conference of the International Socialist League (ISL) accepted the industrial, social and political colour bar. Some delegates thought Africans 'biologically inferior' (H.J. Simons, *Class and Colour in South Africa, 1850–1950*, London, 1969); *International*, ISL organ of 17 March 1916 blamed capitalism for breaking down the 'ethnological tendency' to a 'natural social apartness of white and black' (ibid., p. 193). Racist articles appeared in October 1915 to December *International* issues (from 1921 it was an organ of the Communist Party of South Africa [CPSA], founded by left Zionists and ISL leaders, like Ivor Jones and W.H. Andrews, a leader of 'White' skilled anti-African workers).

4. C. Kadalie, *My Life and the ICU*, London, 1970 (his widow, Eva, thanked the author for a sympathetic review); for defence of liberals and British trade unions, see M. Ballinger, *From Union to Apartheid*, London, 1969

5. The rejection of the ICU affiliation application, signed by CPSA

officers, W.H. Andrews and Weinbren, was reported in the *Star*, Johannesburg, 16 January 1928.

6. Photographs of Fordsburg and Johannesburg banners calling for a 'White Socialist South Africa' in 1922 (Radio Hilton Library, London). The *International* of 13 January 1922, calls for industrial segregation; after the pogrom-strike, it published 'So It Seems' and other racist articles. March 1922 press photographs (reproduced in H. Jaffe, *Africa*, op. cit., p. 249) show funerals of Africans killed by the 'White' strikers. The CPSA officially supported the 'White' strike, in a Manifesto of 30 January 1922 (reprinted in A. Lerumo, *Fifty Fighting Years — The South African Communist Party, 1921–71*, London, 1971, pp. 119, 120) and republished in *International* of 3 February 1922.

7. M. Kumaliza, 'Tanganyika's View of Labour's Role', *East Africa Journal*, April 1964; C.K. Lubembe (Kenya TUC), 'Trade Unions and Nation Building', *East Africa Journal*, April, 1964; J.K. Tettegah, *Towards Nkrumahism — The Role and Tasks of the Trade Unions*, Accra, 1962; Sekou Touré, 'L'Action du P.D.G. au Lutte pour L'Emancipation Africaine', *Présence Africaine*, 1959; HMSO, London, 1955 on Sierra Leone strike-wave.

8. H.C. Armstrong, *Grey Steel* (J.C. Smuts), London, 1937; 'The religious sect was driven home with rifles and machine guns; 300 were killed and wounded.' (p. 246).

9. S. Pankhurst, *Ex-Italian Somaliland*, op. cit.

10. J. Ngugi, 'On Didan Kimathi, Mau Mau leader; 'The Martyr', in *Modern African Prose* (ed. R. Rive), London, 1964.

11. H. Jaffe, *Kenya — from Direct to Indirect Colony*, Milan, 1968.

12. G. Mbeki, *The Peasant Revolt*, London, 1964; I.B. Tabata, *The Rehabilitation Scheme — A New Fraud*, Cape Town, 1955.

13. Blaise Diagne, in *Notes Africaines, 1872–1972*, IFAN, Dakar; and, with W.B. du Bois: 'Statutes of the Black Race', for 1919 Pan-African Conference, Paris.

14. I. Davies, *African Trade Unions*, London, 1966.

15. W. Burchett and H. Jaffe, *Una Democrazia Confezionata? Il Caso del Portogallo*, Milan, 1975.

16. S. Amin, 'The Future of Southern Africa' (introduction to report of 1975 Dar-es-Salaam conference organized by Institute for Development and Planning (IDEP) and the Committee for the Liberation of Southern Africa). Amin cites H. Jaffe, *Processo Capitalista*, Milan, 1973 against South African Euro-Marxists.

17. F. Engels, Appendix to K. Marx, *Capital*, vol. 3.

18. H. Stanley, Manchester addresses cited.

19. C.J. Rhodes, 'Speeches', in *Cape Hansard*; also Plomer, Sarah G. Millen biographies; for details of Rhodes' policies: Mnguni, *300 Years*, op. cit., vol. 2, where British imperialism is seen as main founder of 'apartheid'; for opposite view: Bunting, *The South African Reich*, London and M. Benson, *The Struggle for A Birthright*, London, 1966, chapters 9–20; R.W. Rose-Innes, *The Glen Grey Act and the Native Question*, Cape Town, 1903 (including accounts of resistance).

20. H. Jaffe, *Nigeria vs. 'Biafra'*, Milan, 1969.

21. Mnguni, *300 Years*, vol. 3; H. Jaffe, 'Negative Surplus Value', *Economic Register*, Milan, 1978, 1979 and in *Pyramid of Nations*, op. cit. (articles, 1944, 1980; Minutes of 'Quale Crise?', conference, Milan, 22–3 April 1983.

PART FOUR

Imperialism — African Emancipation

Imperialism — African Emancipation

Resistance and liberatory struggles and their organizations, if any, had necessarily to adapt themselves to the behaviour and 'national character' of the particular European power dispossessing, enslaving and ruling them. Holland, which had a 17th Century merchant and armed navy greater than that of all other nations added together, gave slaves, tribes and artisans little room for manoeuvre outside of flight or desperate half-armed revolts, such as did occur in Gorée (named by Dutch slavers), and the Cape of Good Hope. Louis XIV, XV and XVI, the Napoleons and the Boufflers and Faidherbes of Bordeaux and Paris, represented an empire grandiose enough until Clive defeated Dupleix in India and Wolfe laid Montcalm low in Canada, to afford a small indigenous petite bourgeoisie in the colonial ports of St Louis and Dakar, to begin with, and this semi-class, in turn, combined militancy with servility in its numerous struggles. By the time of the French Revolution, the French Empire was in decline, but it recovered with 19th Century conquests in Algeria, West Africa, Malagasy, Tunisia, Morocco, Ubangi Shari and the Congo — apart from its new Indo-Chinese colonial seizures. The new and greatest ever power was Britain. The rise to world supremacy of Britain was most probably the force which generated the first of the so-called Kondratief long-waves of capitalist booms and crises. This wave (1789 to 1848) rose up with Britain until about the time of the Congress of Vienna, when the early ascent of the USA and world market problems which put the Industrial Revolution in crisis took the curve downwards again. In this first world-wave of capitalism, the Cape experienced an 'Indian summer' of racial tyranny, rapid conquests of Khoi-Khoin and Bantu and extensive Dutch, British and German colonization, on the one hand, and, on the other, the 1808 Abolition of the Slave Trade, Ordinance 50 of 1828 for 'Free Persons of Colour', Emancipation of Slaves in the British Empire in 1834 and limited property and voting rights for 'Coloured' and non-tribal 'Natives' in 1852, when the first settler representation was allowed by Westminster. In law and fact 99.99% of the Xhosa, Fingo, Tembu,

Griqua, Namaqua, Sotho and other conquered or besieged peoples were without any franchise and had lost their communal lands to settlers or the Crown. The very vastness of the British Empire, despite the loss of the USA in 1783 (thrice compensated from the value viewpoint by the gain of India) left economic and political pores in the Cape political-economy for reformism and negotiation which were to become a long tradition later in the APO, the ANC and, in Natal, in Gandhi's Indian Congress. These organizations, however, were formed after the 'Indian summer' of Cape pseudo-liberalism had come to an end.

The early political movements of the Cape, Natal, Liberia, Sierra Leone, St Louis — Dakar and Monrovia showed birth-marks stamped upon them by the changing nature and role of the colonial powers in Africa during the second Kondratief wave (1849–96) which was drawn upwards at first by the rapid rise of new colonial powers, like the USA, Germany, post-Risorgimento Italy, Belgium and the recovery of France on a world scale under Napoleon III after the 1848 revolution. These new colonialist expansions 'completed the bourgeois revolution' of 1848. Around the 1871 Paris Commune, inter-imperialist rivalry and new international production and market crises, including numerous Panama canal and other burst bubbles on the freshly-born stock exchanges reflecting the world-colonialist nature of capitalism, began to turn the long-wave down again in spite of a sudden expansion of the USA's 'Go West' imperialism, the Kimberley and Johannesburg mining revolution, and the completion of the conquests of the Zulus (1879); the Tswana, Sotho, Matabele and Mashona in southern Africa; and of Namibia, Tanganyika and Cameroons by rising German imperialism; of West, Sudanese and Saharan Africa by Britain or France; of Egypt and the Sudan by Britain; and of Somalia and Red Sea Ethiopia by Italy. Although the downward movement of the world cycle reflected the relative — but not absolute — decline of Britain, in Africa British policy remained in the ascendant, and this, together with the rise of socialism and liberalism in Britain and France, was to have profound effects on the first nationalist and socialist intellectuals and their organizations and methods of struggle.

The swift and brutal rise of Germany, the beginning of the definitive decline of Britain and France, the unquestioned ascent to world supremacy of the USA (hence the power of Garveyism, of du Bois' Pan Africanism and of the American-bred West African nationalists) affected every African struggle and movement during the third Kondratief wave (1896–1939), when conquest was completed on a world, and hence also African, scale, when the question was the repartition of Africa after the 1884 Berlin Agreement, which still broadly defines the national boundaries of Africa, and when no African organization could avoid the political issues raised by the 1914–18 war and the outbreak of the 1939–45 world war. Both of these divided old movements, or else gave rise to new ones with new ideas and methods of struggle, in South, West, East and North Africa in particular.

Finally, the period of decolonization and independence, at least nominally or formally (1945–80, approximately, beginning with Ethiopia, Libya, Egypt and the Sudan, and ending with Guinea-Bissau, Angola, Mozambique, Zimbabwe, and, potentially, Namibia) was that of the fourth Kondratief (1940 to probably about the end of the 20th Century) in the capitalist world of which Africa is a major and literally fundamental part. This fundamentality derives from the place of Africa in the base of the capitalist pyramid of nations (or, in centre–periphery language, as the major outer-peripheral mass in the world central-force system). Independence has increased this basic position and function, and this increase has duly manifested itself politically among African leaders and organizations of every kind.

Early Cape Political Movements

Studies made in most African universities have thrown light on 19th Century political ideas. Work done inside liberation movements in Southern Africa have exposed the early roots of African political organization in the Cape. The Cape African intellectuals arose amidst the final conquest of the Xhosa. Glasgow missionaries produced a Xhosa vocabulary in 1826 at Lovedale, later a famous mission centre in the Eastern Cape. The Wesleyan mission in Grahamstown produced the first published Xhosa grammar, in 1834, after the defeat of Ndlambe, Makanda and Hintsa, with the help of Theophilus Shepstone, later to become Secretary for Native Affairs in Natal and to formulate most clearly the first principles of the policy of indirect rule through 'Bantu chiefs' and retribalization. In 1846, Wesleyans issued a Xhosa vocabulary and in 1850 a Xhosa grammar. In 1859 the first Zulu grammar book was issued by a liberal, Colenso, in Pietermaritzburg, after the defeat of Dingane. The Rhenish missionaries translated their catechism into 'Hottentot' in Cape Town in 1820 and the Wesleyans made a Namaqua–'Hottentot' grammar in 1857. The London Missionary Society leader, Moffat, issued a 'Bechuana catechism' in 1826, and Archbell a Sechuana grammar in 1837, both long before the Anglo-Boer conquest of the Sotho-Tswana confederation of Moshoeshoe. These and other Christian studies in the vernacular brought the sons of chiefs and conquered kings to England, Cape Town and Lovedale, where also the first Xhosa poets, Tiyo Soga and his son, and the political leader Tengo Jabavu,[1] fell under British liberal-missionary influence from the beginning. The first political organizations, such as the Imbumba Yama Africa (Union of Africans), formed in 1882, rose in protest against labour and land laws directed against workers, but missionary-educated intellectuals took charge of them. In 1884 Nehemiah Tile broke away from the Wesleyans to form the separatist Tembu Church in Eastern Cape, opposed to British racial taxes. From this church came the song 'Nkosi sikelel' i Afrika' ('God save Africa'), which is still the national anthem of the South African National Congress and the All African Convention — evidence of the missionaries' influence in the liberation movement, for the song is now over 90 years old. In 1884 the Revd Elijah Makiwane formed a conservative Native Education Association, backed by John Tengo Jabavu (1859–1921), who in 1881 had edited *Isigidimi Sama Xhosa*, a liberal protest journal. In 1884 Jabavu founded the Native Electoral Association to get voters under Rhodes's racial electoral laws to elect a Liberal to the Cape Parliament. The Liberal leader, Rose-Innes, financed Jabavu's paper *Imvo Zabantsundu* (African Opinion). Jabavu pledged loyalty to Queen Victoria, submission to legal authority and non-violent petitioning as a method of struggle. His influence was profound and, although he did not take part in its foundation, he was a pioneer spirit in the founding of the African National Congress in 1912. Such were the British liberal–missionary European beginnings of the first South African modern African political organizations. This liberal and missionary formative influence was itself closely associated with Cecil Rhodes' diamond and gold empire; when he had conquered Lobengula in 1894 he thanked the missionary societies and the abolitionist movement.[2] The Liberals functioned as a safety-valve for 'native opinion' while accepting and operating a parliament and executive for 'Whites' only, with a Native Affairs Department, during the period of Rhodes, Schreiner, Merriman and Jameson, long before Union in 1910, when Cape and British liberals led the anti-Union campaign of Jabavu and Abdurahman into futile legalistic petitioning in Cape Town and London.

In 1887 the all-powerful Chamber of Mines was formed, followed by a Native Labour Recruiting Corporation, both of them working with Native Affairs Departments at the British Cape, in British Natal and in the Transvaal of Kruger and the Orange Free State of Fisher (grandfather of Bram Fisher, Communist Party martyr of recent times). In 1887, too, Jabavu led a conference of no fewer than a hundred delegates in Kingwilliamstown to take up, in the manner taught by the liberals, the demand of landless workers for land, against the land-robbery of the companies and government of Rhodes. Jabavu himself was a teacher and lay minister who had matriculated at Lovedale Mission in 1885 — only the second to do so. The first important African intellectual in the Cape had been Tiyo Soga (1829–71). His father had been a tribal councillor of 'Gaika' and died after Soga, in the 1877–8 war of resistance of Ngqika and Galeka against the British. Soga came from a polygamous tribal family; his father sent him to Lovedale and then to Glasgow, at whose university he graduated in theology in 1856, to return to the Cape in 1857 with a Scottish bride, to preach loyalty to the Queen and the Cape Government as a Presbyterian-liberal convert. Jabavu, also from a tribal background, likewise said that the Africans were the 'English party's devoted allies' and that 'we preach submission to superiors'. In 1887 he petitioned Victoria against the disfranchising Registration Act of Rhodes, and became an election agent of the Rose-Innes Liberals, although they accepted and operated the 1892 anti-Coloured and anti-African Ballot Act and prevented a Moslem, Effendi, from being elected. Among those responsible for Jabavu's political training was W.B. Schreiner, doyen of Cape liberalism, who believed that Africans should be 'represented' in Parliament by 'Whites'; there should be no non-Europeans in Parliament. He followed the Liberals and British Fabian socialists in supporting the British Empire in the Boer War of 1899–1901, as did Gandhi and Abdurahman. The British Independent Labour Party supported the racialist anti-African Boers, of whom the European Marxist E. Sik said in 1966 that they had written 'one of the most glorious chapters in the history of liberation wars'. Both views are rejected by all liberation movements in South Africa today — 'A plague on both your houses!' In October 1902 Jabavu condemned the racial clauses in the Vereeniging Peace Treaty, as did Abdurahman in the April 1903 number of Jabavu's *Imvo*.

Abdul Abdurahman (1872–1940) came from Muslim grandparents who had freed themselves from slavery with their own savings. They opened a fruit shop on the edge of District Six, the Cape Town 'Coloured' location, and financed their son Abdul Rahman to become a student of theology in Cairo and Mecca. 'Hadjie' Abdurahman in turn sent his eldest son Abdul to the South African College (SACS) in Cape Town, at that time non-racial. When the school run by liberals, introduced a colour bar, the father took two other sons to qualify in Britain. Abdul matriculated at SACS and then graduated in medicine in Glasgow in 1893, returning in 1895 with a Scottish bride. He soon linked up with an ex-Ghanaian, F.Z.J. Perigrino (1853–1919), John Tobin and Collins to inspire the formation of the APO in 1902 and to become its president after the expulsion of Tobin and Collins for supporting 'White' parties in elections in 1904 — a policy that Abdurahman was at once to follow himself. He remained President from 1905 until his death in 1940. The founders of the APO came from the small traders, artisans and free workers among the former slave and Khoi-Khoin 'Coloured' of the Western Cape.

The Indian leader Gandhi[3] came to Natal as a legal adviser in 1893, founded the Indian Congress in 1894 and remained in South Africa until 1914. Of Indian professional middle-class origin, like so many of the Indian leaders in South Africa, he held a paternalistic view of Africans, whom he saw as naive tribalists to whom civilization was a danger. He formed a stretcher corps for Britain in the Boer War and again when Britain crushed the Bambatta workers' revolt in 1906. It was during this repression of a great peasants' uprising by 10,000 'White' and over 5,000 African troops that Gandhi formulated his ideas of

Satyagraha and Passive Resistance. In his 1906 campaign against Smuts's anti-Indian Registration laws he went to Downing Street. Later, after imprisonment by Smuts, he signed a 'compromise gentlemen's agreement' under which he agreed, in 1908, that a majority of Indians would voluntarily register if no compulsory legislation was passed. (It was, none the less.) Gandhi, Abdurahman and Jabavu went separately, under the Liberal leadership of none other than the old racialist W.P. Schreiner, to London between 1906 and 1909, when the Act of Union passed in Westminster finally denied access to Parliament to any of them or their descendants. He had a mass following of workers and peasants, but he was part of a merchant and professional class, leading the Indian Congresses, a group tutored politically by British and South African liberalism, interested in bargaining for commercial and professional concessions and taking a 'constitutionalist' stand in a country where the people had no constitutional rights.

In December 1912, Gandhi wrote in Abdurahman's APO newspaper in defence of passive resistance, which was 'as pure as the ideal itself. Suffering is the panacea of all evils. It purifies the sufferers'; and the policy was best suited to 'illiterate natives'.

Among the anti-Jabavu forerunners of the South African Native Congress — later the African National Congress — were Seme, who announced the formation of the Congress in 1911, Mangena, Msimang, Dube and Molema. Pixley ka I. Seme, father of the ANC, was related to the Zulu royal house. He graduated at Columbia University, entered the Middle Temple in London and had a law practice in Johannesburg. Alfred Mangena came from Lincoln's Inn, and Msimang also received an excellent education in England. Molema was a chief, member of the Montsioa Baralong council of chiefs. Another ANC forerunner was Rubusana, who followed the Liberals even after his election to the Cape Provincial Council had caused him to be condemned by the Liberal, Rose-Innes, for daring to use a first-class compartment on a train, so breaking the rule of social apartheid. No other African ever won a Provincial Council election, or could even stand for one. The Sotho king, Letsie II, was represented in the first ANC Congress held in Bloemfontein on 8 January 1912 to protest against the colour bar in the Act of Union of 1910 and the pending 1913 Land Act, framed by the Liberal Sauer, whom Jabavu still followed even at that point. The royal houses of the Zulu, Pondo, Baralong, Kgatla, Lozi, Sotho and Ngwato 'tribes' had their chiefs as honorary presidents of the ANC. They found it possible to hold this office at the same time as they carried out their role as indirect rule puppets of racial colonialism. In his *Class and Colour in South Africa*, Jack Simons has rightly reproved the Russian historian I.J. Potekhin[4] for confusing this function with that of 'feudal compradores', which never existed in South Africa, or indeed in Africa generally. The contradiction within themselves between their conflicting roles was a late carry-over of the conflict between the communal and the despotic elements in the old society before colonialism transformed that society into an integral part of capitalism.

Dube, founder of the Natal Native Congress, had come under the liberal, church and Negro middle-class influence of Booker T. Washington at Tuskegee University during his studies in the USA in 1889. The American Negro and liberal influences on South African ANC founders was considerable, though not so great as the British influence. But the American factor gave African nationalism a greater 'identity' element, whereas English education at that time tended to stress assimilation into liberalism rather than political separatism. The South African equivalent in either case was to become electioneering and political appendages of the Liberals. Ex-tribal and middle-class origins and upbringing combined to make this adaptation to the racial system possible, even easy, whatever the motives and intentions of the African 'nationalists' concerned. These for the most part believed it to be the best way of achieving reform, having been taught by British followers of Montesquieu that total change was disastrous. They could do little but 'use' the Liberals to achieve their reforms. For the same reason Dube, Rubusana, Seme and others agreed to go to London after the ANC conferences of 1913 and 1914. When elected, Rubusana said he accepted 'White' superiority.

Such were the personal and social origins of the first South African liberation movements, the APO, ANC and Indian Congress, the last two of which still exist; the ANC, though outlawed in 1960, is still the major South African national movement more than 70 years after its foundation. Abdurahman summed up the fruits of their deputations and petitions in the APO newspaper on 22 August 1914: 'The coloured races could not possibly be worse governed when left to their own resources than they were governed under British rule'. On 5 September 1914, after the war had begun, he stated: 'The only question we have to ask ourselves is how we can best serve the Empire'.[5] The ANC and Indian leaders were in complete agreement with both statements.

West African Socialism

A similar war-time dénouement took place among the early national movements in French West Africa and British West Africa. The social background of early African political thinkers and organizers depended ultimately on the general 'social formation' in the particular colony in which they grew up. After abolishing the slave trade in 1807, Britain declared Sierra Leone a Protectorate and then a Crown Colony, wrested from the local people by slaving, violence and false treaties. Between that time and 1864, British colonial ships landed some 70,000 'Prize Negroes', former slaves, to function as a divide-and-rule mediating caste between the British planters and state and the indigenes. It was largely from this oppressed upper caste that the Sierra Leone nationalist and socialists came. In 1821 the American liberals brought socially corrupted ex-slaves to begin the settlement of Monrovia in Liberia, against the wishes and actual resistance of the indigenes. Out of some 15,000 ex-slaves came an upper caste that ruled over the 'natives' with a generally arrogant or patronizing attitude taken over from 'White' Euramericans. Out of this upper caste came one of the few real bourgeois classes in Africa, but one utterly servile to its colonialistic fathers, the 'White' Americans. This upper class sitting on top of the indigenes gave rise in turn to the pioneers of West African socialism. From 1844, following up missionary land-seizures in Gabon, French 'anti-slave' forces set up Libreville, which for a while became the capital of the French African empire. An attenuated repetition of the Freetown–Monrovia social formation also occurred there, but the main French settlement area creating African socialism was not there but around St Louis, Dakar, and Rufisque in Senegal.

The elitist layers in the West African coastal towns were born in and bred by a non-tribal, yet tribally linked, subordinate and dependent society serving European traders, officials, armies and missionaries. They soon became mediators between the expanding companies, states and churches of Europe and the working poulations of the locations in the towns and of the interior and the growing numbers of landless and unemployed crowding the reserve villages. In South Africa the APO and ANC cadres had become attached by liberal and missionary strings to monopoly capital, drawn in particular to the promises by industrial, commercial and mining monopolies that employment colour bars would be lowered, even if wages would not be raised, so that Africans, 'Coloureds' and Malays might do skilled work such as mine blasting, albeit at unskilled — i.e. not 'White' — rates of pay. In 1907 the ANC had clashed with the early socialists and founders of the Communist Party in evidence before the Native Affairs Commission, and sided with the 'liberal' Chamber of Mines against the open racialism of the 'White' workers.[6] The Chambers of Mines had given donations to the pre-ANC organizations, as in much later years the US Information Services, Central Intelligence Agency, Ford Foundation, Anglo-American Corporation and certain German churches were to give money and material support to the Pan African Congress and the Black Consciousness movement particularly.[7] The West African intellectuals found themselves in similar circumstances, favouring the 'home' government to protect itself against the rabid open racialism of the local *colons*, including the 'White' workers. The same happened later in Kenya in the struggle between the 'White settlers', who included British missionaires and aristocrats, and the British government.

The British in Sierra Leone and the Americans in Liberia exploited the ex-slave Christian 'settlers' as a ruling caste over the 'natives' — as it were a reconstruction of the old clan domination of pre-colonial society. The Liberian upper-caste 'clan' was more American than African, patronizing the 'Africans' and itself patronized by 'White' America, before and after Lincoln. The Liberian settlers came from colonialist, expanding America, with ideas of 'civilizing' Africa and expanding into it. Liberia itself was founded in 1821 by the American Colonization Society, an organ of American colonialism after US independence from Britain in 1776. 'White' Americans promoted the idea of a 'Negro' nation in Liberia. Harvard University's Professor Greenleaf wrote the Constitution. During the 'independence' declarations of 1847, the 'White' American sponsors had to put down a minor rebellion, led by Beverley R. Wilson, who declared that 'Liberia belongs to the citizens of Liberia, as an inheritance from their forefathers' and rejected the 'transfer' of power by the Colonization Society. Wilson was supported by Hilary Teage; but Teage, who had helped to draft the Declaration of Independence,[8] praised 'American benevolence and philanthropy' and recalled that the settlers had come from 'the land of their nativity' — America, not Africa — 'to form settlements on this barbarous shore'. The founder-settlers were imbued with a slave mentality from slavery in America, and asked the Americans and Europeans 'to regard us with the sympathy and friendly consideration to which the peculiarities of our condition entitle us'. In the end Beverley Wilson himself signed the Declaration. Thereafter the 'settlers' were a social-political, economic and cultural middle of a sandwich between the Colonization Society and the 'natives'. Their role has remained unchanged to this day and was decisive in their nationalism and socialism. The Constitution actually laid down that 'none but persons of colour shall be admitted to citizenship' — the first constitutional 'Black Power' law. In his 1856 inaugural address the second president, Benson, expressed the hope that the 'aborigines' would eventually take part in 'our civilization and Christianity'.

Benson advocated not so much equality as 'assimilation' through missionary work; so too did Blyden. Alexander Crummell,[9] a product of Queen's College, Cambridge, preferred settlers brought from slave-boats, without local knowledge — known as 'Congoes' — to the local people as future workers, because, he wrote in New York in September 1861,

> the neighbouring natives . . . know well how to inconvenience our planters [on sugar plantations] by a demand for higher wages and by irregularity in labour. The Congoes are apprenticed to our citizens; are remarkably pliant and industrious, and peculiarly proud and ambitious of being called 'Americans' . . . Its influence upon surrounding tribes is equally manifest. They dislike the Congoes, and as a consequence the Congoes are thrown upon us. This leads them to the adoption of American habits . . . They go to

our schools; they adopt our dress; they crowd our churches; they speak English; they are trained with our militia. I have no hesitation in saying that our native wars are now at an end.

But in 1870, three years before he returned to America after 20 years in Liberia, he wrote:

As a people we were 'ferried over' in a month, or little more, from a state of degradation to a position of independence and superiority. In a little more than a monthly change of the moon, we were metamorphosed from the position of underlings to one of mastery, with a vast population of degraded subjects around us . . . It has led too many to look down on the native as an inferior . . . I know the smallness of our means. I feel too the need of aid in carrying on fully the processes of successful civilization . . . For help we need. There is nothing humiliating in such an avowal. It is the common need of new nations.

These creeds became unseen, hidden thoughts in many independent African states a century later, when nearly 50 African countries had been granted the independence that America had granted to Liberia in 1847.

Crummell denied that there had ever been a free government in Africa, before or after conquest, other than Liberia. But he now called for independence under an American 'protectorate', including 'naval guardianship', to 'enable us to enter vigorously upon that regenerating policy, in this part of Africa, which I will now endeavour to point out. And first, I would suggest the duty of rising to a higher appreciation of the native man' — a reversal of his former stance against the 'native' and for the 'Congoes':

Here is a man who, however rude and uncultivated, is sure to stand. The hardihood of the race through long centuries, its quiet resistance to the most terrible assaults upon its vitality; its resurrection to life and active duties, after a ghastly burial of centuries in the caves of despair, in the graves of servitude and oblivious degradation, are all prophetic of a lasting future. Other races of men, as in America and New Zealand, fall before an incoming emigrant population. But this is not our mission here; and, if it were, it is not in our power, that is, we have not the ability to destroy the native. With all his simplicity he thoroughly feels this. You see that he does not lose his countenance in your presence; and he knows no fear. In his character you see nothing stolid, repulsive, indomitable. On the other hand, he is curious, mobile, imitative. He sees your superiority and acknowledges it by copying your habits. He is willing to serve you . . . Our position and our circumstances make us the guardians, the protectors and the teachers of our heathen tribes . . . All historic fact shows that force, that is authority, must be used in the exercise of guardianship over heathen tribes. Mere theories of democracy are trivial in this case, and can never nullify this necessity . . . it should be the force of restoration and progress.

He then spoke of the 'restoring' work after the crushing of the Sinou revolt in 1861 and the 1866 struggle against 'King Boyer', whom Crummell would have preferred to see as a chief under 'indirect rule', after the model of the English 'Negritude' policy of Venn and Grey. He admired the 'clergymen, doctors, merchants, councillors — native men — who have risen to a position at Sierra Leone' and praised Earl Grey for his policy of 'native self-government'. He called for 'the regeneration of Africa' by 'this grand opportunity, given by God to men of the African race'.

The racialistic 'Africanism' of Crummell, expressing an American 'Negro' ruling-class attitude as mediators of American colonialism, was an unmodulated echo of the 'White' missionary's and liberal's racialism. Economically, it rested on the need for a stable force of docile cheap labour. Benson (1816–65),[10] President of Liberia from 1856 to 1864, denied the 'incapacity of the coloured race for self-government' in his 1856 Inaugural Address and admired

> the facility with which most of the chiefs rule their subjects . . . and but for the accursed slave trade of bygone years, by which they have been greatly corrupted, and which had contributed so much to the subversion of their domestic and social happiness, those very heathens would set a pattern of governing talent and governable disposition, by which several of the proud civilized nations of the earth might be profited.

He advocated that they be 'raised to a perfect level and flow in one common channel with us, socially, politically and religiously'. In his annual message to parliament, December 1858, Benson referred to his good relations with 'several native chiefs'. He feared any development of a hostile 'native' working class:

> I shall ever regard with suspicion any system of education and training for the aborigines, provided by law, that does not equally apply to ourselves, lest it should prove an introduction — though not intended — to a state of things that will cause them to be regarded as intended to permanently sustain the relation to us of hewers of wood and drawers of water, while our own sons and daughters may be encouraged to live in idleness, luxury and affluence. In a word, it would be encouraging a

> dangerous line of demarcation, that should have no existence in Liberia.

He maintained that the 'aborigines' had a greater 'productive consumption', added more 'value' to exports, than the 'Americo-Liberians' in oil, ivory, wood and other articles. He wanted legislation to force 'at least three quarters of our youth' — of the Americo-Liberians — to enter the working class, while their 'missionaries are, as a general thing, labouring among the aborigines', Benson's 'Africanism', paternalistic and imbued with 'White' American racial prejudices, had a solidly middle-class, anti-proletarian, base. It wanted, at the same time, to have a working class so compounded as to act as a buffer against the 'tribes', until the process of detribalization was complete. Unlike Crummell, he was an advocate of detribalization and not of retribalization, of integration rather than indirect rule. Their Africanism had common social and religious components, but were only superficially alike. In practical policy, they differed. In the end both policies 'won', as we see from the later social structure of Liberia, a century and more after the country 'won' its 'struggle for independence', a 'struggle' that lasted from 1821 to 1847. There was a working class, and at the same time all the worst relics of tribalism remained, both of them subordinated to an Americo-Liberian or an 'Afro-American' clan–caste–class acting as mediators between the 'native productive consumers' of Benson and the American and European rubber, oil and shipping imperialists.

From Liberia too came the more politically independent Africanism of Edward Blyden (1832–1912), who took part in the abolitionist and early 'self-government' exercises in Liberia from 1851 to 1871, and then in Sierra Leone and other British West African territories. Blyden was the most coherent and important of the pioneer African nationalists and socialists before Horton and Casely Hayford. He rejected the common liberal slave-mentality acceptance of the superiority of the 'White' race, but accepted the 'White'-created myth of races, including that of an 'equal but different' Negro 'race'.

The Liberian Constitution, Article I, Section 11, said: 'Every male citizen, of 21 years of age, possessing real estate, shall have the right of suffrage.' Article III, Section 2, required real estate of $150 for eligibility for the Legislature. Article V, Section 14, prohibited land-purchase from 'aborigines', who were not explicitly defined as citizens. Only citizens could hold real estate, with the exception of colonization societies, missionary societies etc. (Article V, Section 12.) These were the constitutional property and franchise laws at the time of Blyden's arrival and work in Liberia. They gave land to the colonialists of America and the 'Americo-Liberians' and the franchise effectively only to the latter. The Africans were treated as 'tribalists' in communal reservations, outside the pale of civic society, as the Indians and Negroes had been in the American Constitution of Jefferson and Washington after independence in 1776. This Liberian constitution and all it represented formed the groundwork for Blyden's ideas, standing as he did in the ex-American class with America over and behind him and Africa before and below him. It was this Blyden, in this position, who wrote down practically the whole of the 19th and 20th Century 'African' thought until the arrival of 'African Marxism' about a century after he landed in Monrovia.

Blyden was born in the Danish West Indies, where he was educated under the patronage of the Calvinist, racist Dutch Reformed Church. He matriculated at Alexander High School, Liberia; in 1858 he became its headmaster, and in 1860 a minister of the West African Presbytery. In 1862 he became Greek and Latin Professor in Liberia College, and he studied Arabic in Asia Minor in 1865 during a two-year period as Secretary of State. When Roye's True Whig government split in 1871 he was accused of having seduced Roye's wife and fled to Sierra Leone with the help of Henry Venn, for whose missionary society he worked as well as being Agent for the Interior in the Sierra Leone colonial government. Later he also worked for the Liberian government. His activities, educational and practical, were thus always under colonialist and 'White' patronge. He knew this; in 1857 he addressed the Common Council of Monrovia and told them: 'We are, as a nation, upheld by foreigners. We are entirely dependent upon foreigners for schools, for churches, for preachers, for teachers. Most of the talent of the country is in the employ and at the control of foreigners ... Where is our independence? Where?'[11]

Blyden understood also that he was part of an intermediate social group exploiting the Africans for American interests: 'We purchase the palm oil and camwood and ivory from the natives, giving them in exchange articles of foreign production. We receive the product of their industry ... Foreigners on the one hand, and the natives on the other, are our supporters.' He believed in the European concept that 'Nature intends that Africa shall be an agricultural country.' He likewise accepted the European and American concept of the 'African race' in this address, given at the age of 24 while he was completing his school studies. He repeated both concepts, fundamental to his African socialism, in his Annual Address to the Common Council on 26 July 1865, 18 years after independence. He regarded the 'people of Liberia' as, firstly, the 'citizens' — that is, the non-natives, for under the Constitution the natives were not citizens, might not own 'real estate' and were thus disfranchised in their homeland. But he saw a wider unity: 'We must cultivate pride of race. Longfellow has sung of the "dead past"; but we must allow him such an assertion as a poetic privilege. In reality the past is not dead.'[12]

After Venn brought him to Sierra Leone his early 'Negritude' became integrated with British policies of indirect rule, as formulated by Earl Grey, Lord Russell's Colonial Secretary from 1846 to 1852, and Henry Venn, Church Missionary Society Secretary. In 1853 Grey referred to a meeting of kings and chiefs at Cape Coast Castle as

> a rude Negro Parliament . . . suited to the actual state of society . . .
> In a climate so uncongenial to European constitutions, it is not
> desirable that the maintenance of order and the progress of
> civilization should continue to depend on the exercise of authority
> by white men, or that the duty of governing and protecting the
> inhabitants of Western Africa should be thrown upon this country
> [Britain] longer than can be avoided.

It was a long-range forecast of independence which Britain was to
'grant' a little more than a hundred years later. George Nicol, a Sierra
Leonian middle-class preacher, already in April 1844 called for 'native
agencies', at the same time as Shepstone was clearly formulating his
'Bantustan' policy in Natal. On the other hand, the Baptist missionary
T.J. Bowden wrote in 1857:

> In these nations [Central Africa] we find no class of eminent men
> whose attainments may give unity, force and direction to society;
> no middle class . . . With the single exception of political chiefs,
> themselves barbarians, the whole society of the Sudan rests and
> stagnates on a dead level, and the people remain poor, ignorant
> and wretched, because they have no superiors. I need not say that a
> second and a third higher class must be added before we can
> regenerate African society.

Henry Venn summed up the policy expressed by Grey, Nicol, Bowden
and Shepstone, in a statement of 31 June 1868: 'Study the national
character of the people among whom you labour and show the utmost
respect for national peculiarities . . . let a native church be organized as a
national institution ... the proper position of a missionary is one
external to the native church.' He elaborated detailed procedures for
'indirect rule' in the churches, in 1851, 1861 and 1866, showing the clear
development already made of a 'native' class of pastors as part of
Bowden's rising 'middle class'. On 26 June 1865 a House of Commons
Select Committee proposed that 'the object of our policy should be to
encourage in the natives the exercise of those qualities which may
render it possible for us more and more to transfer to them the
administration of all the Governments'.[13]

Blyden and James Africanus Horton (1835–83) fell fully and deeply
into the Grey–Venn system. Horton qualified as a doctor at Edinburgh
University in 1859 and then served in the Army Medical Service,
spending a long time in the Gold Coast. Horton's Fanti Federation plan
of 1868 was an anti-Ashanti move and at the same time a form of 'native
assembly' as seen by Grey. Britain repressed the Fanti leaders before
crushing the Ashanti in the 1873–4 war. The Federation became a

starting point for the discussion of 'independence' by Horton, Blyden, J. Mensah Sarbah, Bishop Aggrey and, later, J.E. Caseley Hayford.

In his *West African Countries and Peoples* of 1868, Horton outlined the Niger–Sudanese 'despotisms', dividing them into 'the monarchical and the republican'. The commoners in Dahomey and Ashanti, he wrote, quoting Merivale's *History of the Romans under the Empire*, 'have acquiesced in their own immemorial despotisms to which they have been abandoned'. He did not see the anti-colonialist resistance aspect of the two despotisms. He admired many of the hereditary chiefs, whose successor was 'not the eldest son of the chief, but the son of his sister' (explaining this by 'the plurality of wives' and not by its real nature, the matriarchal *gens* lineage, the sister being from a common mother, not a common father). He asked Britain to give 'to the educated natives experience in the form of government', taking Liberia's 'training' from 1821 to 1847 as a model. He had little time for the pre-colonial society of the ex-slaves taken to Sierra Leone:

> Prior to their being kidnapped they were governed by kings or chiefs who had a complete sway over life and property ... they were extremely cruel to each other; polygamy was carried on to a fearful extent; the lower class were kept in a state of slavery; warfare was carried on in a most cruel style, and all conquered populations were enslaved.

He praised the missionaries for 'elevating' the Creoles in Sierra Leone, Gambia, Lagos and Gold Coast to

> lucrative subordinate positions of trust in both the military and the civil service of the government. [He says that the ex-slaves] ... are to be found in every part of the coast sighing after gold in the capacity of merchants, traders and clerks — in the French colony of Senegal; in the Rivers Gambia, Casamanza, Nunez, Pongas, Sherbroe and Galinas; in the Liberian Republic; on the Gold Coast; in the Kingdom of Dahomey in Lagos and Abeokuta; in the Niger; at Bonny, Old and New Calabar; the Cameroons, Fernando Po, the Gaboons, and the Islands of St Helena and Ascension ... But unfortunately, in Western Africa there are no prizes held out to ambition.

He cited Hannibal, 'the African Euclid', the 'African poet' Terence, Origen, Tertullian, Augustine, Clemens Alexandrinus and Cyril to show that Africa had 'her heraldry of science and fame' to which she could return. He raised the call of 'Africa for the Africans as a Political as well as a Biological Truth.' He praised Britain for having by 1860 had 'nearly one-fifth of the whole of the inhabitants at school, which is an unusually large proportion in any country ... in Prussia the percentage was 16 and in England 13'. At the time he proposed a constitutional monarchy, with an assembly and senate, based on a property qualification suffrage, under a king-elect. He proposed this for a 'civilized' nation like Sierra Leone; for the 'uncivilized' Gold Coast there had to be a king appointed by the British governor, as head of a Fanti federation of kings in charge of 'men of education and good, sound common sense, residing in the Coast towns, . . . and responsible chiefs as representatives of the various kings within the kingdom' as a temporary stage towards self-government.

Horton's writings[14] show that the basis of his nationalism was a rising middle class, then relatively and in some ways also absolutely stronger than after his death, before the Berlin Conference and the total domination of Africa, including such middle classes, by imperialistic monopoly capital. A secondary basis was the retribalized 'native authorities', which he saw as temporary. His nationalism was combined with absolute collaboration with British colonialism.

When he came to Sierra Leone, Blyden shared Horton's political views, but in 1872 and 1874 he went further in evaluating the 'great Mandingo and Foulah tribes, who are Mohamedans, and the principal rulers of central Africa'. A student of Arabic, he saw Arab and Islamic culture as African, not as alien. In 1880 he told the American Colonization Society that

> great Negro warriors have risen from the ranks of Islam, and, inspired by the teachings of the new faith, which merges all distinctions in one great brotherhood, have checked the arrogance of their foreign teachers and have driven them, if at any time they affected superiority based on race, from their artificial ascendancy.[15]

Christianity had not achieved the same 'brotherhood' nor become so much part of Africa.

On the question of race, Blyden declared that no argument was necessary or effective. 'Argument may be necessary in discussing the methods or course of procedure for the preservation of race integrity, and for the development of race efficiency, but no argument is needed as to the necessity of such preservation and development.' In a lecture in his home in Free Street, Freetown, on 19 May 1893, he said:

> It is sad to think that there are some Africans, especially among those who have enjoyed the advantages of foreign training, who are so blind to the radical facts of humanity as to say, 'Let us do away with the sentiment of Race. Let us do away with our *African personality* and be lost, if possible, in another Race [my emphasis].

Blyden regarded the alternative as absorption by 'a dominant Race': he regarded race as a natural law. 'The duty of every man, of every race, is to contend for its individuality — to keep and develop it'. He turned to Christianity to justify his belief in race-identity. 'Remember, then, that these racial peculiarities are God-given.'[16] In 1908, in *African Life and Customs*,[17] Blyden found some of his 'African personality' and 'identity' in 'the Family, which in Africa, as everywhere else, is the basic unit of society . . .', and in the communal land and water, the communal social life. 'This is communistic or co-operative. All work for each and each works for all.' The 'individualistic' Liberian settlers, he said, 'could not understand and hardly yet understand that there is an African Social and Economic System most carefully and elaborately organized, venerable, impregnable, indispensable.' He praised Mary Kingsley, as did the Gold Coast lawyer John Mensah Sarbah (1864–1910), whom Britain took into the Gold Coast Legislative Council in 1900. Mary Kingsley had studied Africa and come back with the conception of the African personality or identity and the need to replace the old system of direct colonialism by one based on indirect rule. Blyden's later work is based on that of this European liberal 'discoverer' of African personality. Aimé Césaire, Sartre, Basil Davidson, Senghor and Nyerere, some half a century later, were to revive the concepts of 'Negritude', the 'African personality' and 'African identity' of Blyden, Horton and Sarbah and their British mentors, Grey, Venn and Kingsley.

In between these generations of thought lay the work and thinking of Caseley Hayford and Macauley in Nigeria, of du Bois and Garvey in America and the early writings of Azikiwe, in a period between two world wars characterized more by a world outlook than by 'Africanism'.

Caseley Hayford (1866–1930) was educated at the Wesleyan High School, Cape Coast and Fourah Bay College, Sierra Leone; he qualified as a barrister in Britain and returned to the Gold Coast in 1896. In 1903 he published *Gold Coast Native Institutions*, as a disciple of British liberalism and its new-found 'identity cult', of Blyden and of a Liberian revivalist, Harris, who preached an 'Ethiopian' liberation creed in the Ivory Coast and Gold Coast.

Imperialism, with its vast and rapid continental conquests, its seizure of land, its concessions, mines and plantations, railways and cities, exports of raw materials and sales of manufactures, investment by finance capital, monopolistic chartered and other companies, its racialism and its totalitarianism, had little time in that period for Mary Kingsley. Her time came soon afterwards, when the policies of Grey, Lyautey and Lugard became practicable, in the reserves of cheap labour and in the European-dominated legislative councils. The interregnum saw a compromise between Kingsley and Mill. John Stuart Mill, the leader of British Victorian liberalism, wrote in *Fraser's Magazine* in December 1859 that nations which are still barbarians have not got beyond the period during which it is likely to be for their benefit that they should be held in subjection by foreigners . . . A violation of great principles of morality it may easily be, but barbarians have no rights as a nation.

Cecil Rhodes followed Mill's dictum by applying Shepstone's policy of 'native authorities', and Goldie brought Lugard from India and East Africa to conquer Nigeria completely and set up his 'Native Councils' there. Mary Kingsley's concept of 'identity' was not a principled or practical obstacle to Mill's imperialist policy. Blyden combined her idea of 'racial integrity' with the idea of independence, and Hayford's *Ethiopia Unbound* (1911) called for all 'Negroes' (nowadays called 'Blacks') to maintain and defend their identity. He based this identity, as did Blyden, on the traditional communistic African society. Hayford combined this Africanism with collaboration: in 1920 he entered the British Legislative Council set up by Lugard in Lagos in 1914, as overseer of his Native Authorities. At the same time he formed the National Congress of British West Africa. Such was the dual outcome of his call to Britain in 1903: 'Allow us to make use of our own Native Institutions, which we understand, and which from experience are adapted to us.' These institutions were 'the fastest bond with the Mother Country'. But he suspected European intentions: 'When, in history, has the Caucasian approached the Negro, or the Mongolian — the black, the yellow or the brown man — in the spirit of full brotherhood . . . and not because of its markets and rich natural products?' Nevertheless, he is subordinated to Europe — 'Surely we can look to England for a certain amount of fair play' — and asks the British, for one thing, not to 'divide and rule' Ashanti and Fanti, but 'that the two peoples should be merged into one'.

Hayford predicted that Europe's old civilization would 'be torn asunder by communism and socialism', but that Africa's new civilization, as he advocated it, 'will enjoy rest and quietness, for the foundations of society are here based upon a rock, and that rock is the native law of inheritance' — i.e. the system of communism based on the *gens*. He asks Britain to rule by allowing 'the educated Native' to 'take the Native System as he finds it, and develop and improve it on aboriginal lines, and on scientific principles . . .' The first of these principles is: 'Every member of the Gold Coast or Ashanti is a member of a family . . . There is a community of interest among the members of such family who, as a rule, trace their ancestry from a common materfamilias'. He then went on to 'the higher orders of development', the Village Council of 'Panins or Elders' and upwards to the 'king'. He asks, finally: 'Will British capital, energy and intelligence do it, or will the millionaire from the other side of the Atlantic, in these days of combines, come along and sweep the stakes?'[18]

Hayford opposed both the adaptive servility of Booker T. Washington and W.E. Burghart Du Bois's attempt at 'social enfranchisement amid surroundings and in an atmosphere uncongenial to racial development'. He went back to Edward Wilmot Blyden's independence based on the African 'as a race among the races of men'. He regarded Blyden as the real leader of the Pan African Conference held in the Gold Coast in 1905.

Collaboration and reform were the common tenets of the Cape and West African leaders of the late 19th Century — Abdurahman, Gandhi, Jabavu, Dube, Martin Luthuli, Rubusana at the Cape and Benson, Blyden, Horton, Sarbah and Hayford in West Africa. All believed in the European-created myth of races, but the West Africans accepted racial inequality less than did Jabavu's group. The Cape 'nationalists' worked towards integration and equality, the West Africans towards 'native institutions', 'identity', the 'African personality'. All believed in the British Empire and served it loyally. All came from the ex-slave or ex-tribal middle classes, which were then, in the Indian summer between slavery and imperialism, freer and larger than they became later.

This caste created a unified 'African traditional socialism' or liberal-nationalism out of the elements of ideas and policies made by Europeans and Americans and comprising collaboration, constitutionalism, 'identity', 'personality', 'Negritude' and 'tradition'. These reappeared intact in the African socialism which unfurled a banner of independence after the Second World War, half a century later.

Senegal: From Diagne to Senghor

In French West Africa there developed a third form of 19th Century African nationalism and socialism. There, as in the Cape and British West Africa, a small bourgeoisie had grown up subserving French colonialism; it was old in origin and existed in Gorée during Boufflers's time, when Britain was trying to solve her 'Black problem' by settling ex-slaves in Sierra Leone, in and after 1787. This class or upper caste of ex-slaves and retribalized *evolués* acted as mediator between metropolitan France, with its Bordeaux merchants dominating the Dakar region, and the retribalized Islamic and 'heathen' peoples, then still only half-conquered. Standing between French conqueror and semi-conquered Africa, they produced political ideas suited to their mediating situation. Their political development began not long after that of the Cape African and Coloured movements, but considerably later than the Liberian, Sierra Leone and Gold Coast movements, partly because of the French policy of not providing higher education to Africans in Africa, but sending them to Paris for their education, partly because of the slower development of French industrial capital at the time, compared with British, partly because of the reverses suffered by the French empire in the Americas and Asia in the 18th Century, and finally because of the social changes provoked by the French Revolution — changes which did not affect Britain, since there the landed feudal aristocracy itself became the colonialist capitalist class.

As early as 1848, in the first elections for a Senegalese deputy in the French Assembly, Durand Valentin, a *metis*, was elected by a restricted electorate. The seventh deputy, in 1902, François Carpot, was also a *metis*. These were products of the small bourgeois groups thrown up in the oldest communes, Gorée and St Louis, which became free with the French Revolution in 1789 (while the slave traffic continued) and in Dakar and Rufisque before they became communes in 1887 and 1880 respectively. Certain Africans had voting rights from 1833, Blaise Diagne (1872–1934),[19] with Mandingo and Debou ancestors, was adopted by a wealthy Catholic 'Creole', Crespin, who sent him to a primary school in Senegal, then to Aix-en-Provence and finally to St Louis, where he qualified as an officer in the French customs service, in which both he and Sangue N'Diaye served in Dahomey in 1892. This was before France enabled Africans to enter the higher ranks of the public service. Diagne served in Dahomey, Congo, Gabon, Réunion, Madagascar and Guyana, under colonial governors like Galliéni, Augagneur and the liberal senator Alex André Isaac of Guadeloupe. He returned to Senegal via Marseilles in January 1914, after criticism of French Governors and of the merchants of Bordeaux who dominated Senegal, including the 'Creoles', and suffocated African middlemen and petty officials through the monopoly of groundnut plantations and export, still the monoculture of Senegal to this day. More and more 'Creoles' entered the political service of the Bordeaux colonialists in the Senegal communes, and were condemned as traitors by Diagne and the general African populace. On a non-racial platform, in the face of racial attacks by the Bordeaux groups, 'White' and 'Creole', Diagne stood successfully for election in 1914 and became the first African to enter the French Assembly. He had the backing of incipient 'nationalist' movements, like the Jeunes Sénégalais of 1910, led by T. Diop and M. M'Baye, and the Mouridistes, led by Mamadou Moustapha M'Backe, son of Amadou Bamba and friend of Diagne. The Young Senegalese produced Africanists like Lamine Gueye, A. Duguay-Cledor, A.K. Diallo and M.M. Gaye. Diagne believed he could free Senegal from French racialism from the rostrum of the French Assembly in Paris, whereas British policy confined Herbert Macauley, 'father of Nigerian nationalism', to the straitjacket of British bodies in Lagos. But Diagne's first major act was to recruit massively for France in the First World War, and soon he was accused of capitulation to his former enemies of Bordeaux. After presiding over the first Pan African Congress in Paris in 1919 and taking part in the next in 1921, he broke with Pan Africanism, spoke in defence of forced labour in the French colonies at the International Labour Organization in 1930 and became assimilated in high French social and political life, together with a growing number of West Africans, later condemned at home as 'collaborators'.

In 1914 Diagne was supported by the French Socialists of Jaurès and worked through them in the Assembly. He served as High Commissioner of African Forces in World War I, was President of the Colonial Commission in the Chamber of Deputies and served in eight cabinets, including those of Clémenceau and Laval, under whom he was Colonial Secretary — the highest position in the French Colonial Executive. In 1915 he launched a campaign for the extension of citizenship to all the inhabitants of the colonies. He wrote *The Statutes of the Black Race* for the 1919 Pan Africanist Congress, demanding that the mandatory powers of Versailles 'safeguard the indigenous peoples'. He defended Johnson, the mayor of Monrovia, and Marcus Garvey against charges of being 'Bolshevik' in September 1920.

The young Léopold Senghor, who was studying in France in 1930, was introduced to French politics by Diagne. Diouf represented Diagne's politics in Rufisque from 1920 to 1928 through the Republican Socialist Party.

Diagne was followed by Lamine Gueye, mayor of St Louis in 1925 and Senegalese deputy after Diagne's death. There were many collaborators in his circle — Abdel Kader Mademba Sy, grandson of the old grand resister El Hadj Omar, B.A. N'Diaye, Amadou N'Doye. Lamine Gueye founded the Senegalese Socialist Party with Armand Angrand in 1934 and ensured a considerable French Socialist influence among the post-Diagne generation. Diagne, his followers and his rivals, personified the combination of African nationalism and collaboration with French colonialism.

The entry of the 'collaborator' Diagne into European socialism was nothing out of the ordinary. Even before the First World War 'White' socialists were calling in de Leon, Keir Hardie, the Fabians, Kautsky, even Marx to justify an anti-African internationalism. This too had old precedents. The Utopian Communist experiments of Cabet, Weitling and others in North America were, after all, colonialist, land-robbing exercises completely unconcerned with the dispossession of the Amerindians or the enslavement of Negroes; the movement was a 'White' colonialist one. Jack London, author of *The Iron Heel* and many 'socialist' novels was an avowed anti-African racist. Socialists quoted Abraham Lincoln's opposition to slavery, but not his racialism:

> There is a natural disgust in the minds of nearly all white people at the idea of indiscriminate amalgamation of the white and black races, ... [and in Illinois, on 17 July 1858:] What I would most desire would be the separation of the white and black races.[20]

South Africa: 'White' Communism

In South Africa, British socialists in the 'White' miners' Knights of Labour demanded the industrial colour bar from Rhodes in the 1870s and 1880s. The ANC, APO and ICU often accused the South African Labour Party, the trade union leaders and the Communist Party of 'White' racialism.[21] They preferred the Chambers of Mines and Commerce to socialist trade union secretaries like Bob Stuart and CPSA trade unionists like Solly Sachs who ran segregated 'White' or non-African garment worker unions in the inter-war years.

South African Second International-style socialists and early Communists came mainly from the racialist 'White' workers, who were employed but not exploited: they lived off surplus value produced by non-European cheap labour, but did not produce surplus value themselves. Their resulting 'class' interests were, therefore, racialistic. The 'White'-worker and also 'White' middle class 2nd and later 3rd Internationalists belonged to the generation described in Hobsbawm's *Revolutionaries*. They hated the big capital and feared African competition in the labour market (in the case of the 'White' workers) or the rise of an African bourgeoisie (in the case of the 'White' lower middle class), particularly during the inter-war crisis decades. They feared falling into the bottomless pit into which they or their forebear-settlers had plunged the non-Europeans. Caught between European capital and African labour, they hoisted the red flag of European socialism and looked for 'a White socialist South Africa' as a result of the Russian 1917 Revolution. Communism, after all, was part of 'European civilization' and not, at least for a long time, for 'backward peoples', like the non-Europeans of Africa. Like the Fabian Webbs (as Lord Passmore, he became a Colonial Secretary under Macdonald's labour-imperialist government), they admired not the revolution but the 'order', of 1917; like the Webbs, therefore, they became ardent admirers of Stalin, and they eulogized the Moscow Trials denounced as frame-ups by Kruschev in 1956. 'Nation–class' interests made them subordinate the 'bourgeois' question of colour oppression to 'Collective Security' against Hitler. Like the missionaries and liberals they placed social welfare inside the reserves and locations above the (class) struggle against these segregated reservoirs of cheap African labour; and thought they were helping the African workers by organizing them into Euramerican-style unions, even though this meant working the anti-African IC Act of 1924. Likewise they cited European models, like the Russian Duma of 1905, which discriminated on grounds of class, not 'race', to justify their policy of working the politically segregatory and racist 1936 Native Representation Act. The struggle for non-racial equality, and the anti-imperialist struggle, were secondary to their 'Communism', as it had long been for Euramerican trade unionists and social-democrats. Their Stalinism, with its 'Socialism in One Country' and 'peaceful coexistence' with imperialism, was a logical sequel to their rejection-in-practice of the Leninism to which, like the Stalin bureaucracy, they paid lip-service. It was equally logical for the 'European' elite governing the CPSA, after being outlawed (together with Trotskyism) by the 1950 Suppression of Communism Act, to move towards the anti-USSR and social-democratic stance of French, British, Spanish and Italian Eurocommunism.

When the early racist founders of the CPSA supported the 1922 pogrom-strike, it was partly because of material class interests within the South African racist political economy; but partly because of their ideology that the 'White worker' was the 'vanguard of the revolution' (a view the author has heard expressed also by an old leader of the British Workers Revolutionary 'Trotskyist' party). When the CPSA *International and South African Worker* newspapers wrote in favour of 'tribalism' for the Africans,[22] and when, as the literature of the CPSA discussion on the 'Black Republic' (1928–35, officially) shows, leading members spoke of 'several' such 'Republics' — i.e. socialist Bantustans — it was in the Euro-missionary belief that in these ways they were 'saving the Africans from the horrors of capitalism'.

Together with British Labour and Liberal trade-unionists, they rejected the unregistered, non-racial ICU,[23] in 1928. In 1926 S.P. Bunting, who had hailed the 1922 strike as 'revolutionary', began a CPSA policy of 'Native Representation' — by Europeans — in the Cape and of taking part in 'elections' to the Location Advisory Boards through which the regime ran its reservoirs of cheap urban labour. The CPSA working through the ANC operated the Quisling 'toy telephone' Native Representative Council set up by the 1936 Native Representation Act, against opposition from Moses Kotane, later general secretary of the CPSA.[24] The party leaders persuaded Gomas and la Guma, veteran trade unionists and co-founders of the National Liberation League in 1938, to collaborate with Zionists and Liberals in terms of their Europeanist policy of 'collective security'; when their members, including the Cape Town City Councillor, Cissie Gool, daughter of Dr Abdurahman, accepted the policy of non-collaboration put forward by her brother-in-law, Dr Goolam Gool, the CPSA sacrificed first the NLL and then the NEUF on the altar of the Eurocentric 'fight against Nazism and Fascism' — in Spain, Italy and Germany, not in South Africa or in the Nazi-like African colonies of the 'peaceloving democracies', Britain, France, Portugal and Belgium.

The CPSA had joint meetings with the present National Party (in power today) and published an Afrikaans paper, *Ware Republikeiner*, during the Hitler–Stalin Pact period of the War;[25] but after the Nazi invasion of Russia told the non-Europeans to support and join the Nazi army of Smuts in the Churchill–Roosevelt–de Gaulle 'war for democracy'.[26] The CPSA credo continued after the War into 'Native Representation' by European Communists (Khan, Bunting, Alexander, among others). Their creed was not peculiar to them, but an extension of what had long been a hidden form of Eurocommunism abroad. The British CP, for example, helped British imperialism against the Indian Congress struggle for independence during the War; the French CP backed de Gaulle's retention of the African and Indo-Chinese French colonies during the War.

In South Africa the struggle between Trotskyism and Stalinism in the 1930s and 1940s centred not on inner-USSR persecutions and trials, but on the colonial question: was the banner of 'socialism' higher than the 'bourgeois democratic' fight against colour racialism in South Africa? Or, was the anti-imperialist struggle for land and a non-racial democracy the road to socialism, which, according to Trotsky's 1905 'Permanent Revolution' theory, would come out of and also satisfy these 'bourgeois' demands? Was the fight against an abstract 'capitalism' or 'real imperialism', in terms of Lenin's works? Did Bolshevism triumph because it called for socialism, or because it fought for 'land, bread and liberty' — purely bourgeois democratic slogans? What was the essence of political action, 'socialist' campaigning and the 'class struggle', or anti-imperialist and anti-racialist class struggle through a policy of non-collaboration? In South Africa Stalinism was regarded as a form of liberalism by several Non-European United Front, and later Non-European Unity Movement, leaders. The Trotskyists themselves increasingly ceased to function as such, and became critical of the Fourth International(s) after Trotsky's death in 1940, as they became more Europeanistic and less anti-imperialist and internationalist.[27] The issues fought out in South Africa were widely different from those fought out in Europe. Bordiga, Gramsci and Nenni treated the issue of Italy's colonies as secondary. Even in Spain, the Communists and POUM were not concerned with the independence of Morocco — which provided Franco's shock-troops. In Germany the Communists were little different from the Social Democrats, and both collapsed into a 'death without battle' before National Socialism, which certainly had a mass working-class as well as middle-class support. The French Popular Front of Blum-Thorez did not free the French colonies. But in West and South African liberation circles in those days the question was the colonial Nazism of Britain and France, the Japanese war on China, the Italian invasion of Ethiopia, India's struggle for independence, opposed during the War by the British Labour and Communist Parties, which stood to the right of Gandhi and Nehru.

Between the Wars: An African 'Indian Summer'

The entry of Marxism and Leninism into South African liberatory thought was more a reaction against the Europeanist non-African 'Marxism' and 'Leninism' of 'White' racialist Communists than a direct response to the Russian revolution of 1917. Things were not altogether different in East Africa, where the early Indian and African leaders like Thiku and Kenyatta were under heavy pressure from the constitutionalism and Fabianism of British socialism, or in French West Africa, where African trade unions and political parties reacted against the racist patriotism of the French Socialist and Communist Parties. In British West Africa, Azikiwe, Balewa and Awolowo laboured under the double yoke of British Fabianism and liberalism and of the fruit of Casely Hayford's policies working for 'change from inside the system'. Exile contacts with European socialists and Communists, as well as a flood of literature, including the works of the West Indian George Padmore (who finally called for Pan Africanism as the only alternative to Communism), introduced European Marxism into British West Africa and French West Africa. The battle of ideas in Africa between the wars was centred round the various brands of socialism, their adaptability or otherwise to the real situations of imperialism — land-hunger and colour bars in Kenya, South Africa, Nigeria, Ivory Coast, Senegal or Gold Coast. Such struggles, against a background of deep interest, and many actions of solidarity, by the Chinese, Indian and Ethiopian peoples in the 1930s, divested the liberatory movements of some of their former Africanism and imbued them with an anti-imperialist internationalism. The old questions of race, identity and personality posed by Blyden, Horton, Hayford, Garvey and Du Bois, and also by Diagne, had largely fallen away in the tide of trade union, land and anti-imperialist struggles and the new world situation. It was a sort of Indian summer, albeit in an exceptionally dark world, in which Nazism, Fascism and Stalinism threatened the future, the wars in China and Ethiopia dragged on and independence was not yet in sight in Asia or Africa. But this interregnum was not to survive the Second World War.

During the war the Anti-Coloured Affairs Department movement rose against Smuts' racialist, pro-British government in South Africa. This movement was formed in 1943 after a conference called by the New Era Fellowship, a kind of South African Jacobin-Cordelier Club which became famous in the late thirties and forties for the high level of its discussions and lectures. Its leaders, like B.M. Kies, R.O. Dudley, S.A. Jayiya, I.B. Tabata, G. Gool, A. Fataar, and, later, Victor Wessels, and many others came from non-European workers, artisans, teachers and clergymen, but rejected every racial classification and concept. Like the African teachers and professional people who came to lead the All African Convention at this time, they were taught by a previous generation of non-Europeans. The Teachers League of South Africa and the Cape African Teachers Association were divided on the question of collaboration: it was largely from this body of workers that the government took its NRC and CAD 'Quislings'. In nation-wide struggles the TLSA and CATA ousted the old leadership in 1943 and set about re-educating the people in non-collaboration and against retribalization such as was intrinsic in the Bantu education laws of 1952 and the Bantustan laws. The new teachers created a new environment for the next generation. It was the political re-education of the Non-European Unity Movement, against Bantustan, against retribalization, demanding full democratic rights, that led to the students' uprising at Soweto in 1976. The movement, formed in 1944 out of the AAC and the Anti-CAD, was led by anti-war anti-imperialists. In India Nehru's anti-war groups were in gaol for their anti-imperialist struggles. Tilak, Gandhi, Nehru and Bose were studied and well known in South Africa. The CPSA and ANC were pro-war, recruiting for Smuts in the Springbok Legion and other bodies that helped to keep Haile Selassie out of his own country, even out of his palace, to apply South African race laws to Ethiopia and to forcibly prevent the Ethiopian national resistance from reaping the harvest of its own bitter toil against Italy. The war saw smaller anti-imperialist struggles, against the Vichy and de Gaulle imperialists in French Africa and against the British in Tanganyika and Kenya. Zambian copper miners struck, and were massacred.

The war years were formative periods in Marxism, socialism and 'nationalism' for Azikiwe, who published his *Economic Reconstruction of Nigeria* in 1943, for the Ghanaian Kwame Nkrumah, studying abroad, for Tom Mboya and Kenyatta and Koinange from Kenya (the first a son of a poor labouring family in a Nairobi location, the last two of retribalized *kulak* origin near Nairobi) for Léopold Senghor, Sekou Touré and Modibo Keita. British Fabianism guided by Harold Laski, West Indian socialism of the Padmore and Eric Williams variety, itself schooled in Fabianism, French socialism and Communism and Anglo-American liberalism all played large roles. The future 'Africanist' schools were arising, too, from the Existentialist school of Jean-Paul Sartre, of France, with its revival of the old West African ideas of 'Negritude' and 'identity', now furthered by Catholic academics with post-war Vatican blessing. But during the war the socialist and nationalist wings were stronger than the Africanist tail. In South Africa neither played any role; the struggle centred round the anti-racialist struggle for full equality, interpreted by the Tabata wing of the NEUM in an increasingly formal way and by the Kies–Jaffe group more and more as real democracy and equality. Difference on the agrarian question led to a rupture between the two opinion-groups in the NEUM in 1958-9; the Tabata–Jordan–Tsotsi section was charged with making concessions to African nationalism, which was still anathema to non-collaborationist and non-European unity thought and action. At the same time the openly 'Africanist' Pan African Congress was formed as a breakaway from the ANC in 1957–8 under the leadership of Robert Sobukwe, later to be gaoled on Robben Island after the 1960 Sharpville massacre. Until that time Africanism had been a non-starter in South

Africa. By 1976 it had become a major issue of division with the rise of the anti-ANC and anti-NEUM 'Black Consciousness' movement — from the 1957 PAC to the 1983 National Forum, which represented a return to 19th Century West African thought and to European liberal-missionary 'Negritude' and 'identity' theories.[28]

In India (carved in half by Britain in 1948) the anti-British independence movement, the Indonesian independence struggle against Holland in the vacuum left after the Japanese defeat; the defeat of the French at Dien Bien Phu, the emancipation of North Korea from Japan and from Europe, above all the Chinese revolution of 1949, a social revolution against imperialism, profoundly changed the strategy of imperialism in Africa. It has often been said that Europe was forced to 'grant' independence in Asia but did so voluntarily, as a deliberate policy, in Africa. But the 'granting' of independence, via self-government, beginning in Ghana in 1954, had behind it a long mass struggle against imperialism and for independence. Britain, after her Indian experience, and France after her Indo-Chinese losses and the great national liberation war in Algeria from 1954 onwards, knew that if they did not step aside physically and turn the independence movements into their own shields, they would be destroyed by social revolutions against imperialism. They chose the lesser — and clearly useful — evil of political independence, not from choice but as a response to real, mass liberation movements involving workers' strikes, peasant uprisings, of which the most powerful and effective was the Mau Mau peasant rebellion led by the heroic Dedan Kimathi, executed by the British, and, finally, well organized political movements which synthesized these struggles in demands for independence which unified the causes of the diverse layers of the oppressed peoples. What gave independence the appearance of having been granted rather than forced was the ultimate constitutional nature of the proceedings, whether at Lancaster House or in Paris or Brussels — or in the formal withdrawal of Italian imperialism from Somalia after the resumption of Fascist tyranny there during the UN-imposed 10-year 'Trusteeship' from 1952 to 1962.

National Wars — Nigeria, Algeria, Egypt, Morocco

While having a common anti-colonialist denominator, the armed struggles of Ethiopia, Egypt, Algeria, the Angolans, Mozambicans, Guineans, Zimbabweans, and Namibians were led by movements covering a wide political spectrum. Haile Selassie was head of a compradore 'feudal' class while other leaders came from the loins of the oppressed petite bourgeoisie, colonial bureaucracy, peasants or urban workers. Gamal Abdul Nasser (1918–70) was the son of a post office worker in the poor Bacos area of Alexandria — that ancient Ptolemaic city which did not allow non-Hellenized Egyptians to enter, except to warm the baths or bring in animals and meat for the Greek, Roman and Jewish merchants, land-owners and officials. His uncle was gaoled by the British. After school and law college he entered the Military Academy in 1937 and in 1942 served in the Sudan where, with Amer, Mohieddine and the later 1980 Camp David collaborator, Sadat, he formed the anti-British Free Officers. In the 1948 war with Israel, in which King Farouk was objectively more progressive than the 'socialist', Ben Gurion, Nasser wrote part of the *Philosophy of Revolution*.[29] The Islamic socialism of this work was made a mass credo by Gaddaffi in Libya after his overthrow in 1968 of King Idris I, who had led the war-time resistance movement in Libya against Italy and then fought off demands at UNO by the Italian Christian Democrats, Socialists and Communists for the recolonization of Libya by Italian settlers after the war. The Free Officers toppled Farouk on 23 July 1952, setting up a militarized African Socialist Republic. The existence of such military or one-party regimes in Africa reflected the weakness of the local bourgeoisie, which was suspended between foreign capitalists and the local fellaheen. Such regimes consequently failed to reverse the process of anti-labour persecution of Wafdist, Ba'ath, Muslim Brotherhood and monarchist governments in pre-Nasser, British-dominated Egypt.

The Algerian leadership was more 'bourgeois' than the Rasses and Negus who led Ethiopia to victory against Italy, but less 'bourgeois' than Nasser's Free Officers. Abd el Krim or Muhammad Ibn'Abd Al-Karim Al-Khattabi (1882–1963) led an armed resistance in Morocco, formed the Rif Republic from 1921 to 1926, and became a hero of Magreb anti-imperialism to such an extent that Ho Chi Minh once called him 'the precursor of the armed struggle for independence'.[30] Abd el Krim was of Berber tribal origin, educated in Spanish and Arabic and employed by Spain in an 'Indirect Rule' Bureau of Native Affairs in which he was, in 1915, the Chief Muslim Judge. He understood that this was a Spanish form of retribalization, protested, was gaoled, escaped, and after reappointment as Judge in 1918, left his post and formed the Rif Army in 1919. His troops defeated Spain at Annoual in July 1921 and 1924 and in 1925 his tribally-confederated men drove a French army to the gates of Fez. France and Spain joined forces, Spanish troops landed in force near Adjir, Krim's birthplace, while Marshal Pétain (who, like Spain's Franco, had his fascist base in the North African colonies) led 160,000 French troops in support of the 90,000 Spanish army. Abd el Krim had to surrender on 27 May 1926. He was exiled to Reunion and given 'permission' by the de Gaulle–Socialist–Communist government of 1947 to return to France in 1947. He scorned the offer and asked asylum from Farouk. In Cairo he became head of the Maghreb Bureau, was invited back to Morocco by King Muhamed V, but refused to go as long as a single French soldier remained in North Africa.

Many Maghreb nationalists were inspired by Krim. Ahmed Messali

Hadj (1898–1974) in 1937 began the Algerian Movement pour le Triomphe des Libertés Democratique, from which, after 1946, arose the Mouvement National Algérien and the Front de Libération Nationale (FLN) led by Ben Bella to victory. During the Franco–Algerian war (1952–62), Messali Hadj was charged by the FLN, including Fanon, with collaboration, but some 'leftist' groups, including a British and French 'Trotskyist' one, supported him materially and ideologically. Ahmed Ben Bella (b.1918),[31] after serving in the French colonial army in 1937 and 1919–45 on de Gaulle's side, and rejecting offers by Hitler and Pétain, joined an illegal armed movement, and was gaoled by the Gaullist–Socialist regime of France in 1950. He escaped to Cairo in 1952. There he met the circle of Abd el Krim and in 1954 was a co-founder of the FLN. He was captured in 1956 and imprisoned until 1962. In 1965 he was ousted by a coup led by Boumedienne. He was a founder of the Organization for African Unity (OAU) at Addis Ababa in 1962. His 'bourgeoisie' stood socially between the Tunisian and Egyptian level and the non-bourgeoisie (unfairly called 'lumpen-bourgeoisie' by some Marxists) of FRELIMO, MPLA, ZAPU–ZANU, SWAPO (or the South African ANC, and PAC), whose bourgeoisie is a foreign and European-settler one, and not a 'national bourgeoisie' akin to Sun Yat Sen's or Nehru's.

Constitutional Nationalism — East and West Africa

The 'peaceful' constitutional process was made possible by the prior political education of African nationalism by the liberal, Church, socialist and Communist wings of European imperialism. It was this that enabled Nkrumah to come out of gaol and work amicably with the British Governor, Arden-Clarke; which made Kenyatta the sole possible choice for Whitehall after defaming him for a decade as the Mau Mau 'leader to darkness and death', in the Corfield report and later; which led Britain towards Nyerere in Tanganyika and de Gaulle towards Senghor, Houphouët, Boigny, Touré and Keita in French Africa. Both sides realized that the distance separating them had been shortened by the bridges built previously, mainly in exile, by European liberal, missionary, socialist and Marxist training and co-operation. None the less many were surprised at the ease with which first de Gaulle and then Macmillan conducted their voyages round Africa about 1960 — the mean year of generalized independence.

Independence represented a fusion of European liberalism, social-ism and Marxism with African nationalism, socialism and Marxism, which were mirror images, sometimes laterally inverted, of the European counterparts. Near the centre of the African Socialist spectrum, both Nyerere and Agostino Neto have declared that they are part of the 'West'. The policy of non-alignment adopted by African governments is in theory one of free choice in foreign affairs. From another theoretical viewpoint this implies 'neutralism' between capitalism and socialism — a position that few accept, the few being 'conservatives' like Bokassa, Mobutu, Houpouet Boigny, the late Seretse Khama, Hastings Banda and, in practice, despite official KANU policy, the late Jomo Kenyatta. Nevertheless the socialists, like the Ugandan leader Milton Obote, Nyerere, Barre of Somalia, Senghor, Touré, Keita, Oginga Odinga,[32] Stevens, Nkrumah, Neto, Andrade, Pereira, the Cabral brothers, Machel, the SWAPO president Sam Nujoma and the ZANU president Mugabe, like Ben Bella and the late Nasser, have all at one time subscribed to 'neutralism' in foreign policy and have associated themselves with the Western, anti-Communist EEC imperialist bloc through the Lomé Convention. The parties striving for independence realized political power soon after their formation, within 10 years in Uganda, Kenya, Tanganyika, Guinea, Ivory Coast, Senegal, Mali, Gabon, Cameroons, Rwanda, Burundi, Zaire, Zambia, Ghana, Malawi, and Libya and within 20 in Nigeria, Algeria, Sudan, Tunisia, Egypt, Somalia, Guinea-Bissau, Angola and Mozambique, Zimbabwe and (by all indications) Namibia. In 1956 the French still preserved an all-'White' top administration in Africa, a few small high schools and Dakar University. The British considered only Ghana as ripe for 'self-government in 1954, with Sierra Leone, Nigeria and the Gambia as probables and decades in mind for East Africa. There was a thin layer of high schools, and university colleges only in Sierra Leone, Nigeria, Uganda (serving all British East Africa) and Khartoum. In 1956 the Belgian policy-maker Belsen foresaw a preparatory period of 30 years before independence for the Belgian colonies. Within a decade, under the impact of Asian independence (the Bandung Conference included African independence movements), of Algeria's war of liberation, of Mau Mau, mass strikes and student upheavals, all were independent.

The New Dependence — Independence

But the shape of imperialism was changing: German imperialism, rising rapidly by means of massive colonialist loan capital and the contract system in South America, Asia and North Africa, needed both a united Europe and an 'open' Africa. The British, French, Belgian, Dutch, Italian, Japanese and American imperialists wanted a freer capital export and raw material market and mutual access to each other's former colonies and spheres of influence. The old, closed, direct colonial relationship no longer suited the post-war multinationals of the old colonial powers, of Germany and Switzerland (whose hidden imperialism has recently been neatly exposed by Ziegler's book), of the USA–Canada bloc and the world's greatest multinational, the European

Economic Community. The EEC, founded in Rome in 1957 before any African state other than Egypt, Ghana, Liberia and Ethiopia had become independent, had already embroiled Sékou Touré, the leading African Marxist, in a pre-Lomé treaty in 1958, and had begun to do the same with other self-governing states approaching independence. The days of direct, open, political colonialism were drawing to a close in Africa. The sun of the new, indirect, hidden neo-colonialism, of multinational colonialism, with the old masters everywhere remaining dominant, was rising very rapidly. With it came new forms of rule, and new forms of socialism.

European Democrats and African Despots

Nearly every new, independent state moved in the direction of one-party and military dictatorships, which gave European liberals and socialists new grounds for pointing to the 'backwardness' of Africa, Europe and North Africa, like 'White' South Africa, Israel and Australasia, became richer and more democratic, while Africa, Asia and Indo-Negro America became steadily poorer and subject to dictatorships. The economic and political gaps widened together. The 'White' world became richer and more democratic, the non-European world poorer and more totalitarian. Nowhere was this more so than in Africa; for here the whole of its past fused into the modern reality.

The regimes of Amin Dada in Uganda, of 'Emperor' Bokassa in the Central African Republic, of the military dictators in Tchad, Ghana, Zaire, Nigeria and the Sudan are all examples of the more extreme form of a general tendency: a return, in modern bureaucratic form, of the old pre-colonial 'communal despotism', or 'African despotism'. So weak is the 'national bourgeoisie', after a century and more of denial by the retribalisation policy of colonialism, that there does not, generally, exist a middle class strong and able enough to run the complex imperialist economy of nationalised mines, plantations, banks, transportation and infra-structure of our times. It is too weak to afford the luxury of democracy. It cannot attain anything like the living standard of the European working class, whose social-economic-political level is a great deal more affluent than that of, say, the Indian bourgeoisie, on average. With Africa the situation is incontestably worse. The absence of a bourgeoisie has caused many states to be run by bureaucratic clan-despotisms.

The return to 'African despotism' is, however, only an apparent phenomenon, whose essence is something else altogether. The clan-despotism of an Amin clan, or a Bokassa clan, or even the tight family governing circle of Guinea during Sekou Touré's Presidency (akin, mutatis mutandis, to that of the Hoxha family in Albania), the Burundi and Rwanda clan dominions of Tutsi or Hutu over their opposite clans, the Kenyatta-Kikuyu tribal trend in Kenya, ousting the Odinga Luo groups, the Mobutu clan domination in Zaire, that which followed on the deaths of Ngoubi in Congo and Keita in Mali, the Ibo, Yoruba and Hausa regional regimes in Nigeria, the ruling clans of Haut Volta, the long reign of the Khamas in Botswana, the open clan despotism in Swaziland, the absolutely retribalised family Quislings managing the Transkei, Venda, Bophuthutswana and Ciskei Bantustans for the South African Herrenvolk — all these, as well as the tribal divisions inside liberation movements in Zaire, Zambia, Zimbabwe, Nigeria and among Peuls, Ouolofs, Cereres, Mandingos and other 'tribes' in former French West Africa, are not returns to the old past. They are the practical and logical developments of the colonialist destruction, inversion and perversion of 'communal despotism' by the retribalization political economy of 'indirect rule' as the *modus operandi* of racialist imperialism. It is this 'false past' that expresses itself in these dictatorships with their clan or tribal appearance.

This recreation of colonial 'African despotism' is less manifest where a bourgeoisie of some proportions has developed — in Senegal, Ivory Coast, Tunisia, or in newly independent 'African Marxist' states like Guinea-Bissau, Angola and Mozambique, or where all classes are weak, as in Guinea and Tanzania. Between the two ends of the political spectrum lie non-military one-party states like that in Kenya. Even in Ethiopia the weakness of the bourgeoisie threw up a military 'Dergue', the present African Marxist government, which has clashed with workers, peasants and students in spite of having nationalized the land and led a war against the Italians and Germans, who arm and finance the Eritrean and Somali secession movements and whom the 'Leninist' movements of Western Europe fight in the name of 'self-determination' — yet another European 'Marxist principle' which, in Africa and Asia, means the European partitioning of nations.

The general trend towards 'African despotism' arises not only from the subsequent final stage of capitalism–imperialism. The totalitarian character of the African economy, run by foreign monopolies, multinationals, states and banks, with industry-backed armies always at the ready, rapidly subjected and even de-classed the small middle class which had struggled through retribalization into the bigger colonial towns. Imperialism totally excluded this inhibited and puny layer from industry, mining and plantations and, with the partial exception of Indian merchants, from banking and wholesale and foreign commerce as well. The new class had less breathing space than its ancestors had had in the 'Indian summer' between slavery and imperialism. Even in the post independence period, the bourgeoisie remained half strangled at birth by this foreign dominion. The practical continuation of locations and reserves, in which no bourgeoisie could arise properly, restricted this already confining process to the major cities and economic junction-points.

In trying to define the economy of independent Africa, the fundamental criteria are not those of 'property relations' as they are in European Marxism. Clearly, there is private landed and urban productive property in Senegal, Ivory Coast, Tunisia, Sudan, Kenya, Zimbabwe, Zambia and Zaire, as there is, obviously, in 'White' South Africa. But even in these countries all major sectors, and the overwhelming bulk of the capital, is in the hands not of the local 'Boers' and settlers, but of foreigners. But in a number of other states — Algeria, Ethiopia after the Dergue victory over feudalism in 1975, Tanzania even before the 1967 Arusha Declaration of Nyerere's African socialism, in Guinea under Touré, Mali under Keita, Congo under Ngoubi, Guinea-Bissau, Angola, Mozambique — private landed property was illegal or negligible, except for surviving imperialist leaseholds. In these states, as well as in Libya and Zambia, partial or total nationalization has taken place in mining, banking and insurance. A large part of Africa has returned to communal land ownership and has communal or state ownership of the means of production, distribution and exchange. By mechanical European Marxist definitions they are already socialist and hence in no need of a social revolution, since no expropriation is possible.

The International Relations of Production

Just as pre-capitalist Asia, America and Africa did not conform to the 'Marxist' concept of classes of Europe, but, according to Marx and Engels, were communally based despotisms, so much of independent Africa defies definition by European criteria. Instead of a bourgeois class there is a bureaucratic caste; instead of a private property base there is communal property. But these combinations of bureaucracies and communal property are also found in the USSR, China and Eastern Europe; yet these are not capitalistic countries, for they have experienced unreversed social revolutions and have less than 10% of their economy in the capitalist world market. Independent Africa, in contrast, is 100% in the capitalist world market; and this is a basic criterion. Secondly, and more importantly, there is imperialistic capital in all the independent African states, in the form of investments — on freehold or leasehold or in nationalized enterprises — or in loans. Thirdly, through foreign commerce and the Lomé convention, Africa is in a subject position, as a primary producer transferring 'hidden surplus value' by exporting raw materials to imperialist countries and importing their finished industrial products. Fourthly, these three economic criteria have political and cultural reflexes such as membership of the British imperialist Commonwealth (so named by the racialist Smuts himself) or the French Union, or cultural agreements with the former 'mother countries'. And finally there is a foreign policy of 'neutralism' such as is not held by the USSR or any East European state except Yugoslavia, which is 'transitional' but not capitalist, by North Korea, Vietnam, Cuba or China. These are the basic criteria by which we can decide whether or not a former colony is capitalist or socialist. Neither the formal property relations, nor public declarations, are scientific judgments. Most imperialist states have had or have 'socialist' governments, which have waged many racialist colonialist wars, against Indo-China, Vietnam, the Mau Mau in Kenya and others. Nearly all African states declare themselves to be socialist or Marxist — 'African' Marxist as well as 'scientific' — as are nearly all independent Asian states. But the ultimate defining factor is the imperialistic nexus, and in terms of this criterion none of Africa is 'socialistic' yet, all property forms and policy declarations notwithstanding.

A social, anti-imperialist revolution clearly involves the expropriation and nationalization of all imperialist property and investments. In much of Africa these have already been nationalized, which in 'European Marxist' terms reduces the social revolution to the expropriation of the small, inhibited, non-industrial, non-banking, non-exporting colonial bourgeoisie. But such a revolution is pathetic, meaningless, and would leave the entire imperialist domination intact. It would be meaningless to define as bourgeoisie the non-property-owning bureaucratic caste in Tanzania, where state officers may not own property in production, or shares, or investments, and thus cannot be capitalists. There are comparable restrictions on the bureaucratic caste in Ethiopia, in Guinea, Guinea-Bissau, Angola and Mozambique and similar trends in Nigeria, the most populous country in Africa. Since there is no real bourgeoisie in these states, expropriation would be meaningless.

A social revolution in Africa — South, East, West, Central as well as North — has these days to do not only with formal property relations but with the real economic domination of imperialism, including that of European South Africa. That is what must be abolished. When it has gone, no bourgeoisie can exist. There are only two types of capitalist state, the imperialist and the colony or semi-colony. Since no former colony in these days can do what the USA, Canada and Australasia did in the 19th Century — convert themselves from colonial to colonialist countries — the anti-imperialist social revolution in Africa would destroy the very foundations of capitalism. For without colonialism, its very base, capitalism cannot exist.

The social anti-imperialist revolution requires not only expropriation, where that situation arises, but attention to the newer forms of imperialism, the EEC Lomé Convention and loan-capital. It calls for a grand 'Boston Tea Party' all around Africa. Conversely, it calls for an end to all agreements to export raw materials cheaply, cutting Europe and North America off from those materials that Africa and Asia need for their own rapid industrialization. It means reversing the international social division of labour. It means annulling and cancelling the public external debt as a necessary pre-revolutionary step; had Lenin or Mao stood in awe before the external debt of the Czars or Chiang Kai-shek, there would have been no revolution in Russia or China. Leasehold concessions would be cancelled without compensation. Foreign contracts would be under national control, at rates that did not reflect cheap labour, free from subsequent dominion by foreign technology, aimed at economic independence from tool-making and power machinery. But without an African Cuba — the dream of Che Guevara — without the permanent anti-imperialist revolution, 'planning' must fail.

Imperialist exploitation, the transfer of surplus value from Africa to, mainly, Europe, will end. The transfer takes place in two major ways: first, through investments and loans. Loans, for example, enable European banks to give loans to African states — these loans never leave Europe, but go to multinationals and states which undertake construction and projects in Africa and earn super-profits by super-exploiting African cheap labour. Most of the loans go to European salaries and wages, always 20 or more times higher than African wages, to the purchase of European steel and other products, to European shipping and air companies and insurance companies, and finally to the profits of the contractors. The African states, which have received no money except some for local wages and materials, then have to repay the loan with interest. They are left with some fixed capital installations — generally non-industrial, for European capital and labour agree not to export heavy machine industry, atomic power equipment, computer units, electronics to Africa. Africa remains unindustrialized, predominantly agricultural — the reverse of what its deserts and thin top-soil call for. The myth that Europe, with its rich top-soil, poverty in minerals and in water power, is made for industry and that Africa, with its poor top-soil and abundant minerals and water-power, is made for agriculture, has even been endorsed by Nyerere, whose Arusha Declaration of 1967 declares agriculture to be the base of Tanzania's economy. The loan system preserves the fundamental world division of labour between industry and agriculture. It leaves Africa with a debt equal to a year's production. The whole semi-colonial world today owes nearly 1,000 billion dollars to the advanced West. In repaying the capital and paying the interest Africa has become poorer and poorer, as its surplus value is drained off in debt and capital repayments.

Secondly, Europe imports African minerals and agricultural raw material crops at cheap labour prices, below their true value. Not that African productivity in mining and export farming is lower than European; for the most part different products are mined and grown, and figures for productivity are not comparable, but where they are, as in gold, copper, uranium and coal mining and oil and iron extraction and in the manufacture of textiles, car assembly, processing and even in certain heavy industry, African productivity is higher than European. Productivity and wages are unrelated quantities. The low selling price of African products has behind it 500 years of European undervaluing of African lives, African lands and African labour and wealth. Marx drew attention once to European undervaluing of American gold and silver. The undervaluing of African production in the pre-independence period was standard practice — used also for tax and customs evasion. But when the imported raw materials are sold as part of a European manufacture, they are sold at full world value. They are costed not at import but at world prices. The general rate of profit may be in the region of 100%, but the profit on the colonial products is 200%, even 1000%, as shown by recent research into British imports of electrical products from Hong Kong. The surplus value transferred in this manner I have called 'hidden' surplus value: colonial imports to the imperialist countries make up about 10% of total national incomes, and the hidden super-surplus value some 10% or more, so that it comprises the entire declared surplus value in the gross national products of those countries. To this major element we must add the surplus value made either through direct investments or through the German-developed loan-contract system; and the Lomé Convention[33] guarantees to Europe a regular supply of cheap, undervalued raw materials and at the same time preserves the character of the independent African countries as primary producers and the colonialist world social division of labour. The combination of the two methods of super-exploitation, through loans and through undervalued imports, has frustrated every ambition of independence. About 10 years after most African states had won independence, Kwame Nkrumah declared them to be still 'neo-colonies' of Europe and the United States. And there is still the enormous capital market of Anglo-European owned South Africa, whose economy sprawls over the major area of sub-equatorial independent Africa with mining, banking, export, transport and other investments and operations, including the recruitment of cheap labour.

One third of independent Africa labours directly for this system of imperialism. The other two thirds is unemployed: its production counts for little; it is auxiliary to wages, helping cheap labour to survive, preserving the system of cheap labour with a pressure of mass unemployment a hundred times greater than any known in Europe. The capitalist system in Africa is not the same as that in Europe: it is the hell below the European heaven. But it is the heaven, not its hellish underworld, that the Solzhenitsyns and other pro-Western defectors from Eastern Europe have seen. Over two-thirds of Africa's production is drained away to Western Europe via the Lomé Convention, loan repayments and profits on investments. What is left is termed the gross national product. The bureaucratic castes and neo-bourgeoisies take at best an increasing (from nearly zero) share of this profit, but the major share goes abroad and the capitals of Europe have ways of recovering the bulk of what even the oil kingdoms keep, through property and financial investments which they and not the 'sheikhs' own and control and which give them access to Iran, Libya and other states. Nationalization has had the same effect. The giant multinationals of South Africa, Holland, America, Belgium, Britain and France that have been nationalized remain powers in their old states and, through 'aid', loans and 50-50 nationalization, also in the new states. This fusion of monopoly capital with independent states much weaker than this capital has been the economic-political basis of 'African dictatorships' which mask, and are inversions of, those European despotisms that underlie European democracy. It is this imperialistic totality, combined with the retribalization of indirect rule, that has produced the modern 'African despotisms'.

Despite, and under cover of, African socialism and, more and more, of African Marxism, independence is the ultimate form of indirect rule fused with the ultimate form of monopoly capitalism, the imperialist, multinational companies and multinational treaties like the EEC. This reality was never the intention of African nationalism, socialism or Marxism, which aimed at freedom and self-determination. The converse has happened; the independence movements acted as catalysts in processes to which they were in principle opposed.

Sekou Touré and Senghor have reflected the underdevelopment of a colonial bourgeoisie in writing about the classless nature of African society and a Marxism without the class struggle, apart from that against imperialism. European Marxism, in contrast, self-interestedly undervalued imperialism and explained world surplus value more through 'productivity' in the 'metropoles' than through colonial super-exploitation. The historic objectivity of these two leaders places them as the finest representatives of an African bourgeoisie which never had the chance to become a proper class. They represent the 'bourgeois-democratic' revolution in the age of imperialism as Robespierre and Cromwell, for instance, did in the age of feudalism.

Paradoxes and Accidents: the African Revolution

Given the special conditions in Africa (communal land, nationalization of foreign interests, a singularly weak bourgeoisie and a strong proletariat, it cannot be excluded that a few independent states may, like Cuba under Castro, become socialist countries without the political replacement of the bureaucratic caste. In the case of Cuba, a national bourgeoisie, after the defeat of the Batista regime, found itself impelled towards the Soviet Union by an error of American political strategy. This accident took Castro and Che Guevara from a bourgeois into a social revolution without being themselves overthrown by a

Communist or other 'workers'' party, whose place was actually taken by their own party of revolt. China had its social revolution, under different post-war conditions, because the party of Mao turned away from its previous agrarian course on to one of agrarian revolution, and broke with Stalin over collaboration with America. Hungary, Yugoslavia, Bulgaria, Romania, Albania and Czechoslovakia had social revolutions as a result of the combination of resistance movements in semi-colonial countries with the Red Army's crushing victories over Nazism, and East Germany and Poland became 'socialist' by force of the Soviet army's victory and not by any internal resistance movement. North Korea and Vietnam went from national liberation to social revolution under ex-Stalinist parties. There are thus no golden rules for social revolutions, however desirable the Leninist rule may seem. What was once regarded as an exceptional path has become common. There is no reason why, in quite an unexpected way, through some 'accident' or other, Mozambique, Angola, Guinea-Bissau, Ethiopia, the Congo or even Tanzania should not be transformed from a semi-colony, a member of some European Commonwealth or EEC convention, into a member of the 'socialist bloc'.

Such accidental social transformations, however, cannot be the norm. In the case of South Africa, the Evian–Lisbon–Lancaster House type of 'independence' solution is ruled out by the social, economic and political structure of the country. It is a bastion of the West in minerals, gold, uranium: a third of the Western investments in, and 24% of the trade, 50% of the industry and 66% of the energy-supply of, all Africa are concentrated there; it is of great strategic importance militarily to NATO and the EEC, and 'majority rule' cannot be risked there. The five million Europeans will not give up their racial stance and privileges without a war. The non-Europeans possess no bourgeoisie in the reserves or locations, or indeed anywhere, strong enough to manage the vast imperialist mining, banking and industrial undertaking. There is a politically unbeaten proletariat, utterly non-'European', unclassical, totally revolutionary.

The course of the revolution against racialism seems to be directed not to a Lancaster–Zimbabwean agreement, nor to a Pretoria–Bonn–Washington–London deal on Namibia, but towards a Vietnamese type of international confrontation, but one such as Vietnam never, even in the midst of the revolution and the napalm, knew. The southern arm of the EEC-apartheid 'nutcracker' will burst the shell of Sam Nijoma's hopes for a really independent Namibia,[34] whose independence requires the repatriation of Angolan-Cubans, freedom for German capital, in particular, and the closing down by all African states of the guerrilla camps and bases of the ANC of South Africa. The EEC, Whitehall, Pretoria, the UNO, liberals, World Council and other Church bodies, social democracy and Eurocommunism, will try repeatedly to engage the liberation movement in political talks with the

Quislings of apartheid. Talks such as these occurred in October 1979 when ANC leaders met Buthelezi's 'Inkatha' (strongly backed by West Germany and USA parties and finance) and agreed on a 'United Patriotic Front' against the Pretoria regime which had, with the Thatcher government of the time, arranged this meeting with the foremost 'anti-apartheid' Bantustan-type collaborator with apartheid,[35] at the same time as Lord Carrington was, with the help of the 'Front Line Presidents' (of Tanzania, Zambia, Mozambique and Botswana) preparing the Lancaster House agreement for the continued economic dominion of British capital and settlers in Zimbabwe. While British capital's private police murderously put down a massive African miners' strike in September 1984, its two main political vehicles in South Africa — the Liberals and the Anglican Church — stepped up a proto-Lancaster House policy. Hence the opening up of the Oppenheimers' Progressive party to non-Europeans in November 1984. Hence, too, the appointment by the Canterbury Church-within-a-State of one, Naidoo, as Cape Town archbishop, and of the avowedly anti-Communist 1984 Nobel Peace Prize winner, Tutu, founder, in 1983, of the Black Consciousness National Forum, as archbishop of the Golden City, Johannesburg.

While imperialism spreads the illusion of a 'negotiated solution', *à la* Lancaster House, for South Africa, NATO has rearmed South Africa as a member of the secret South Atlantic Treaty Organization (for which, inter alia, the British went into the Malvine or Falkland Islands in 1982). France, the USA and, since 1972, German firms, backed by the Socialist–Liberal Government of Schmidt and the government of Kohl, have made South Africa an atomic power, producing West Germany's first A-bomb since President Carter informed the world of an A-bomb test on 22 September 1979.[36] Parallel with this EEC–NATO nuclear potential is a German-backed plan, first elaborated by Kauffmann in 1962, and refined by Natorp, Van der Ropp and other admirers of 'Black Consciousness' and of the apartheid principle, to partition South Africa into a consolidated Bantustan, to be known as Azania, including the Eastern Cape and Natal, and a 'White'–Asian–'Coloured' South African Republic.[37] All this is very different to the process of constitutional negotiations used for the rest of Africa. The difference lies in the fundamental role of racialism as the cement of imperialism in South Africa, in the dual nature of the country as being, in Trotsky's words, 'A colony for the Blacks and a Dominion for the Whites',[38] i.e. as being the only imperialist nation in Africa itself.

This dual character of the South African political economy locates it as a bridge between the imperialist 'centre' and the semi-colonial 'periphery'. It has its 'West' and its 'South' in juxtaposition with each other. Its conflicting 'race'–class poles are inside one geo-state, as in the USA and, to a much lesser degree, in the EEC states with their relatively smaller 'internal colonies'. This South African duality is an internalization of the general international social relation of production: namely that the exploited/oppressed classes are in the semi-colonial 'periphery' and the exploiting/oppressor classes are in the imperialist 'centre'. The conflicting classes belong, generally, to different nations, but in South Africa they belong to one race-class-divided 'nation'. The world-dominant capitalist system has a fundamental self-negating contradiction:the international nation–class relations of production, namely that 'the world is divided into oppressed nations and ruling nations',[39] form a barrier known as the 'gap' which obstructs the worldwide development of the forces of production. These forces are situated largely in the 'West'. The semi-colonial 'South' pays tribute in labour and natural wealth to this 'West', but is itself starved of developed forces of production by the international division of labour, which itself is the most direct expression of the international class relations of production. This international contradiction of capitalism is largely internalised in South Africa. However, through its own Southern African Customs Union and virtual Common Market, South Africa has the same external contradiction between relations and forces of production as other imperialist powers have in relation to their respective spheres of influence.

This twofold contradiction of South Africa takes the form of conflicts between the European 'race'–class with both its internal and its external non-European cheap-labour antithesis: the racially oppressed in South Africa and the exploited and dependent neighbouring peoples of Namibia, Lesotho, Botswana, Swaziland, Zimbabwe, Malawi, Mozambique, Angola, Zambia and even Zaire, Tanzania and Kenya. This proletarian-peasant antithesis, in the context of an impending Guevarist awakening of Africa, is the nemesis of 'White' South Africa. It is bound by its very mode of existence to be the major force in the resolution of the irreconcilable conflict between relations and means of production in Southern and thence in most, if not all, of Africa. As the experience of Guinea, Mozambique, Angola and Ethiopia has confirmed, neither 'aid' nor economic planning — which, at best can be a holding operation for the Permanent Revolution in Africa — can secure independence and transform it into socialism. This permanent revolution is the 'nation-class' struggle against the international relations of production.

When the illusions have been dispelled by the anti-imperialist and international nature of the final 'solution of the South African problem', when the tears have dried and the clouds lifted over this seemingly inevitable clash of classes and nations, Africa may well not recognize itself in any Africanist mirror; certainly not in any European one. Certain it is, at any rate, that every concept and practice of tribe and race, from Crummell to Black Consciousness, will have long been sloughed off by the actual struggles of the liberation movements. Certain, too, that the communal society that will emerge will be a non-racial, multicultural, cosmopolitan and non-European one. It will de-Europeanize also Europe, help to reagriculturalize, deindustrialize and humanize it, closing the material and cultural gap. No one can say whether this will happen before the year 2000. History, however, has shown often enough that novelty can very quickly be born out of conflict in Africa.

Notes

1. T. Soga, T. Jabavu, op. cit; Jabavu's paper 'Imvu Zabantsundu'; H. Jaffe, *Storia del Sudafrica*, Milan, 1980, ch. 7, parts 1, 2; Milner Papers, vol. 2 (on Liberals, Boers, 'Native Policy'), London; C.J. Rhodes, *Vindex* (speeches), 1887–1900, Cape Town.

2. Mnguni, *300 Years*, vol. 2 (on Zimbabwe conquest).

3. M.K. Gandhi, *Satyagraha in South Africa*, Madras, 1928.

4. I.J. Potekhin, op. cit.; *Formirovanie Natsionalnoi Obschnosti Yuzhnoi Afrikanskich Bantu*, Moscow, 1955.

5. APO Newspaper, 22 August 1914 and 5 September 1914, Cape Town.

6 M. Benson, op. cit. (history of ANC); W.H. Andrews, *Class Struggles in South Africa*, Cape Town, 1941.

7. *Korrespondenz*, vol. 1, Hamburg 1973; *Black Review*, 1974–5, p. 123.

8. C. Huberich, *The Political and Legislative History of Liberia*, 1947.

9. S.A. Crummel, *Africa and America*, New York, 1891.

10. S.A. Benson, *African Repository*, XXXII, and H.S. Wilson (ed.), *Origins of West African Nationalism*, 1969.

11. E.W. Blyden, in Wilson (ed.), op. cit., p. 79–86.

12. E.W. Blyden, ibid., pp. 94–104.

13. Henry Venn and Grey, op. cit.

14. J.A. Horton, *West African Countries and Peoples*, London, 1868.

15. E.W. Blyden, *Christianity, Islam and the Negro Race*, 1887.

16. E.W. Blyden, in *Sierra Leone Times*, 3June 1893, Freetown.

17. E.W. Blyden, *African Life and Customs*, London, 1908.

18. J.E. Casely Hayford, 'Gold Coast Native Institutions, with Thoughts upon a Healthy Imperial Policy for the Gold Coast and Ashanti', London, 1903.

19. Blaise Diagne, in *Notes Africaines*, op. cit.

20. A. Lincoln, *Addresses*, op. cit.

21. APO Newspaper, 1917–22; E. Roux, *Time Longer than Rope*, London, 1948; J.H. Simons and Ray Alexander, *Class and Colour*, op. cit. (but absent in M. Benson, op. cit.).

22. S.P. Bunting, *Red Revolt and the Rand Strike*, Johannesburg, 1922; defended by I. Jones at 3rd International; E. Roux, S.P. Bunting, self-published, 1944; *International*, 22–3; A. Lerumo, op. cit.; Simons, op. cit.

23. C. Kadalie, *My Life and the ICU*, op. cit., chapters 9, 10, 12.

24. I.B. Tabata, *The Awakening of the People*, Johannesburg, 1950; *The Boycott, A Weapon of Struggle*, Cape Town, 1955; H.J. Simons, op. cit., pp. 591–4, on December 1947 ANC and CPSA pro-boycott resolutions, reversed in 1948; (*Freedom*, CPSA organ, November–December 1947, vol. 6); Moses Kotane,

CPSA Secretary, condemned 'Native Representatives' as 'Traitors to Africa' and 'Representatives of White Supremacy' in *Freedom*, September–October 1947, pp. 14–17.

25. *Ware Republikaner*, issued by CPSA groups in 1939–40; H. Snitcher spoke with Nazi-Nationalists at Railway Hall, Adderley Street (author's recollection); Non-Europeans were organized in separate social functions so as to court Afrikaner 'comrades' in this period.

26. CPSA cadres helped organize the pro-Smuts, *Springbok Legion*; the *Guardian* (CPSA weekly) was pro-war from 1941–5.

27. The post-Trotsky 4th International officially admitted its 'error' in supporting the (CIA and Mao backed) FLNA and not MPLA in *Inprecor*, Brussels, no. 46 of 18 March 1976, p. 27. The MPLA was 'recognized' only at the 10th Congress, in 1974, one year before its final victory; *Inprecor*, 10 November 1977, proposed unity between the ANC of the Quisling, Muzorewa, and the Patriotic Front of Nkomo and Mugabe. Post-Trotsky 'Trotskyism' accepted, as a 'fact' the British partition of India, the Pentagon–Whitehall sub-partition of 'Pakistan' India known as Bangladesh; like the whole Euramerican 'Left', it either stood with 'Biafra' or was 'neutral', and supported the EEC-armed and propagandized 'Eritrean' and Ogaden violation of Ethiopian national unity. But, it stood for the 'United Socialist States of Europe' and put up candidates for the 'European Parliament', talking shop of the world's major multinational.

28. S. Biko, *Black Consciousness in South Africa* (testimony), London, 1979; *Black Review*, 1974–5, 1975–6, Lovedale; *Handbook of Black Organisations*, Durban, 1973; *SASO on the Attack*, 1973; *National Forum* (Hammanskraal Conference, 11–12 June 1983), are among indigenous 'Black Consciousness' source-material.

29. G.A. Nasser, *The Philosophy of the Revolution*, 1955, 1959; United Arab Republic official biography, *President G.A. Nasser*, 1965.

30. D.S. Woolman and R. Furneaux, op. cit. on Abd el Krim.

31. R. Merle (authorized biography), *Ahmed Ben Bella*, 1965 (1967 in English); TV programmes from France after release.

32. Oginga Odinga, *Not Yet Uhuru*, London, 1968.

33. H. Jaffe, 'The Lomé Convention', in *Pyramid of Nations*, op. cit.; G. Martin (Yaounde), 'Africa and the Ideology of Eurafrica: Neo-Colonialism or Pan-Africanism', *Journal of Modern African Studies*, 20 February 1982, pp. 221–38, Cambridge, England. The domination of the OECD countries is shown in a 1983 *OECD Observer* statistic of the ratio of profits to wages in the leading seven OECD countries. The ratio fell from 32% in 1961 to 28% in 1981. This ratio — the 'degree of exploitation' for Marx — is the inverse of the African ratio of 300% (i.e. 2 hours 'necessary labour time' and 6 hours 'surplus labour time' in a working day of 8 hours on mines, farms etc.).

34. Sam Nujoma, interview, *Panorama*, Milan, 12 March 1984, pp. 113–4.

35. ANC statement by O. Tambo, 5 November 1979; The *Star*, Johannesburg, 3 November 1979; The *Guardian*, 7 November 1979. The meeting was between 'Inkatha' and ANC executives and agreed to parallel action 'regardless of secondary differences'. (O. Tambo, circulated press statement, London.)

36. 'Atombome mit Deutscher Hilfe?', *Der Spiegel*, 29 October 1979, with photograph of Palindaba A-plant; H. Jaffe, 'Una Bomba "Made in Germany"', *Panorama*, Milan, 19 November 1979. On earlier German work: 'Going Nuclear', in *Economic and Political Weekly*, 29 January 1977; 'South Africa's

Mysterious A-Plant', in *Herald Tribune*, 7 May 1977.

37. Details of the West German Partition Plan in H. Jaffe, *Germania*, op. cit.; and H. Jaffe, *Storia del Sudafrica*, op. cit. The German plan has the support inside Botha's cabinet of at least two policy-making members; the German plan was worked out in Bonn's Stiftung Wissenschaft Und Politik, in the *Aussenpolitik* journal, and by Frankfurt and traditional Hamburg African-Studies centres. Von Der Ropp's contacts with *Black Review* and other 'Black Consciousness' bodies was paralleled by meetings with the South African Ministry of Foreign Affairs in 1976. The German plan rejects the separate Bantustans as well as the 'liberal' solution of 'one man one vote' (subscribed to by the EEC and by Kissinger–Mondale only after Soweto, 1976.)

38. L. Trotsky, 'Letter to South Africa', reproduced in *Workers Voice*, Cape Town, 1944. (Trotsky wrote two letters, the one referred to being April 1935. They were written to the Lenin Club and Workers Party, Cape Town. Like Engels (in articles on Morocco, 1957 and to Storckenberg, 25 January 1894) and the 3rd International 'Resolutions on a Black State' in America and South Africa, but unlike Marx and Lenin, on the evidence, Trotsky accepted the concept of 'race' and wanted the 'Black race to ascend, hand in hand, with the White race, to new cultural heights'. The New Era Fellowship, during the rise of the Non-European Unity Movement, rejected the concept of 'race' which B.M. Kies described as a 'myth' in his *Contribution of the Non-Europeans to World Civilization*, Cape Town, 1953.

39. V.I. Lenin, speech, 6 December 1920, in *Collected Works*.

Select Bibliography

Africanus, Leo, *De Totius Africae Descriptione*, Antwerp, Venice, 1556.

Ahmad Ibn Mohammad (Tippoo Tib), *Autobiography*, Royal African Museum, Brussels.

Alexander, R. and Simons, J., *Class and Colour in South Africa*, London, 1969.

Al Masudi, *Muraj el Dhabab (The Meadows of Gold and Mines of Gems)*, Trans. Spenger, London, 1841.

Alvarez, F., *Travels (1540)*, London, 1890.

Amin, S., *Quale 1984?* (with A.G. Frank, H. Jaffe), Milan, 1975, Madrid, 1976.

——, *Histoire économique du Congo*, Dakar, 1969.

——, *The Future of Southern Africa* (Preface), Dar-es-Salaam, 1975.

Andrews, W.H., *Class Struggles in South Africa*, Capetown, 1941.

Angola in Arms, M.P.L.A., Bulletin, Dar-es-Salaam, c. 1970.

Annals of the South African Museum, 27/1929.

Anti-CAD Bulletins, Capetown, 1943–7.

Archives Year Books for South African History, Pretoria, 1938–9, 1946, 1952, 1965.

Armstrong, H.C., *Grey Steel* (J.C. Smuts), London, 1937.

Aussenpolitik, Hamburg, 27/4, 1976; 28/1, 1977.

Ayola, G.P. de, *1534 Letter to Charles V*, Copenhagen Royal Library, (Trans. A. Poznansky), 1944.

Azan, M.M. Samba, *Martin Samba*, Dakar, 1976.

Azania News, Vol. 1, London, September 1966.

Badoglio, P., *The War in Abyssinia*, London, 1937.

Ballinger, M., *From Union to Apartheid*, London, 1969.

Bantu Studies, Johannesburg, 1921–2, 5/1931, 9/1935, 1945, 1955, 1963.

Barbosa, de Jao, *Romerugte Scheepstogt van Francisco D'Almeida na Oost-Indien*, Leyden, 1706.

——, *The Book of Duerte Barbosa (1500, 1517–8)*, Hakluyt Society, London, 1918.

Barrow, J., *An Account of Travels into the Interior of Southern Africa*, 2 vols, London, 1801.

Barth, H., *Travels and Discovery in North and Central Africa*, 5 vols, London, 1857.

Bartnicki, A., Mantel-Niecko, J., *Geschichte Äthiopiens*, 2 vols, Berlin, 1978.

Battuta, Ibn, *The Travels of Ibn Battuta*, London, 1929, 1962.

Bekri, El, (Tr. V. Monteil), *IFAN Bulletin*, Dakar, 1968.

Bell, J.S., and Morrell, W.P., *Select Documents on British Colonial Policy*, Oxford, 1928.

Bella, Ben, *Ahmed Ben Bella* (authorized biography, R. Merle), 1965, 1967.

Bell, R.M., 'The Maji Maji Rebellion', in *Tanganyika Notes and Records*, 28/1950.

Benson, S.A., *African Repository*, in *West African Nationalism* (Ed.) H.S. Wilson, London, 1969.

Bent, J.T., *The Ruined Cities of Mashonaland*, London, 1902.

Bergh, P.L. van der (Ed.), *Africa — Social Problems of Change and Conflict*, San Francisco, 1965.

Biko, S., *Black Consciousness in South Africa*, London, 1979; and in: *Black Review*, Durban, 1974–5; *Handbook of Black Organisations*, Durban, 1973; *S.A.S.O. On The Attack*, 1973.

Biobaku, S.O., *Lugard Lectures*, Lagos, 1955.

Bird, J., *The Annals of Natal, 1495–1845*, 2 vols, Pietermaritzburg, 1888.

Bleek, W.H.I., *Specimens of Bushman Folklore*, London, 1911.

Blommaert, W., *Het Invoeren de Slavernij*, Cape Records, 1938.

Blyden, E.W., *Christianity, Islam and the Negro Race*, 1877.

——, *Sierra Leone Times*, 3 June 1893.

——, *African Life and Customs*, London, 1908.

Bokassa, J.B., Interview in *E.E.C. Courier*, Brussels, February 1977.

Bolshevik, The, Capetown, October 1919 to September 1920.

Boufflers, Chevalier de, *Memoires*, IFAN and Gorée Museum, Dakar.

Braudel, F., 'Monnaies et Civilisations' in *Annales: Economies, Sociétés, Civilisations*, Paris, 1969.

——, *La Mediterranée et le Monde Mediterranéen à l'Époque de Philippe II*, Paris, 1966.

Breasted, J.H., *Ancient Records of Egypt*, Vol.4, Chicago, 1906.

Bretout, F., *Mogho Naba Wobgho*, (Haute Volta resister-king), Dakar, 1976.

Brey, de D., in Lopez, D., *Relazione de Reame di Congo* (Tr. Pigafetta), Rome, 1591–1601.

——, *Beschreibung des Konigsreiches Kongo in Afrika*, Frankfurt, 1597.

British Foreign Office, *Somaliland*, London, 1920.

Broadbent, S., *A Narrative of the First Introduction of Christianity amongst the Baralong Tribes of the Bechuanas, South Africa*, London, 1865.

Broome, R., *The Natives of South Africa*, 1923.

——, *The Missing Link*, 1950.

Brosselard, *Report on the Capture of Lamine and Bokar*, Lille, 1888.

Bruce, J., *Travels in Ethiopia*, London, 1768, 1773, 1813.

Buganda Nyaffe, Kampala, January–February, 1945.

Bulletin Cultural da Guinea Portuguesa, Lisbon, to 1973.

Bulletin d'Etudes Camerounaises, Douala.

Bunting, S.P., *Red Revolt and the Rand Strike*, Johannesburg, 1922.

Burchett, W., and Jaffe, H., *Una Democrazia Confezionata, Il Caso del Portogallo*, Milan, 1975.

Burger, C.P., and Hunger, F.W.T., *Itenerario, Voyage ofte Schipvaert van Jan Huygen van Linschoten Naer Oost Ofte Portugals Indien, 1579–1592*, The Hague, 1934.

Burton, R.F., *The Lake Regions of Central Africa*, 2 vols, London, 1860.

——, *Lands of Gazembe*, London, 1873.

——, *First Footsteps in Africa*, London, 1910.

Cabral, A., *Declaration of Principles*, Cuba, in *La Vittoria o la Morte*, Milan, 1971.
——, *Die Theorie als Waffe*, Berlin, 1968.
——, *Die Ekonomie der Befreiung*, Frankfurt, 1969.
Cadbury, *Labour in Portuguese Africa*, London, 1909.
Caillé, R., *Rapport sur son Voyage à Tombouctou*, Paris, 1828.
Cameron, V.L., *My Tanganyika Service*, London, 1939.
Campbell, J., *Travels in Southern Africa*, London, 1815.
Campbell, R.A., *A Pilgrimage to My Motherland*, New York, 1961.
Cape Colony Chronicles of Commanders, Capetown, 1882.
Cape Colony Records (Ed. G.M. Theal), 36 vols, London, 1897–1905.
Cape Hansard, Capetown, 1853, 1857, 1875, 1877, 1883–5, 1888, 1894.
Carter, G., Karis, T., and Gerhart, G.M., *A Documentary History of South African Politics, 1882–1964*, 4 vols, Stanford, 1974–77.
Castenshosa, *Portuguese Expedition to Abyssinia in 1541–3*, Hakluyt Society, 1902.
Caselis, E., *My Life in Basutoland*, London, 1889.
Caton-Thompson, G., *The Zimbabwe Culture*, Oxford, 1931.
Cavazzi, da Montecuccolo, G.A., *Istorica Descrizione dei Tre Regni Congo, Matamba et Angola*, Bologna, 1687.
Challenge (Alemakef Ethiopian Journal), New York, August 1967, February 1968.
Charter of the British East Africa Company, London, 1889.
Churchill, Lord R., *Men, Mines and Animals*, London, 1892.
Churchill, W.S., *My African Journey*, London, 1908.
——, *Memoirs on the Second World War*, London, 1948–52.
Ciano, G., *Ciano's Diary, 1939–43*, London, 1946.
Cissoko, M., *Tombouctou et l'empire Songhay*, Dakar, 1975.
Clark, J.D., *The Stone Age Culture of N. Rhodesia*, Capetown, 1950.
——, *Background to Evolution in Africa*, Chicago, 1972.
Clapperton, J., and Denham, D., *Narrative of Travels and Discoveries in Northern and Central Africa*, London, 1826.
Collins, R., *Journal*, Capetown, 1809.
Colonisation of Central Africa, in *Royal Colonial Institution, Vol.7*, London, 1895.
Compagnie du Congo, Assemblée Générale, 21 March 1891, Brussels.
Compagnie du Katanga, *Statutes*, Brussels, 1891.
——, *History 1906–1956*, Brussels, 1957.
Congo: *Code Penal*, Brussels, 1888.
Congo: *Hansard*, London, 1901, 1903, 1908.
Congo: *Jesuit Reports*, Brussels, 1906.
Conscience Africaine, Brussels, June 1956 (Ileo, Zaire, vs., Belsen, Belgium).
Contenson, H. de, in *UNESCO General History of Africa*, vol.2, California, 1981.
Cook, A., *Uganda Memories, 1897–1940*, London, 1945.
Corriere UNESCO, Rome, November 1973 (B. Davidson, A. Cabral).
Courier, EEC/ACP/Lomé Bulletins, 24/1974, 32-3/1975, 41-2/1977.
Cresques, A., *Catalonian Map of Africa, 1375*, copy, IFAN, University, Dakar.
Corfield Report on Kenya, H.M.S.O., Cmnd. 1030, London.
Cranforth, Lord, *A Colony in the Making* (Kenya), London, 1912.
Crowder, M., 'Indirect Rule – French and British Style', in *Africa*, 24/1964,

Oxford.

Crummell, A., *Africa and America*, New York, 1891.

Curtis, L., *With Milner in Africa*, Oxford, 1951.

Dapper, O., *Beschreibung von Afrika*, Amsterdam, 1670; trans. London, 1968.

Dart, R., in *International Anthropological and Linguistic Review*, 1/201–8; see L.S.B. Leakey and R. Broome.

Davidson, A.B., 'African Resistance and Rebellion against the Imposition of Colonial Rule', in T.O. Ranger (Ed.), *Emerging Themes in African History*, Nairobi, 1968; and in R.O. Collins (Ed.), *Problems in the History of Colonial Africa, 1860–1960*, New Jersey, 1970; see Potekhin, I.J.

Davidson, B., *Portuguese Africa*, London, 1954.

——, *Old Africa Rediscovered*, London, 1959.

——, *Guide to African History*, London, 1963.

——, *The Liberation of Guinea*, London, 1969.

——, 'Dans les Maquis de Guinée-Bissau', in *Le Monde Diplomatique*, February, 1973.

——, *Angola*, London, 1961.

——, *In The Eye of the Storm: Angola's People*, London, 1974.

Davies, I., *African Trade Unions*, London, 1966.

De Bono, E., *The Conquest of an Empire*, London, 1937.

De Chavonnes, M.P. and Baron Von Imhoff, D.E.I.C., *Reports* (17th century), Capetown, 1918.

D.E.I.C., *Journal, 1660–1795*, Cape Archives, Capetown.

De Kiewiet, C.W., *The Imperial Factor in South Africa*, Cambridge, 1937.

——, *Social and Economic History of South Africa*, Oxford, 1941.

De Kock, V., *Those in Bondage* (from Cape Archives), London, 1950.

Delafosse, L., *Maurice Delafosse le Berrichon Conquis par l'Afrique*, Paris, 1976.

Delafosse, M., *Negroes of Africa*, London, 1931.

Delaney, M.R., *Official Report of the Niger Valley Exploring Party*, N.Y., 1861.

Del Boca, A., *The Ethiopian War, 1935–41*, Chicago, 1970.

De Mist, J.A., *Memoranda, 1802–6*, Capetown, 1920.

Deschamps, H., *Les Méthodes et les Doctrines Coloniales de la France du XVIme Siècle à nos Jours*, Paris, 1953.

Diagne, B., in *Notes Africaines, 1872–1972*, IFAN, Dakar.

——, *Statutes of the Black Race* (with W.E.B. du Bois), Paris, 1919.

Diame, Aba Mago, *Voyage dans le Soudan Occidental, 1863–6*, Paris, 1866.

Dike, K.O., *Trade and Politics in the Niger Delta, 1830–85*, Oxford, 1956.

Diop, C.A., *Nations Nègres et Cultures*, 1954.

Diop, D.M., *Hammer Blows*, London, 1977.

Dorman, M.H., *The Kilwa Civilization and Mines*, 1936.

Drummond, H., *Tropical Africa*, London, 1889.

Du Bois, W.E.B., *The World and Africa*, London, 1947.

——, *The Birth of African Unity*, London, 1963.

——, 'My Last Message to the World' (26 June 1957), in *Revolution*, Paris, after his funeral on 29 August 1963.

Dunne, S.P., *The Fall and Rise of the Asiatic Mode of Production*, London, 1982.

Duyvendak, J.J.L., *China's Discovery of Africa*, London, 1949.

East African Chronicle (Ed. Desai), Nairobi, 1920–1.

East African Standard, Nairobi, 1965–6 issues.

ECA Reports, 1963 et seq., Addis Ababa.

Echo, The, Accra, 13 February 1977 (on Nkrumah).

Egharevba, J.V., *A Short History of Benin*, Ibadan, 1960.

Eiselen, W.M., *Commission on Bantu Education*, Pretoria, 53/1951.

El Idrissi, *Description of Africa and Spain* (Trans. K. Dozy, M.J. de Goede), Leiden, 1866.

Elliott, C., *The East African Protectorate*, London, 1903.

Empire Review, London, 1910.

Encyclopédie de l'Empire Français, Paris, 1948.

Engels, F., *The Origins of the Family, Private Property and the State*, Moscow, (1st edition, Zurich, 1884); in *Marx–Engels Correspondence* and *Marx on Colonialism*, N.Y., 1972; and Appendix to K. Marx, *Capital*, Vol.3.

Ethiopian Observer The, London.

Ethiopian Ministry of Justice, *Report*, Addis Ababa, 1949 (Italian war atrocities).

Ethiopian Government, *Memorandum to UNO*, Paris, July 1946 (on Italian post-war demands for Somalia, Eritrea).

Eybers, G.W., *Documents Illustrating S. African History*, London, 1918.

Fage, J.D. and Oliver, R., (Eds.), *Cambridge History of Africa*, 5 vols, Cambridge, 1972-7.

Fagg, N.A.B., 'The Nok Culture in Prehistory', in *Journal of the Historical Society of Nigeria*, December, 1959.

Falconbridge, A., *An Account of the Slave Traffic on the Coast of Africa*, London, 1788.

Fanon, F., *A Dying Colonialism*, London, 1965.

——, *The Wretched of the Earth*, London, 1961.

——, *Toward the African Revolution*, London, 1970.

——, *Black Skies, White Marshes*, New York, 1967.

Fernandez, V., *Description de la Côte Occidentale l'Afrique, 1506–10* (Ed. R. Mauny, Monod, de Mota), Bissau, 1951.

Findlay, G.C., and Hodsworth, W.W., *The History of the Wesleyan society*, 5 vols, London, 1921-4.

Fisher, Bram, *What I Did was Right*, London, 1966 (Christian Action, Ed. P. Altman).

First, R., *South West Africa*, London, 1963.

Flint, J.E., *Sir George Goldie and the Making of Nigeria*, London, 1960.

Foreign Affairs Institute, New York, Vol.55/1,1976 (Africa and OPEC).

Fort Jesus Handbook, Mombasa, 1965.

Frankel, H.S., *Capital Investment in South Africa*, Oxford, 1938.

Fraser, D., *Primitive Art*, London, 1962.

Freedom, Johannesburg (CPSA organ), Sept. 1942; Sept–Oct. 1947; Nov. 1948; Feb. 1950.

FRELIMO: The Mozambique Revolution, Special Issue, 25 September 1967, Dar-es-Salaam.

Frobenius, Leo, *Kulturgeschichte Afrikas*, Vienna, 1933.

——, *History of African Civilization*, Berlin, 1909.

——, *The Childhood of Man* (Trans. Keane), 1909.

Furneaux, R., *Abdul Krim, Emir of the Rif*, 1967.

Fynn, H.F., *Diary* (Natal, 1820–30s), London, 1950.

Galvao, A. de, *Tratado dos Descubrimentos (1563)*, Oporto, 1944.

Gambuze (old Uganda journal).

Gamitto, A.C.P., *King Kazembe*, 2 vols (1854), Lisbon, 1960.

Gann, L., and Duignan, P. (Eds.), *The History and Politics of Colonialism*, Vol.1, Cambridge, 1969.

Garrido, *Historia de las Clases Trabajadoras (1871)*, Madrid, 1970.

Gautier, E.F., *L'Afrique Noire Occidentale*, Paris, 1935.

Gandhi, M.K., *Satyagraha in South Africa*, Madras, 1928.

Gide, A., *A Report on French West Africa*, Paris, 1927.

Gizenga, A., 'Hier, Aujourd'hui, Demain', in *Remarques Congolaises*, Brussels, August, 1964.

Godinho, V.M., *L'Economie de l'Empire Portuguais aux XV et XVI Siècles*, Paris, 1969.

Goodwin, A.J.H., in *South African Journal of Science* (on 'Stone Age'), 1925.

Goris, J.A., *Etude sur les Colonies Marchandes Méridionales à Anvers de 1488 à 1567*, Paris, 1925.

Gould, S.J., *The Mismeasurement of Man*, Harvard, 1980.

Greenberg, J.N., *Studies in African Linguistic Classification*, New Haven, 1955.

Green, T.W., *Account of Bushmen Paintings*, August, 1885.

Grey, *The Colonial Policy of Lord John Russell's Administration*, London, 1853.

Grossmann, H., *Il Crollo del Capitalismo*, Milan, 1967 (Frankfurt, 1967).

Guerrilhero, London (irregular Angolan–Mozambique–Bissau paper).

Hailey, Lord, *African Survey*, London, 1938, 1957.

Hakem, A.A., 'The Civilization of Napata and Meroe', in *UN General History of Africa*, Vol.2, California, 1981.

Hakluyt, R., *The Principal Navigations, Voyages, Traffiques and Discoveries of the English Nations*, London, 1598.

Haouqal, Ibn, *Description de l'Afrique* (Trans. by Slane), Paris, 1842.

Hayford, Casely J.E., *Ethiopia Unbound*, London, 1911.

——, *Gold Coast Native Institutions*, London, 1903.

Hiernaux, J., in 1968 *Annales du Musée Royal de l'Afrique Centrale*, Tervuren, 1968.

'History of Historiography', 4/1983, 5/1984, *International Review*, Milan, 1984.

H.M.S.O., *Abbysinian Campaigns*, London, 1942.

Hobson, J., *Imperialism*, London, 1902.

Hofmeyr, J.H., *South Africa*, Capetown, 1933.

Hollingsworth, L.W., *Zanzibar under the Foreign Office, 1890–1913*, London, 1953.

Horton, J. Africanus, *West African Countries and Peoples*, London, 1868.

——, *Letters on the Political Condition of the Gold Coast*, London, 1870.

Huberich, C., *The Political and Legislative History of Liberia*, 1947.

Huxley, E., *White Man's Country: Lord Delamere and the Making of Kenya*, 2 vols, London, 1953.

Ibn Madjid, A., *Tres Roteiros Desconhecidos* (Trans. Jirmounsky), Moscow, 1957, Lisbon, 1960.

Ingrams, W.H., *Zanzibar, Its History and People*, London, 1931.

——, *Uganda*, London, 1960.

Jabavu, D.D.T., 'Bantu Grievances' in *Western Civilization and the Natives of S. Africa* (Ed. I. Schapera), London, 1934.

——, *The Black Problem*, Lovedale, Cape, 1920.

——, *The Segregation Fallacy*, Lovedale, 1928.

Jabavu, T., in *Imvu Zabantsundu*, Cape newspaper.

Jaffe, H., *Fascism in S. Africa*, Cape Town, 1946.

——, *300 Years, A History of S. Africa*, Cape Town, 1952.

——, *Colonialism Today*, London, 1962, Milan, 1972, Madrid, 1976, Luxembourg, 1980.

——, *Africa — From Tribalism to Socialism*, Milan, 1971, Mexico City, 1976.

——, *Africa — Movimenti e Lotte di Liberazione*, Milan, 1978.

——, *Kenya, 1968; Uganda, 1969; Nigeria, 1969, Tanzania, 1970* (Milan).

——, *Rhodesia*, Milan, 1971.

——, *Ethiopia*, Milan, 1971.

——, *Neo-Imperilaismo Portugues*, Bilbao, 1976.

——, *Storia del Sudafrica*, Milan, 1980.

——, *The Pyramid of Nations*, Luxembourg, 1980.

——, *Zimbabwe Memo*, Luxembourg, 1982.

Jalée, P., *Il Terzo Mondo in Cifre*, Milan, 1971.

Jamaladinni, A.K., *Maji Maji Rebellion*, Arusha, 1957.

James, T.G.H., in *Encyclopaedia Britannica*, 15th Edition, Vol.6, pp. 468–70.

Johnston, H.H., *England's Work in Central Africa*, London, 1897.

——, *Uganda*, London, 1902.

——, *Journal of African Studies*, Vol.3/12, London, 1904 (on Belgian Congo).

Journal de la Société des Africanistes, Paris.

Journal of the Historical Society of Nigeria, Ibadan, 1956 et seq.

Journal of African History, Cambridge, 1960, 1964.

Journal of the Royal Anthropological Institute, London, 1962, 1963.

Kadalie, *My Life and the I.C.U.*, London, 1970.

Kamal, Y., *Monumente Egyptae et Africae.*

Kamara, C.M., *La Vie d'El Hadj Omar* (Trans. Amar Samb), IFAN, Dakar.

Kariuki, *Mau Mau Detainee*, Oxford, 1963.

Kati, M. (Trans. M. Delafosse), *Tarik El-Fattach*, Paris, 1913.

Kaunda, K., Speech, Mulungushi, 19 April 1968.

Keita, M., 'The Foreign Policy of Mali', in *International Affairs*, 37/4, October, 1961.

Kenyatta, J., *Kenya, Land of Conflict*, London, 1945.

——, *Facing Mount Kenya*, London, c.1936.

——, *Speeches, 1963–77*, Nairobi.

Kenya Workers News, Nairobi, Mombasa, 4 April 1958; 6 and 13 June 1958.

Khaldoun, Ibn, *History of the Berbers*, 4 vols, 1925–56.

——, *The Muqadimmah* (Trans. Rosenthal), London, 1958.

Kies, B.M., *The Contribution of the Non-Europeans to World Civilization*, Cape Town, 1953 (address, 29 September 1953 in St. Georges Cathedral Hall).

——, *The Basis of Unity*, Address 4–5 January 1945, at 3rd NEUM Conference, Capetown.

Kierman, J.A., and Ogot, B.A., *Zamani*, Dar-es-Salaam, 1969.

Kingdon Report, *Disturbances in Uganda during April 1949*, Entebbe, 1950.

Kizerbo, J., *Histoire de l'Afrique*, Paris, 1971, Turin, 1977.

——, in *UNESCO General History of Africa*, Vols.1, 2, California, 1981, 1982.

Klarwill, Von V., (Ed.), *The Fugger Newsletters, 1568–1605* (Trans. P. de Chary), 1924.

Knight, W., *The Missionary Secretariat of Henry Venn*, London, 1880.

Kobishanov, Y.M., 'Aksum', in *UNESCO General History of Africa,*, Vol.2, California, 1981.

Kolb, P., *Caput Bonae Spei Hodiernum*, Nurnberg, 1719.

——, *Beschrywing van de Kaap de Goede Hoop*, Amsterdam, 1727.

Krapf, J.L., *Travels in East Africa*, London, 1860.

Kubbel, L. and Matveev, V.V., *Treatises for USSR Academy of Sciences*, Moscow,

1960, 1965.

Kumaliza, M., 'Tanganyika's View of Labour's Role', in *E. Africa Journal*, November 1944.

Kurtze, M., *The German East Africa Company*, Jena, 1913.

Lacerda, F.J.M., *The Lands of Gazembe, 1798* (Trans. R.F. Burton), London, 1873.

Lagos Weekly Record, Lagos, 1891–8.

Leakey, L.B.S., *Science News*, September 1950.

——, *Olduvai Gorge*, Cambridge, 1951.

——, *A Preliminary Report on Olduvai Gorge*, 1964.

——, *The Progress and Evolution of Man in Africa*, London, 1961.

——, *The Stone Age Races of Kenya*, London, 1935.

League of Nations, *Reports*, Geneva, May 1935; *Journal* No. 11, Document 1571, November 1935 (on Ethiopia and Italy).

——, British report on mandates, London, 1921.

Le Herissé, A., *L'Ancien Royaume de Dahomey*, Paris, 1911.

Lebeuf, J.P. and Masson-Deterbet, A., *La Civilisation du Tchad (les Sao)*, Paris, 1950.

Leclant, J., 'The Empire of Kush', in *UNESCO General History of Africa*, Vol.2.

Lenin, V.I., *Imperialism*, 1916.

——, *Collected Works*, Vol.21 (on war and working class parties), Vol.23 (idem). Speech, 6 December 1920 (on self-determination).

Lerumo, A., *Fifty Fighting Years — The S. African Communist Party, 1921–71*, London, 1971.

Lestrade, G.P., *The Bantu Speaking Tribes of S. Africa*, Cape, 1949.

Lewis, M., *Race and Culture, UNESCO*, Paris, 1952.

Lewis-Williams, J.D., *Rock Art in Southern Africa*, Milan, 1983.

Liberator, The, (N.L.L. organ), Cape Town, 1937.

Linschoten, J.H. van, *Descriptio Totius Guineae Tractus Congi, Angolae et Monomotapae*, The Hague, 1599 (Ed. Burger, C.P.).

Livingstone, D., *Missionary Correspondence* (Ed. I. Schapera), London, 1961.

——, *Private Journals* (Ed. I. Schapera), Berkeley, 1960.

——, *Missionary Travels and Researches*, London, 1857.

Lopez, D., *Relazione de Reame di Congo* (Trans. Pigafetta, F.), Rome, 1591–1601.

Lubembe, C.K., 'Trade Unions and Nation Building', in *E. Africa Journal*, April 1964.

Ludolphus, *Ethiopia*, Frankfurt, 1631, London, 1684.

Lugard, F.D., *Dual Mandate in British Tropical Africa*, Edinburgh, 1922, London, 1929.

——, *The Rise of Our East African Empire*, London, 1893.

Lumbroso, A., *Carteggi Imperialie Reali, 1870–1918*, Vol.4, Milan, 1931.

Luthuli, A., *Let My People Go*, London, 1962.

——, *Nobel Prize Address*, Oslo, 10 December 1961.

Luxembourg, R., *The Accumulation of Capital*, 1913, Ch.27 (Algeria), Ch.29 (S.Africa).

Lyautey, L.H., *Choix de Lettres, 1882–1919*, Paris, 1947.

Lyautey, P., 'La Politique du Protectorat en Afrique Marocaine, 1905–18', in *Convegno Volta*, Royal Academy of Italy, 4–11 October 1938.

Mabuza, A., 'The Ethiopian Monarchical System', in *Challenge*, NY, February, 1968.

Machel, S., *Mozambique: Sowing the Seeds of Revolution*, London, 1974.
——, *Message to the Nation*, Maputo, 25 June 1975.
Majeke, N., *The Role of the Missionaries in Conquest*, Johannesburg, 1952.
Mandela, N., *I Am Prepared to Die*, London, 1965.
——, *What I Did Was Right*, London, 1966.
Marsh, Z.A., *East Africa through Contemporary Records*, Cambridge, 1961.
Marx, K., *Abstract of Morgan's Ancient Society*, Moscow, 1945.
——, *On Colonialism*, New York, 1972.
——, *Grundrisse* (London edition, pp. 475–7), 1973.
——, *Letters to Meyer and Vogt*, 9 April 1870 and from Engels, F., 7 October 1858.
Maspero, J., *New Light on Ancient Egypt*, 1908.
Matanzima, K., *Independence My Way*, Pretoria, 1977.
Mauny, R., *Tableau Géographique de l'Ouest Africain au Moyen Age*, Dakar, 1961.
Mbeke, G., *The Peasant Revolt*, London, 1964.
Mboya, T., *The Kenya Question*, London, 1956.
——, *Freedom and After*, London, 1963.
Meek, C.K., *Land, Law and Customs in the Colonies*, London, 1946.
Mekouria, T.T., 'Christian Aksum', in *UNESCO General History*, Vol.2.
Michelet, R., *African Empires and Civilizations*, Paris, 1933.
Millin, S.G., *Rhodes*, London, 1952.
Milner Papers, Ed. C. Headlam, Vol. 2, London, 1931–3.
Missionary Society Transactions (Van der Kemp Report), London, 1804–13.
Moffat, R., *Missionary Labours and Scenes in Southern Africa*, London, 1842, 1894.
——, *The Matabele Journals of Robert Moffat*, 2 vols, London, 1894.
Mofolo, Th., *Tshaka*, Morijo, S.Africa (Trans. V. Ellenberger), Paris, 1940.
Molema, S.M., *The Bantu Past and Present: An Ethnographical Study*, Edinburgh, 1920.
Molteno, P.A., *The Life and Times of Sir Charles Molteno*, 2 vols, London, 1900.
Mondlane, E., *The Struggle for Mozambique*, London, 1969.
Moodie, D., *History of Battles and Adventures of the British, Boers and Zulus in Southern Africa*, 2 vols, Cape Town, 1888.
Moodie, J.W.D., *Ten Years in South Africa*, 2 vols, London, 1835.
Moodie, R.N., *Native Tribes of South Africa*, Cape Town, 1838–42 (Amsterdam, 1960).
Morel, E.D., *King Leopold's Rule in Africa*, London, 1904.
Morgan, L.H., *Systems of Consanguinuity and Affinity of the Human Society*, Washington, 1871.
Morrell, W.P., *British Colonial Policy in the Age of Peel and Russell*, Oxford, 1930.
Mugabe, R., Addresses, Parliament and at Independence, Harare, 1980–4.
Mulele, P., in *West Africa*, 1968–9 and Milan, 1969 (after his murder by Mobutu).
Nachtigal, G., *Sahara und Sudan*, 3 vols, Berlin, 1879–89.
Nasser, G.A., *The Philosophy of the Revolution*, 1955, 1959; and United Arab Republic Official biography, *President G.A. Nasser*, 1965.
Nationalist, The, Dar-es-Salaam, January 1964–July 1965.

Native Affairs Commission, *Reports*, S. Africa, 1903 (on Chinese labour), 1921.

Ndlovo, S.G., *Zimbabwe*, Lusaka, 1974.

Needham, J., *Science and Civilization in China*, Vol.1 (1954), Vol.2 (1956), Cambridge.

Nesturck, M., *The Races of Mankind*, Moscow, 1962.

Neto, A., *Speeches*, in M. Albano; *Angola*, Milan, 1972.

——, *Un Popolo in Rivoluzione*, Milan, 1971.

——, *Colonialismo, Cultura e Rivoluzione*, Milan, 1972.

New Age, Cape Town, 1950s.

New Times and Ethiopian News, May 1936–1944, London.

Newton, J., *Diary from "The Duke of Argyle", 1750–5* (Eds. B. Martin and M. Spurrel), Epworth Press, private.

Ngai, M., *Aimé Césaire*, Dakar, 1977.

Nhlapo, J.M., *Nguni and Sotho*, Cape Town, 1945.

Nkrumah, K., *Address to African Heads of State*, Addis Ababa, 24 May 1963.

——, *I Speak of Freedom*, London, 1961.

——, *Autobiography*, London, 1957.

——, *Conscienscism: Philosophy and Ideology of Decolonisation*, London, 1964.

——, *Rhodesia File*, London, 1965, 1966.

—— *Challenge of the Congo*, Conakry, June 1969.

Nujoma, S., in *Panorama*, Milan, 12 March 1984.

Numeiri, G., in *Courier*, Brussels, May–June 1977.

Nyasaland Commission, *Report*, Zomba, 1916.

Nyerere, J., *Freedom and Unity*, January, 1966, Dar-es-Salaam.

——, *Freedom and Socialism*, Dar-es-Salaam, 1969.

——, *Arusha Declaration*, 29 January 1967, Arusha.

Ogot, B.A., and Welbourne, F.B., *A Place to Feel at Home* (on Ethiopian Churches), London, 1966.

——, (with Kierman), *Zamani*, Dar-es-Salaam, 1969.

Oginga Odinga, *Not Yet Uhuru*, London, 1968.

Okuma, T., *Angola in Ferment*, Boston, 1962.

Oliver, R., *The Missionary Factor in East Africa*, London, 1952.

Oliver, R. and Fage, J.D., 'Collaboration as a Form of Resistance', in *Problems in the History of Colonial Africa, 1860–1960* (Ed. Collins, R.O.), New Jersey, 1970.

Orde-Browne, G.St.J., *Labour Conditions in E. Africa*, London, 1946.

——, (with Bryant, W. and Mumford), *Africans Learn to be French*, London, undated.

Ormsby-Gore, Commission on East Africa, Cmd.2387, London, 1925.

——, Commission on West Africa, London, 1926.

Ottenberg, Simon and Phoebe (Eds.), *Cultures and Societies of Africa*, New York, 1960.

Owen, W.F.W., *Narrative from Voyages to Explore the Shores of Africa, Arabia and Madagascar*, London, 1833.

Owen, F., *Diary of Rev. Francis Owen, Missionary with Dingane in 1837–8* (Ed. G. Cory), Cape Town, 1926.

Padmore, G., *Africa, Britain's Third Empire*, London, 1949.

——, *Pan-Africanism or Communism?*, London, 1956.

Palmers, H.R., *Sudanese Memoirs*, London, 1928.

Pan Africa, Nairobi, January 1964–August 1965.

Pan African Congress (S. Africa), *Conference Reports*, 1959, 1964, 1969.
Pankhurst, R., *Kenya*, London, c.1956.
——, *An Introduction to the Economic History of Ethiopia from Early Times to 1800*, London, 1961.
——, *State and Land in Ethiopian History*, Addis Ababa, 1966.
Pankhurst, S., *Ex-Italian Somaliland*, London 1951.
——, (Editor) *Ethiopian Times*.
——, 'Lalibela Churches etc.', in *A Culture History of Ethiopia*, London, 1955.
——, *British Policy in E. Ethiopia, Ogaden and the Reserved Area*, London, 1948.
Park, M., *Travels in the Interior Districts of Africa, 1795–7*, London, 1798, Paris, 1820.
Pereira, D.P., *Esmeraldo de Situ Orbis (R. Mauny, Journal 19)*, Bissau, 1956.
Perham, M., *Lugard*, London, 1956.
——, (with Simmons, J.), *An Anthology of Exploration*, London, 1942.
Person, Y., *Samori*, 2 vols, IFAN, Dakar, 1971–5.
Peters, K., *New Light in Darkest Africa*, c.1895.
——, *Das Deutsch-Ostafrikanische Schutzgebiet*, Munich, 1895.
——, *Die Grunding von Deutsch-Ostafrika*, Berlin, 1906.
Philip, J., *Researches in South Africa*, 2 vols, London, 1828.
Plaatje, S., *Native Life in South Africa, c.1916* (on 1913 Land Act).
Plomer, W., *Cecil Rhodes*, Cape, London.
Portal, G., *The Mission to Uganda*, London, 1894 (after death of Rev. Hannington amidst Christian–Islam 'divide and rule' missionary activity).
Potekhin, I.I., 'Land Relations in African Countries', in *Peoples of Asia and Africa*, No.3, Moscow, 1962.
——, *Formirovanie Natsionalnoi Obschnosti Yuzhnoi Afrikanskich Bantu*, (The uniform national communal (lands) of the Southern African Bantu), Moscow, 1955.
Poznansky, M., 'The Iron Age in East Africa', in *Background to Evolution in Africa* (Eds. Bishop, W. and Clark, J.), Chicago, 1972.
——, on 'Igbo Ikwu', in *Archaeology*, 25 April 1973.
——, in *UNESCO General History*, Vol.2, California, 1981.
Pretoria Convention, The, August 1881.
Prior, J., *Voyage along the Eastern Coast of Africa*, London, 1819.
Radcliffe-Brown, A.R. and Forde, D. (Eds.), *African Systems of Kinship and Marriage*, London, 1950.
Ranger, T.O. (Ed.), *Emerging Themes in African History*, Nairobi, 1968.
Ravenstein, E.G., *A Journal of the First Voyage of Vasco da Gama*, 1898.
Rebman, J., *Travels, Researches and Missionary Labours*, London, 1860.
Rennel, Lord of Rodd, *British Military Administration in Africa, 1941–7*, H.M.S.O., London, 1948.
Rhodes, C.J., *Vindex (Speeches), 1887–1900*, Cape Town.
Rinchon, D., *L'Esclavage des Congolais par les Européens — Histoire de la Déportation de 13 Millions de Noirs*, Brussels, 1929.
Roberts, H., *The History of French Colonial Policy*, London, 1929.
Robinson, K.R., *Khami Ruins*, Cambridge, 1959.
Rohlfs, G., *Quer Durch Afrika, Reise vom Mittelmeer dem Tscad-See und zum Golf von Guinea*, 2 vols, Leipzig, 1874–5.
Roncière, C. de la, *La Découverte de l'Afrique au Moyen Age*, 3 vols, Cairo, 1924–7.

Rose-Innes, R.W., *The Glen-Grey Act and the Native Question*, Cape Town, 1903.
Rosenthal, E. and Goodwin, A.J.H., *Cave Artists of S. Africa*, Cape Town, 1953.
Rossetti, C., *Storia Diplomatica*, Rome, 1908.
Rotberg, R.I., 'The Lenshina Movement in N. Rhodesia', in *Rhodes-Livingstone Journal*, London, June, 1961.
——, *Plymouth Brethren and the Occupation of Katanga, 1856–1907*, London, 1964.
Roth, Ling, H., *Great Benin, its Customs, Art*, London, 1968.
Roux, E., *S.P. Bunting*, 1944.
——, *Time Longer Than Rope*.
Royal Geographic Society, *Proceedings*, 16/1872 (Limpopo expedition), et altri.
Royal Society of Africa, London, *Transactions*, 1935, 1945 (30/4, Leakey, M.D.), 1962.
Rutherford, J., *Sir George Grey: A Study in Colonial Government*, London, 1961.
Salmon, P., *Insurrection de Mopoie Bangezegine*, (Congo), 1916, Brussels, 1969.
Samuel, A.E., *Ptolemaic Egypt*.
Schapera, I., *The Bantu Speaking Tribes of South Africa*, 1936, New York, 1952.
——, *The Khoisan Peoples of South Africa*, London, 1930.
——, *The Early Cape Hottentots*, Cape Town, 1933.
Schleicher, A.W., *Geschichte der Galla* (of 16th century et seq.), Berlin, 1893.
Schweinfurth, G., *Im Herzen von Afrika*, Leipzig, 1874.
Sekou Touré, 'Cos'e la Rivoluzione Guineana', in *Relazioni Internazionali*, 1/1 January 1972.
——, *Discours* with de Gaulle, Conakry, 25 August 1958.
——, *Experience Guinéenne et Unité Africaine* (forward by A. Césaire).
Senghor, L.S., *Discours*, Dakar, 19 April 1962.
——, *Negrita e Politica Africana*, Rome, 5 October 1962.
——, *Théorie et Pratique du Socialisme Sénégalais*, Tunis, 1–7 July 1975.
——, *For an African Re-Reading of Marx and Engels*, Dakar, 1976.
——, *Selected Poems*, London, 1977.
Shaw, T.S., *Igbo Ikwu*, 2 vols, London, Ibadan, 1972.
Shaw, W., *The Story of My Mission to S.E. Africa*, London, 1865.
Shepstone, Th., *Memoranda*, November 1864, Durban, 1874.
Shepperson, G., 'The Politics of African Church Separatist Movements in British Central Africa, 1892–1916', in *Africa*, July 1954.
Shinnie, M., *Ancient African Kingdoms*, London, 1965.
Sik, E., *The History of Black Africa*, 2 vols., Budapest, 1966.
Simons, J., (see Alexander, R.).
Smith, W., *A New Voyage to Guinea*, London, 1744.
Soga, J.H., *Amaxhosa Life and Customs*, Lovedale, Cape, undated.
——, *The South East Bantu*, Lovedale, 1930.
Soga, T., *Gxulwe and the Bushmen*, Cape, undated.
South African Archaeological Bulletin, 1952–3, 1959, 1963–5 (iron-working Bantu).
South African Journal of Science, 1915, 1931–2, 1938, 1942, 1956, 1965.
South African Worker, (CPSA organ) Johannesburg, 13 August 1926 (S.P. Bunting on Bantu Councils).

Soyinka, W., *Myth, Literature and the African World*, London, 1977.

Speke, J.H., *Journal of the Discovery of the Source of the White Nile*, London, 1863.

Stamp, L.D., *Africa*, London, 1953.

Stanley, H.M., *In Darkest Africa*, London, 1886, New York, 1890.

——, *Address to Anti-Slavery Society*, Manchester, 23 October 1884.

——, *Address to Manchester Chamber of Commerce*, 21 October 1884.

——, *Letters to King Leopold II, 1881–2* (published only in 1957).

——, *The Congo and the Founding of its Free State*, 2 vols, New York, 1885.

Star, The, Johannesburg, on 1922 strike; on 16 January 1928 (W.H. Andrews, CPSA leader, rejects ICU affiliation to 'White'-dominated Trades and Labour Council).

Staudenraus, P.J., *The African Colonisation Movement, 1816–1865*, New York, 1961.

Storme, M., *Les Mutineries Militaires au Kasai en 1895*, Brussels, 1970.

Strong, A.S. (Ed.), 'Chronicles of Kilwa', in *Journal of Royal Asiatic Society*, London, 1895.

Stuart, J., *Fynn's Diary*, London, 1950.

Summers, R. (Ed.), *Zimbabwe: A Rhodesian Mystery*, London, 1963.

Suret-Canale, J., *Les Sociétés Traditionelles en Afrique Tropicale et le Concept de Mode de Production Asiatique*, Paris, 1964.

——, *Afrique Noire, Géographie, Civilisations, Histoire*, Paris, 1962.

Tabata, I.B., *The Awakening of a People*, Johannesburg, 1950.

——, *Education for Barbarism*, c.1960.

——, *The Boycott, A Weapon of Struggle*, Cape Town, 1955.

——, *The Pan African Congress Venture in Retrospect* (after Sharpville, 1960), Queenstown, 1960.

——, *Unity, The Road to Freedom in S. Africa* (address to O.A.U. Committee of Nine), Canada, 1965.

Tarikh es Soudan (Trans. Houdas, O.), Tombouktu, Paris, 1900.

Tambo, O., *Statement on ANC Meeting with Inkatha*, 5 November 1979.

Tas, A., *The Diary of Adam Tas, 1705–6*, London, 1914 (Ed. L. Fouche).

Tettegah, J.K., *Towards Nkrumahism — The Role and Tasks of the Trade Unions*, Accra, 1962.

Theal, G.M. in *Oxford History of South Africa*, Vol.1, 1973.

——, *Basutoland Records*, 3 vols, Cape Town, 1883.

——, *The History of South Africa*, 11 vols, London, 1892–1919.

——, *Important Historical Documents* (trans.), 3 vols, Cape Town, 1896–1911.

Thompson, G., *Travels and Adventures in Southern Africa*, 2 vols, London, 1827.

Thunberg, C.P., *Travels in Europe, Africa, 1770–9*, 4 vols, London, 1795.

Tomlinson, T., *The Congo Treaty*, London, 1884.

Torch, The, Cape Town, weekly, 1945–61.

Townsend, M., *Origins of Modern German Colonialism*, New York, 1921.

——, *European Colonial Expansion since 1871*, Philadelphia, 1941.

Tricontinental, Havana, June–August 1967 (on P. Mulele; Che Guevara on Africa).

Trimingham, J.S., *A History of Islam in West Africa*, London, 1959, Oxford, 1962.

Trotsky, L., 'Letters to South Africa (1934–5)', in *Workers Voice*, Cape Town, 1944.

Tucker, A.R., *Eighteen Years in Uganda and East Africa*, London, 1908.

Uganda Eyogera, Kampala, 1953 (Kabaka crisis).

Uganda Post, Kampala, 1953.

Uganda Star, Kampala, 1949.

Ullendorff, E., *The Ethiopians*, 1960.

Umlilo Mollo (Flame), Johannesburg, Vol.1, No.1, September 1936 to December 1937.

Umzebenzi, Johannesburg (CPSA organ), 28 November 1930, 5 May 1934.

UNESCO, *L'Apartheid*, Paris, 1968.

United Nations War Crimes Commission, *Ethiopian Documents*, 1949.

United Nations at Work: Tanganyika, its Present and its Future, UNO, Geneva, 1952.

United Nations 4-Power Commissions on Libya, Eritrea and Somalia, 1949.

United Nations Trusteeship Council, 15th Session, Supplement 3, 1955.

Unity, Lusaka, 1966 to January–February 1968.

U.N.O. *Treaty Series*, No.8, New York, 1947.

Urvoy, Y., *Histoire de l'Empire du Bornou*, Paris, 1949.

Vandewalle, F.A., 'Mutineries au Congo Belge', in *Zaire*, Vol.1, pp. 488–514, Brussels, 1947.

Van der Horst, S., *Native Labour in South Africa*, c.1939.

Van Riebeeck, J.,*Journal*, Cape Archives, 1652–8; then in D.E.I.C. Journal, 1660–2.

Van Zandijeke, A., 'La Révolte de Luluabourg, 1895', in *Zaire*, Vol.4, pp. 931–63, 1063–82, 1950.

Vedder, H., *Das Alte Sudwestafrika*, Berlin, 1934; Trans. C.G. Hall, London, 1938.

Venn, H., (see W. Knight), *Papers*, July 1861 and 8 January 1866; *British House of Commons Select Committee Report, 1865/V.412.iii* (on 'Indirect Rule').

Verbeken, A., 'La Révolte des Batetela en 1895' (unpublished), Académie Royale des Sciences, Vol.7, Brussels, 1958.

Verhulpen, E., *Baluba et Balubaisés*, Antwerp, 1936.

Villard, U.M., *Storia della Nubia Cristiana*, Rome, 1938.

Von Lettow Vorbeck, P., *My Reminiscences of East Africa*, London, 1920.

Walker, E.A., *Lord de Villiers and his Times, S. Africa 1824–1914*, London, 1925.

Walker, H., (Mss. Rhodes House, Oxford), *29 Diaries in Universities Missions, Congo, 1861–7*.

Wallerstein, I., *Africa—The Politics of Independence*, New York, 1961.

——, *The Capitalist World Economy*, New York, 1980.

Walton, E., *The Inner History of the National Convention* (before S. African Union, 1909–10).

Wangemann, T., *Maleo en Sekoekoeni* (Sotho resister), (Trans. J.F.W. Grosskopf), Cape Town, 1957.

Welbourne, F.B.E., *East African Rebels*, 1961.

Westermann, D., *Geschichte Afrikas*, Cologne, 1952.

White Paper, H.M.S.O.: Withdrawal of Recognition from Kabaka Mutesa II of Buganda, Cmd.9028, London, 1953.

Wilde, V., *The Uganda Mutiny, 1897*, London, 1954.

Williams, E., *Capitalism and Slavery*, London, 1944.

Wilson, E.T., *Russia and Black Africa before World War II*, New York, 1975.

Wilson, H.S. (Ed.), *Origins of West African Nationalism*, London, 1969.

Wilson, M., *Social Structure*, Pietermartizburg, 1952.
——, *Peoples of the Nyasa-Tanganyika Corridor*, Cape Town, 1958.
——, *Divine Kings and the 'Breath of Men'*, Cambridge, 1959.
——, *Good Company*, London, 1951.
Windrich, E., *The Rhodesian Problem: A Documentary Record, 1923–73*, London, 1975.
Wittvogel, K.A., *Oriental Despotism*, New Haven, Mass., 1957.
Woddis, J., *The Roots of Revolt*, London, 1960.
Woolf, L., *Empire and Commerce in Africa*, London, 1920.
Woolman, D.S., *Abd el Krim and the Rif Rebellion*, 1968.
Workers Herald (I.C.U. organ), Cape Town, 1922.
Workers Voice, Cape Town, 1942–7.
Wreh, T., *The Rule of President Tubman in Liberia, 1944–71*, London, 1977.
Wrigley, C.C., 'Speculations on the Economic Prehistory of Africa', in *Journal of African History*, Vol.1, Cambridge, 1960.
Wyndham, H.A., *The Atlantic and Slavery*, London, 1935.

Index

AFRICA TITLES FROM ZED

Dan Nabudere
IMPERIALISM IN EAST AFRICA
Vol. I: Imperialism and Exploitation
Vol. II: Imperialism and Integration
Hb

Elenga M'Buyinga
PAN AFRICANISM OR NEO
COLONIALISM?
The Bankruptcy of the OAU
Hb and Pb

Bade Onimode
IMPERIALISM AND
UNDERDEVELOPMENT IN
NIGERIA
The Dialectics of Mass Poverty
Hb and Pb

Michael Wolfers and Jane Bergerol
ANGOLA IN THE FRONTLINE
Hb and Pb

Mohamed Babu
AFRICAN SOCIALISM OR
SOCIALIST AFRICA?
Hb and Pb

Anonymous
INDEPENDENT KENYA
Hb and Pb

Yolamu Barongo (Editor)
POLITICAL SCIENCE IN AFRICA:
A RADICAL CRITIQUE
Hb and Pb

Okwudiba Nnoli (Editor)
PATH TO NIGERIAN
DEVELOPMENT
Pb

Emile Vercruijsse
THE PENETRATION OF
CAPITALISM
A West African Case Study
Hb

Fatima Babikir Mahmoud
THE SUDANESE BOURGEOISIE
— Vanguard of Development?
Hb and Pb

No Sizwe
ONE AZANIA, ONE NATION
The National Question in South
Africa
Hb and Pb

Ben Turok (Editor)
DEVELOPMENT IN ZAMBIA
A Reader
Pb

J. F Rweyemamu (Editor)
INDUSTRIALIZATION AND
INCOME DISTRIBUTION IN
AFRICA
Hb and Pb

Claude Ake
REVOLUTIONARY PRESSURES
IN AFRICA
Hb and Pb

Anne Seidman and Neva Makgetla
OUTPOSTS OF MONOPOLY
CAPITALISM
Southern Africa in the Changing
Global Economy
Hb and Pb

Peter Rigby
PERSISTENT PASTORALISTS
Nomadic Societies in Transition
Hb and Pb

Edwin Madunagu
PROBLEMS OF SOCIALISM: THE
NIGERIAN CHALLENGE
Pb

Mai Palmberg
THE STRUGGLE FOR AFRICA
Hb and Pb

A.T. Nzula, I.I. Potekhin and A.Z. Zusmanovich
FORCED LABOUR IN COLONIAL AFRICA
Hb and Pb

Jeff Crisp
THE STORY OF AN AFRICAN WORKING CLASS
— Ghanaian Miners' Struggles, 1870-1980
Hb and Pb

Aquino de Braganca and Immanuel Wallerstein (Editors)
THE AFRICAN LIBERATION READER
Documents of the National Liberation Movements
Vol I: The Anatomy of Colonialism
Vol II: The National Liberation Movements
Vol III: The Strategy of Liberation
Hb and Pb

Faarax M.J. Cawl
IGNORANCE IS THE ENEMY OF LOVE
Pb

Kinfe Abraham
FROM RACE TO CLASS
Links and Parallels in African and Black American Protest Expression
Pb

Robert Mshengu Kavanagh
THEATRE AND CULTURAL STRUGGLE IN SOUTH AFRICA
A Study in Cultural Hegemony and Social Conflict
Hb and Pb

A. Temu and B. Swai
HISTORIANS AND AFRICANIST HISTORY: A CRITIQUE
Hb and Pb

Robert Archer and Antoine Bouillon
THE SOUTH AFRICAN GAME
Sport and Racism
Hb and Pb

Ray et al.
DIRTY WORK 2
The CIA in Africa
Pb

Raqiya Haji Dualeh Abdalla
SISTERS IN AFFLICTION
Circumcision and Infibulation of Women in Africa
Hb and Pb

Christine Obbo
AFRICAN WOMEN
Their Struggle for Economic Independence
Pb

Maria Rose Cutrufelli
WOMEN OF AFRICA
Roots of Oppression
Hb and Pb

Asma El Dareer
WOMAN, WHY DO YOU WEEP?
Circumcision and Its Consequences
Hb and Pb

Miranda Davies (Editor)
THIRD WORLD — SECOND SEX
Women's Struggles and National Liberation
Hb and Pb

Organization of Angolan Women
ANGOLAN WOMEN BUILDING THE FUTURE
From National Liberation to Women's Emancipation
Hb and Pb

Zed Books' titles cover Africa, Asia, Latin America and the Middle East, as well as general issues affecting the Third World's relations with the rest of the world. Our Series embrace: Imperialism, Women, Political Economy, History, Labour, Voices of Struggle, Human Rights and other areas pertinent to the Third World.

You can order Zed titles direct from Zed Books Ltd., 57 Caledonian Road, London N1 9BU, UK.

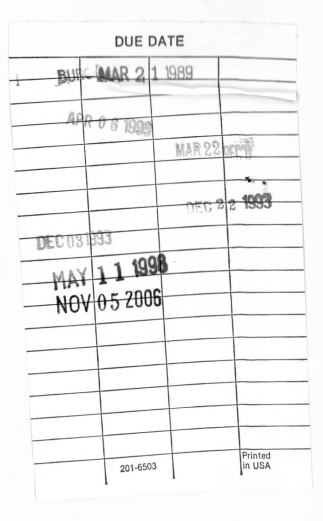